PRAISE FOR PREVIOUS EDITIONS OF

Oklahoma
Off the Beaten Path ®

"It's about time somebody wrote a decent
Oklahoma travel guide. . . .
Oklahoma Off the Beaten Path fills much of the gap."
—*Eagle* (Wichita, Kans.)

"Globe Pequot publishes some fine books in its
'Off the Beaten Path' series. . . . These books cover states
that no other publisher covers thoroughly."
—*Union-Tribune* (San Diego, Calif.)

Help Us Keep This Guide Up to Date

Every effort has been made by the author and editors to make this guide as accurate and useful as possible. However, many changes can occur after a guide is published—establishments close, phone numbers change, hiking trails are rerouted, facilities come under new management, etc.

We would love to hear from you concerning your experiences with this guide and how you feel it could be improved and be kept up to date. While we may not be able to respond to all comments and suggestions, we'll take them to heart, and we'll make certain to share them with the author. Please send your comments and suggestions to the following address:

The Globe Pequot Press
Reader Response/Editorial Department
P.O. Box 480
Guilford, CT 06437

Or you may e-mail us at: editorial@GlobePequot.com

Thanks for your input, and happy travels!

INSIDERS' GUIDE®

OFF THE BEATEN PATH® SERIES

Off the
Beaten Path®

SIXTH EDITION

oklahoma

A GUIDE TO UNIQUE PLACES

DEBORAH BOUZIDEN

INSIDERS' GUIDE®

GUILFORD, CONNECTICUT
AN IMPRINT OF THE GLOBE PEQUOT PRESS

The prices, rates, and hours listed in this guidebook were confirmed at press time. We recommend, however, that you call establishments to obtain current information before traveling.

To buy books in quantity for corporate use or incentives, call **(800) 962–0973, ext. 4551,** or e-mail **premiums@GlobePequot.com.**

INSIDERS' GUIDE ®

Text design by Linda Loiewski
Maps created by Equator Graphics © Morris Book Publishing, LLC
Illustrations by Carole Drong
Illustration on p. 135 from photo courtesy of the Oklahoma Historical Society
Spot photography throughout © Masterfile

ISSN 1540-8876
ISBN-13: 978-0-7627-4207-3
ISBN-10: 0-7627-4207-0

Manufactured in the United States of America
Sixth Edition/First Printing

To all the Oklahoma organizations, foundations, readers, visitors, and citizens for helping make this book possible.

HIGH PLAINS

■ Woodward

BLACK GOLD
AND
GOLDEN PRAIRIES

■ Tulsa

CHEROKEE
COUNTRY

■ Broken
Arrow

SOUTHWEST
PASSAGE

■ Altus

Oklahoma
City
★

CROSS TIMBERS

RIVER COUNTRY

■ Ardmore

McAlester ■

OUACHITA
COUNTRY

Contents

Acknowledgments

Thanks to my writer friends and the Oklahoma Writers' Federation for their support. Special thanks goes to my family for their patience and not taking those blank stares personally when I was working.

Introduction

Finding Oklahoma in a United States atlas sometimes takes a little extra page flipping, but not because of its geographic location. It's right there in the middle of the country, barely south of the exact center of the United States. It's figuring out to which region map makers have assigned the state that can be tricky.

Sometimes considered a southern state, Oklahoma is indeed south of the Mason-Dixon line. You'll find biscuits and gravy on the breakfast table and fried chicken at supper, and we talk slow. Southeastern Oklahoma, where cotton plantations flourished around the Red River, is even referred to as "Little Dixie."

A good case can be made for including the state with the Midwest: Grain elevators and church steeples form the skyline of many an Oklahoma town. The state is the country's fourth-largest producer of wheat, a matter-of-fact statistic that takes on radiant meaning in spring, when ripening grain ripples out to the horizon. There are plenty of southwestern images to be found here, too: Native American trading posts selling turquoise jewelry and cactus candy, red bluffs with chalky stripes of gypsum, and juniper-dotted mesas.

But perhaps the images that most resonate with Oklahomans are western ones. Three major cattle trails crossed through Oklahoma during the nineteenth century, and Panhandle residents still look out on marks made by wagons along the Santa Fe Trail. There are more horses per capita in Oklahoma than in any other state and so many small-town rodeos in July and August that the season is called "Cowboy Christmas." Cowboy boots are ubiquitous: Bankers wear them in the boardroom, lawyers wear them to court, and chefs wear them in the kitchen. In ranching country, saddle shops have been as much a fixture on Main Street as automobile mechanics. But none of those labels—southern, midwestern, southwestern, western—stretches quite far enough to corral all of what's found in Oklahoma. There's just no other place like it.

Oklahoma became the forty-sixth state admitted to the Union in 1907. Before statehood, it was Indian Territory, a world of constantly changing borders and frontier forts where the members of thirty-seven Native American nations eventually came together.

Beginning in the 1830s, the Choctaw, Cherokee, Creek, Chickasaw, and Seminole tribes who lived in the southeastern United States were forced to exchange the farms they lived on for land in Indian Territory, already inhabited by nomadic tribes who hunted buffalo on the plains. (Oklahoman Will Rogers, who never met a man he didn't like, seems to have made an exception for President Andrew Jackson, who signed the Indian Removal Act in 1830. Rogers said: "I am not so sweet on old Andy. He is the one that run us Cherokees out of Georgia and North Carolina.")

The tribes were unjustly uprooted and terribly mistreated, but it is a persistent myth that these were unwanted lands: Choctaw chief Pushmataha claimed that his tribe had received the best remaining U.S. territory west of the Mississippi. The new land wasn't home, but the five tribes cleared land for farms, established newspapers, and built schools that were the envy of surrounding territories.

During the remainder of the nineteenth century, dozens more tribes were moved to Oklahoma, always under tragic circumstances. The federal government flagrantly ignored its treaties with the tribes, outlawed Native American religions, and at statehood, abolished their governments. Against those odds, the tribes have endured, reclaiming their status as sovereign nations and working to preserve their languages and traditions. Anyone who has joined the warm circle of a powwow on a summer evening can attest to the grace and generosity with which the tribes have borne their history. Today Oklahoma is home to more Native Americans than any other state. Thirty-seven tribes have their headquarters here, and flags from each Indian nation fly over the state capitol's lawn.

Other states can say that homesteaders competed for the best claims, but in Oklahoma they literally raced for them. A series of land runs inaugurated in 1889 found would-be settlers lined up on horseback, in wagons, on bicycles, and on foot, waiting for the cannon fire that signaled the start of a pell-mell rush for land. (The temptation to sneak in a little "sooner" than was legal is the source of Oklahoma's nickname, the "Sooner State.") Settlers came from all over the United States and beyond its borders. Czech, Italian, English, Mennonite, and other ethnic communities flourished, making Oklahoma's population wonderfully diverse. A short-lived all-female town was established in the new territory, and promoter E. P. McCabe proposed that a portion of Oklahoma be incorporated as an all-black state, resulting in the creation of dozens of all-black towns.

It comes as a surprise to some visitors that Oklahoma's geography is as diverse as its population. Its image is one of prairie and pasture, and that is partly accurate. In Osage County, where the largest remnant of tallgrass prairie left in the United States is being preserved, the landscape calls to mind the vastness of the ocean. But there are in fact a dozen distinct ecosystems in Oklahoma, more than in any other state except Texas, which also has a dozen. Oklahoma is home to the Ozark and Ouachita Mountains, which lap over the state's eastern borders, covering hills and mountains with forests of hickory, oak, and shortleaf pine. Piñon and juniper dot the mesas in the Panhandle, red-rock canyons hide out in the northwestern plains, and, in southwestern Oklahoma, the blue-and-rose granite of the 500-million-year-old Wichita Mountains forms the backdrop for herds of bison and longhorn cattle.

There isn't a single natural lake in all of Oklahoma, but there are plenty of man-made ones. Flood-control projects, most of them started after the 1930s, have created nearly 200 reservoirs. Many of Oklahoma's springs, waterfalls, lakes, and rivers can be found within the state's fifty state parks, where hundreds of miles of hiking, mountain biking, and horse trails can be found. The strong thread of populism that is part of Oklahoma's history ensures that many attractions remain within the means of every visitor. Admission is charged to only a handful of state museums; there is an entry fee to only one state park; and there are more acres of public hunting lands in Oklahoma than in any other state. Very little of Oklahoma's scenic beauty will reveal itself to the traveler who stays on the interstate. Slow down, and you'll be richly rewarded.

Getting off the beaten track in Oklahoma is a sure way to meet Oklahomans. As a group, Oklahomans are markedly friendly; they are southern in their approach to hospitality. There's a high regard for storytelling here, too, and a certain style of good-natured banter that seems to reach its apogee in small-town cafes. One caveat to travelers: Lighter styles of eating have yet to make much of an impact in all but Oklahoma's larger towns, and many little roadside groceries are more apt to stock pickled hard-boiled eggs than bottled water. Diners may sometimes just have to make do with coconut cream pie, barbecued ribs, and chicken-fried steak.

Route 66, once America's best-known highway, was bypassed two decades ago by the interstate system. There are more drivable miles (426) of Route 66 in Oklahoma than in any other state. Route 66 fans from around the globe have elevated the road to cult status, and it's a favorite in this book, too, making its nostalgic appearance in more than half of the chapters.

There's a good bit of history in this guidebook, which seems appropriate, because Oklahoma history itself is off the beaten path. It's the only state in the Union, for instance, to hold the nineteenth-century capitals of four sovereign nations within its borders (Cherokee, Chickasaw, Choctaw, and Creek). With the stories of thirty-seven Native American nations woven into its own story, Oklahoma's culture is like a bright web, with strands leading back before the time of European settlement. Excepting the Revolutionary War, the entire cast of characters from U.S. history is found here: loggers and miners, explorers and gold seekers, trappers, traders, immigrants, cowboys, crusaders, southern plantation owners, Civil War heroes, outlaws, bootleggers, oil magnates, and Native American chiefs—some of them the same people. The wide character of the state's land and people led Will Rogers to declare that "Oklahoma is the heart, it's the vital organ of our national existence."

Oklahoma Facts

The name *Oklahoma* comes from the Choctaw words *okla* (which means "people") and *humma* (which means "red"); *Oklahoma* means "Red People." The state's population is just over 3.5 million. Oklahoma is home to more Native Americans than any other state: about 275,000.

The highest point in the state (4,973 feet) is Black Mesa, in the extreme northwestern tip of the Panhandle; the lowest spot is 287 feet, east of McCurtain in the extreme southeastern tip of the state.

Oklahoma's land area is 69,919 square miles. It ranks eighteenth in size of all the states.

Oklahoma has more man-made lakes than any other state, with more than one million surface acres of water and 2,000 more miles of shoreline than the Atlantic and Gulf Coasts combined.

Oklahoma was the forty-sixth state to be admitted to the Union. The Oklahoma Constitution is the longest in the country; when it was ratified in 1907, it took eighteen hours to read.

Oklahoma's average high temperature is seventy-one degrees, but in July and August the average high temperature is a searing ninety-three degrees. Spring is warm, autumn is very mild, and summers are hot. Winter temperatures are also mild, with cold periods lasting a few days. Heavy snowfall is rare. Tornadoes aren't uncommon in Oklahoma and are most frequent in April and May. Oklahoma television stations compete with one another to supply the most extensive and reliable information about spring weather conditions, and tornado watches are issued when weather conditions are favorable to the formation of tornadoes; a tornado warning is issued when a rotating cloud has been spotted.

The toll-free number for the Oklahoma Department of Tourism is (800) 652–6552. The department operates an excellent Web site with a database of state attractions at www.travelok.com. Travel information, including a statewide calendar of museum exhibitions, festivals, and other events, appears in *Oklahoma Today,* published by the tourism department and available in bookstores across the state.

Major newspapers are *The Daily Oklahoman,* published in Oklahoma City and distributed statewide, and the *Tulsa Daily World.* Extensive entertainment listings covering central Oklahoma are found in the *Gazette,* a weekly newspaper distributed through restaurants, clubs, and bookstores throughout the Oklahoma City area.

International and domestic airlines are served by the Tulsa International Airport and the Will Rogers World Airport in Oklahoma City. Amtrak rail service has returned to Oklahoma. The Heartland Flyer makes a daily run between Oklahoma City and Fort Worth, Texas, and stops in several small towns along the route. A new trolley system provides transportation in downtown Oklahoma City, but city bus service in Oklahoma City and Tulsa is limited; renting a car is recommended, even in these major cities.

More astronauts have come from the state than any other: Gordon Cooper, Shannon Lucid, Owen Garriott, William Reed Pogue, and Thomas P. Stafford.

Famous Oklahomans include: Will Rogers, aviator Wiley Post, Hopalong Cassidy, writer Ralph Ellison, Paul Harvey, Woody Guthrie, Sequoyah, Charles "Pretty Boy" Floyd, Olympians Jim Thorpe and Shannon Miller, J. Paul Getty, Mister Ed, Johnny Bench, Mickey Mantle, Chuck Norris, Toby Keith, Garth Brooks, Reba McEntire, Vince Gill, and Ron Howard.

Oklahomans are proud of their state's symbols. While visitors may recognize Oklahoma's song/anthem, "Oklahoma," by Rodgers and Hammerstein, they might not readily know some of our more native emblems.

- **Animal (Mammal)**—American Buffalo (*Bison bison*)
- **Bird**—Scissor-Tailed Flycatcher (*Muscivora forficata*)
- **Butterfly**—Black Swallowtail (*Papilio polyxenes*)
- **Colors**—Green and White
- **Floral Emblem**—Mistletoe (*Phoradendron serotinum*)
  Adopted in 1893, this is Oklahoma's oldest symbol.
- **Grass**—Indiangrass (*Sorghastrum nutans*)
- **Insect**—Honeybee (*Apis mellifera*)
- **Rock**—Rose Rock (*Barite Rose*)
- **Tree**—Redbud (*Cercis canadensis*)
- **Wildflower**—Indian Blanket (*Gaillardia pulchella*)

Web Sites Visitors May Find Helpful

www.oklahomaparks.com

This Web site offers information on all state parks and recreational areas. Here visitors will find a description of each park, detailed directions, pictures, fees, contact numbers, and scheduled events for the area.

www.okhistory.org

Click on "Outreach" (middle of page toward the top). This site gives information on many museums and historical sites across the state. Contact numbers and background information can be found here.

www.travelok.com

This is the Web site maintained by the Oklahoma Tourism and Recreation Department. Visitors will find photos of the state, vacation ideas, information about the state's golf courses, and much more. They can also order brochures or find out about "hot deals" on this site.

Black Gold and Golden Prairies: North Central Oklahoma

In 1832 writer Washington Irving traveled to eastern Oklahoma to explore what he called the "Far West" and found "great, grassy plains, interspersed with forests and groves, and clumps of trees. Over these verdant wastes," he wrote in *A Tour on the Prairies*, "still roam the elk, the buffalo, and the wild horse in all their native freedom."

Today's travelers through north central Oklahoma will recognize Irving's expansive plains, find wooded hills and shady groves, and, on a number of preserves and ranches, still find elk, buffalo, and wild horses roaming on the prairie.

Part of the fun of north central Oklahoma lies in the contrasts between the loping, laid-back cowboy way of life, the art, architecture, and other cultural icons that oil money brought to the plains, and the gentle persistence of the Native American cultures of the Osage, Delaware, and other tribes. Some places manage to combine all three at once.

There are a few hundred miles of four-lane roads in the region, excluding Tulsa. U.S. Highway 60 runs east and west and takes travelers to the doorstep of a huge swath of prairie traversed only by county roads. Scenic Highway 11 meanders through the blackjacks and post oaks of the Osage Hills.

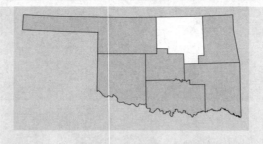

Tallgrass Prairies

Dewey, www.deweyoklahoma.com, 16 miles south of the Kansas border on U.S. Highway 75, is a town built on the Caney River—and a grudge. Jacob Bartles, namesake and founder of bigger Bartlesville to the south, moved to the area in the 1870s and built the first flour mill in Indian Territory. But when a railroad depot was built on the other side of the river, near a competitor's store, Bartles left in a huff. He loaded his entire store on logs and dragged it upriver with mules to a new site, which he named Dewey after Admiral George Dewey. It took Bartles five months—and he stayed open the entire time.

In Dewey, Bartles also built in 1899 a white Victorian structure with wide porches, the twenty-eight-room ***Dewey Hotel Museum.*** The hotel dining room was *the* fashionable place for area residents to have Sunday dinner, and the Saturday-night poker games in the hotel's third-floor cupola became legendary. The hotel, restored and filled with period furnishings, is open year round. Hours are Monday through Saturday 9:00 A.M. to 4:30 P.M. and Sunday 1:00 to 4:30 P.M. The hotel sits at the corner of Delaware and Don Tyler; turn west on Don Tyler from US 75 and travel 2 blocks. Admission is $1.00 for adults. Children are free. Call (918) 534–0215 for information.

Until it burned in 1950, Bartles's wooden store operated across the street at 721 North Delaware. Now it's the local tourist information center and site of the ***Tom Mix Museum.*** Mix, a cowboy movie star in the silent pictures era and the original "King of the Cowboys," worked briefly as Dewey's city marshal, and the third of his five wives, Miss Olive Stokes, was a local girl. Mix, who came to Oklahoma from Pennsylvania, was working at the Miller Brothers 101 Ranch when he volunteered to do some stunts for a film being shot on location there. The moviemakers took the young daredevil back to Hollywood with

---

AUTHOR'S FAVORITES IN BLACK GOLD AND GOLDEN PRAIRIES

Drummond Home	Pioneer Woman Museum
Kaw City	Price Tower Art Center
Marland Estate Mansion	Tallgrass Prairie Preserve
Osage Tribal Museum and Gift Shop	Tom Mix Museum
Pawnee Agency	Woolaroc Museum

Wild Onions and More

For over fifty years, the Bartlesville Indian Women's Club has sponsored an annual Wild Onion Dinner. Held at the Washington County Fairgrounds in Dewey, Oklahoma, members serve guests a traditional dinner of wild onions and eggs, ham, hominy, and coleslaw. Dessert, such as fry bread, blackberry and peach cobblers, and a drink are included. Diners will want to have plenty of time to browse the artwork, baskets, silver jewelry, and arts-and-crafts booths. Tickets are $7.00 for adults and $3.50 for children twelve and under and may be purchased at various locations around town. For more information, call (918) 333–1860.

them, where Mix and his horse Tony continued to do all their own stunts, jumping canyons and riding atop moving trains. Visitors can see the stunts that made him famous by watching the movies that play in the museum's little theater. They can also admire Mix's white linen suits, silver-trimmed saddles and six-shooters, and the leather shoes that Tony the Wonder Horse wore on stage so he wouldn't slip. Hours are Tuesday through Saturday 10:00 A.M. to 4:30 P.M. and Sunday 1:00 to 4:30 P.M. Admission by donation. Call the museum, (918) 534–1555, for additional information.

Downtown Dewey is small, and it's not hard to find *Linger Longer Antiques and Old Fashioned Soda Fountain,* 814 North Shawnee. It's filled with reasonably priced vintage furniture and china, and, after shopping, visitors can order old-fashioned cherry phosphates and sodas at a vintage soda fountain. Open seven days a week, Monday through Saturday 8:00 A.M. to 5:30 P.M. and Sunday 1:00 to 5:30 P.M. Be sure to visit the lunch room, *Kaffe Bona,* while you're there. It serves soups, sandwiches, salads, desserts, and gourmet coffees. For more information, call (918) 534–0610.

The food is good at the *Half Dollar Cafe* (homemade rolls, brown beans and cornbread, peach and apple pie, and cherry cobbler), but what brings diners from miles around is owner John Anthony and his extravagant line of what locals delicately call B.S. and the "Best Chicken–Fried Steak" in the state. The cafe, at 101 South Osage, on the corner of US 75, opens at 6:00 A.M. and closes at 7:30 P.M. Monday through Friday. Call (918) 534–3073.

In the beginning, Marilyn and Kenneth Tate simply wanted to reconstruct an old log cabin to use as a hidden retreat on their 1,400-acre working ranch. But Kenneth Tate enjoyed bringing the cabin back to life so much, he added a frontier barn and filled it with longhorns. Next he added a little chapel, in a grove of oak trees, with pews made of wood from each of the nine types of trees that grow on the ranch. As neighbors, and then strangers, came out to see what the Tates were building, the project kept growing. Now twenty-seven meticulously furnished buildings make up *Prairie Song, I.T.*, including a school, saloon, depot, post and land offices, trading post, covered bridge, doctor's office, general store, tin shop, bank, and cowboy line shack. (Ken Tate's latest project is a 70-foot-long blacksmith's shop.) The village is open to groups and to the general public each Monday, Wednesday, and Friday by appointment only. Tours begin at 10:00 A.M. Flexible tour hours for those from out of town. The tours take about two hours, including the time men generally spend lingering at the tool shed, says Marilyn. "Or if Ken gives the tour, plan to spend three. My husband loves to talk." For groups, the Tates bring in special entertainment, like Sky Shivers, who travels with Miss Kitty, "The Mediocre Cow Dog." Admission to the ranch is $6.00 for adults and $4.00 for children under six. Travelers in self-contained RVs can make arrangements to camp at the ranch. Prairie Song is midway between Dewey and Bartlesville to the south. Take Durham Road east for exactly 5½ miles, and you'll see a sign hanging on the fence on the south side of the road and the silhouette of a longhorn over the gate. Call (918) 534–2662 for information, or visit the Tates' Web site at www.prairiesong.net.

TOP EVENTS IN BLACK GOLD AND GOLDEN PRAIRIES

Mayfest,
downtown Tulsa, mid-May;
(918) 582–6435;
www.tulsamayfest.com

Bi-Plane Expo,
Bartlesville, early June;
(918) 622–8400;
www.biplaneexpo.com

OK Mozart International Festival,
Bartlesville, June;
(918) 336–9900;
www.okmozart.com

Juneteenth Music Festival,
Tulsa, third weekend of June;
(800) 348–9336;
www.okjazz.org

Pawnee Indian Homecoming and Powwow,
Pawnee, starts Thursday
prior to July 4 weekend;
(918) 762–3621;
www.pawneenation.org

Bluegrass and Chili Festival,
Claremore, early September;
(918) 341–2818;
www.claremore.org

Former Bob Wills Texas Playboys Reunion,
Pawhuska, second weekend
in September;
(918) 287–3316

Oktoberfest,
Marland Estate Mansion, Ponca City;
(800) 422–8340
www.marlandmansion.com

Bartlesville, 4 miles south, is a pretty town of about 35,000 spreading out from the banks of the Caney River. Oil was discovered in Bartlesville more than a century ago, and the **Nellie Johnstone No. 1,** drilled on April 15, 1897, was the first commercial oil well in Oklahoma. A reproduction of the wooden derrick stands downtown in Johnstone Park, built along the Caney River. The shady park is a wonderful place for a picnic, a stroll, or a serious walk: A 13-mile-long hiking and biking trail called "Pathfinder Parkway" connects to **Jo Allyn Lowe Park** in south Bartlesville, where there is a tranquil fishing pond and picnic tables.

While visiting Bartlesville, stop in the **Bartlesville Area History Museum.** Located at 401 South Johnstone Avenue, this museum is home to thousands of photographs, artifacts, and documents that educate visitors about the town and surrounding area. Included in the museum's collection is the first glass bottle made in Oklahoma, manufactured by the Great Western Glass Company, and bricks that paved the roads of the early community. Hours are Tuesday through Saturday 10:00 A.M. to 4:00 P.M. For more information, call (918) 338–4290.

Bartlesville's Chamber of Commerce and Convention and Visitors Bureau is located in a vintage Santa Fe Railroad depot just northwest of the downtown business district. SunFest, an arts and entertainment festival, is held the first weekend in June at Sooner Park. Go to www.visitbartlesville.com or call (918) 336–8708 for more information.

Among Bartlesville's downtown treasures is the **Price Tower Art Center,** www.pricetower.org, a nineteen-story glass-and-copper skyscraper designed by Frank Lloyd Wright, which was built in 1956 for the owner of an oil pipeline company. The building is the only skyscraper Wright ever designed for Oklahoma and attracts the architect's fans from all over the world. The American Institute of Architects selected it as one of seventeen Wright-designed buildings that best illustrate the architect's genius. Wright designed the building's interior furnishings as well. After years of renovation, the tower is again open to visitors. Guided tours are available Tuesday through Saturday from 10:00 A.M. to 5:00 P.M. and on Sunday 12:00 to 5:00 P.M. Museum admission is $4.00 for adults, $3.00 for seniors (sixty-five and above), and free for students (sixteen and under). Admission to tower is $4.00 extra. For information call (918) 336–4949. The Price Tower is at Sixth Street and Dewey, Bartlesville. On floors seven through thirteen, overnight guests can stay in the **Price Tower Inn,** www.innatpricetower.com. Twenty-one rooms are available. For inn reservations, call (877) 424–2424. Above the inn sits the **Copper Restaurant and Bar.** Designed for fine dining, this restaurant serves lunch and dinner, featuring such fare as salmon, steak, hummus wraps, and more. Don't leave without trying the Chocolate Lava Cake. Served warm with its hot fudge center, it's a treat you'll not soon forget. For restaurant hours, call (918) 336–1000.

In the 1970s city leaders commissioned architects at Taliesen, the school founded by Frank Lloyd Wright, to design the spiraling, terra-cotta **Bartlesville Community Center,** at Adams Boulevard and Cherokee Street, adjacent to the Price Tower. The acoustics in the center's auditorium so impressed a visiting conductor (Ransom Wilson, of Solisti, New York) that he arranged to bring an orchestra back every summer to play. Wilson now conducts the resident orchestra for the ten-day OK Mozart International Festival, www.okmozart.com, which brings in such heavyweight guest artists as flutist Sir James Galway. Festival organizers, fearing that out-of-town concertgoers might need a little help in amusing themselves between concerts, arrange dozens of tours, lectures, and social events, ranging from rodeos to waltzing lessons at little or no cost. The center is open 9:00 A.M. to 5:00 P.M. For information call (918) 336–2787 or visit www.bartlesvillecommunitycenter.com.

The Greek Revival mansion that was home to Phillips Petroleum founder Frank Phillips has been preserved in the style of the 1930s, the decade when Phillips and his wife, Jane, had the 1909 mansion remodeled. Phillips was a barber before he traveled to Indian Territory from Iowa and amid the crystal chandeliers and gold-and-marble bath is a barber chair where Phillips had a shave every morning. A secret room in the paneled library was a hiding place intended to foil kidnappers. The converted garage now houses an award-winning interpretive exhibit called "The Life and Times of Frank and Jane Phillips." The mansion is owned and operated by the Oklahoma State Historical Society. It is open Wednesday through Saturday from 10:00 A.M. to 5:00 P.M.

Name for New State

In the late 1800s, there was discussion about statehood for Indian Territory and a proposed name. The *Wichita Beacon* reported "Here are some of the names suggested for the new state to be made out of the Indian Territory: Indiahoma, Indianola, Dawestonia, and Sequoyah. Indianola is the sweetest of them all. Someone has objected to it on the ground that it would cause trouble in the mail by abbreviations. 'Twouldn't be half as troublesome as the two Washingtons.'" The abbreviation suggested was Ino.

However, years earlier, at the close of the Civil War, a name had already been chosen. The name was proposed in 1866 by Allen Wright, Chief of the Choctaws, when the draft of the Choctaw-Chickasaw Treaty was being written. The Commissioner of Indian Affairs asked the tribal delegates: "What name would you call your territory?" Wright, a Choctaw delegate, responded: "Oklahoma."

and on Sunday from 1:00 to 5:00 P.M. for self-guided tours. A donation of $3.00 for adults and $1.00 for children is requested. The *Frank Phillips Home* is at 1107 Southeast Cherokee Avenue, Bartlesville. Call (918) 336–2491 for information.

Another fabulous oil mansion is found on an estate a little south of town. *LaQuinta,* built on 152 acres, was the thirty-two-room Spanish Mission–style home built in 1930 by H.V. Foster, one of the first of a long list of men in the area who grew very wealthy leasing land from Indians and drilling for oil. In 1896 Foster traveled to Washington with an Osage chief and got permission from the federal government to lease the mineral rights to land owned by the Osage Nation for ten years, a lease that was renewed in 1905 for another decade. This arrangement made Foster the wealthiest man west of the Mississippi for a time, and the Osage the wealthiest tribe in the nation: A full 2 percent of all the oil found in the United States before 1945 was underneath the Osage-owned land. LaQuinta's grounds now house the Bartlesville Wesleyan College campus. The main house now holds the college library, but enough original features remain to fuel the imagination: a hidden stairway installed to thwart would-be kidnappers; seven fireplaces; terra-cotta–tiled floors; and hand-painted ceilings. LaQuinta is at 2201 Silverlake Road, Bartlesville. Visitors are welcome to tour the house during daylight hours, Monday through Friday. Free admission. Call (918) 335–6234 for information.

Can't decide between a nice glass of wine and salmon or a beer and hickory-smoked bologna? Driving to the little shopping center just east of the Caney River bridge and downtown, where two very different restaurants sit side by side, will give you a little extra time to make up your mind. *Sterling's Grille,* (918) 335–0707, decorated with dark wood and hunting prints, has a full wine list and a menu offering steaks, seafood, and prime rib. Next door, the casual *Dink's Pit Barbecue,* (918) 335–0606, smokes sausage, pork ribs, brisket, and bologna over hickory wood. The Grille is at 2905 East Frank Phillips Boulevard; Dink's is at 2929 East Frank Phillips Boulevard, Bartlesville.

The Hereford on the sign in front of *Murphy's Steak House,* (918) 336–4789, at 1625 Southwest Frank Phillips Boulevard, Bartlesville, is a pretty good indication of what diners find inside. Murphy's has served steaks and hamburgers in Bartlesville in this diner-like location since 1946. Along with steaks, specialties include the garlicky house salad dressing and the Murphy's Hot Hamburger. Consisting of a hamburger patty served on toasted bread, topped with a mountain of French fries and doused with brown gravy, it truly is a guilty pleasure.

As Frank Phillips Boulevard continues west out of town, it picks up the route of US 60 and Highway 123. Two miles west of that intersection is a little blue-and-white sign to the *Keepsake Candle Factory;* turn north and follow the road to the end, then turn back east. Tours of this little factory take only fifteen minutes. Workers turn out an impressive 850 candles a day, but their methods are refreshingly low-tech: Kitchen stoves keep the wax melted as the workers add layers of wax to molds. The factory's signature candles are made from Depression-glass molds and scented with cinnamon, bayberry, and cranberry oils. Open Monday through Saturday 10:00 A.M. to 5:00 P.M. Closed Sunday. Extended holiday hours. Visit www.keepsakecandles.com or call (918) 336–0351.

West of the Keepsake Candle Factory is the ***Red Dirt Soap Company,*** named after the red clay that curses many Oklahoma gardeners. Red Dirt soap, made from vegetable oils and scented with herbs and spices, is mixed, poured into molds, and sold on the premises. The gift shop stocks bath salts and body oils, also made in the factory, along with many other Made in Oklahoma items. Visitors can tour the factory and see soap cuttings Monday through Friday from 9:00 A.M. to 5:30 P.M. Saturday tours are from 10:00 A.M. to 5:30 P.M., but there is no factory activity at this time. Call (918) 338–2276 or visit www.reddirt soap.com for more information.

US 60 takes travelers into the Osage Hills, a rolling wooded area where the many gullies and caves once sheltered outlaws like Henry Starr, who rode with the Daltons. ***Osage Hills State Park,*** 10 miles west of Bartlesville, is tranquil these days, tending to attract birdwatchers and hikers. The park is a sanctuary for migrating waterfowl such as great blue herons and wood ducks, which travel over Oklahoma along the Central Flyway. Eastern bluebirds, bald eagles, cedar waxwings, nuthatches, and four kinds of woodpeckers have been spotted in the park's 1,199 acres.

Many structures in the park, which was started as a Boy Scout camp, were built during the 1930s by Civilian Conservation Corps workers. They quarried sandstone from the hills and built picnic shelters, lined paths and camping areas with the rocks, and constructed cabins. The eight cabins, which have been modernized but still retain their 1930s outlines, are so popular that they must be reserved a year in advance for weekends, except in the heart of winter. To check rates or reserve, call (918) 336–4141. The park has a small fishing lake, a swimming pool and tennis court, hiking and mountain biking trails, and tent and RV campsites.

Eight more miles down the road, travelers find ***Woolaroc,*** a 3,600-acre weekend retreat built by Frank Phillips, founder of Phillips Petroleum Company. Phillips, originally from Iowa, became an honorary member of the Osage tribe and an enthusiastic student of the Old West after his move to Oklahoma. He patterned his rustic log lodge after the El Tovar Hotel at the Grand Canyon and filled it with Navajo rugs, chandeliers made of antlers, and the Western art he had begun to collect. The back terrace of the lodge overlooks Clyde Lake, the setting for an outdoor concert during Bartlesville's OK Mozart Festival each June. The orchestra plays from a pavilion at the lake's edge. The concert, which is preceded by Native American dances and ends with fireworks launched from boats on the lake, is always a sellout.

Not content with just cattle, Phillips added longhorns and bison to the ranch and shipped in exotic animals from around the world, including black swans, yaks, and camels. Most couldn't tolerate Oklahoma's climate, and some of the failures have been stuffed and mounted in the lodge. Animals more suited to the climate, including bison, elk, deer, ostriches, and emu, now roam the preserve and can be spotted during the 2-mile wooded drive from the refuge gate to the lodge and museum. (Visitors must stay in their cars during the drive.)

The focal point of the ranch is the **Woolaroc Museum,** www.woolaroc .org, which holds 55,000 artifacts, including Phillips's art collection displayed in bark-covered frames. The museum started with a small building constructed behind Phillips's lodge to show off his plane, *The Woolaroc*. Phillips sponsored the plane in the 1927 Dole Race after pineapple tycoon James Dole offered $35,000 to the first pilot to fly nonstop from California to Honolulu. *The Woolaroc* won first place. The little blue-and-orange plane still hangs in a greatly expanded museum. As the museum grew, so did Phillips's aim: His goal became to illustrate the history of the development of the southwestern United States. To achieve that end, he collected Native American tools, clothing, and regalia; Colt firearms; Navajo blankets; and a world-class Western art collection, including numerous works by Charles Marion Russell, Frederic Remington, and Thomas Moran. Phillips had a very forceful personality, and museum guides like to tell the story of how, when Thomas Leigh's painting *Custer's Last Stand* arrived, he became livid because one of the horses had a purplish cast. Phillips demanded that the museum director "fix it" by adding paint to make the horse more conventionally realistic looking. The director flatly refused, and Phillips eventually calmed down and grew to appreciate the painting.

Phillips left the museum, lodge, and grounds to the public when he died. A Y-Indian Guide Center, which was built across from the museum, shows a film that tells the story of Phillips and the ranch, along with Native American legends. The trailhead for the 1½-mile Thunderbird Canyon Nature Trail is located near the Y-Indian Center. Picnic tables are near the main entrance, and visitors can buy buffalo burgers, Indian tacos, and other snacks at a concession stand near the museum.

In spring and fall, an **1840s Mountain Man Camp** is set up north of the museum, and during June, July, and August, a children's petting zoo is open in a stone barn near the museum. The preserve, lodge, and museum are open Wednesday through Sunday from Memorial Day to Labor Day from 10:00 A.M. to 5:00 P.M. and are closed on Monday, Tuesday, Thanksgiving, and Christmas during the winter. Admission is free for children eleven and under; $8.00 for visitors ages twelve through sixty-four; $6.00 for senior citizens. For more information call (918) 336–0307 or (800) WOOLAROC (966–5276).

The outlines of Osage County, the biggest county in Oklahoma, are exactly the same as the historic borders of the Osage Nation, who moved from Kansas to Indian Territory to settle on land the tribe purchased from the Cherokee Nation. The Osage were forced from Kansas by western settlement. According to tribal history, the Osage leader and warrior Wah-Ti-An-Ka persuaded the tribe to choose this prairie because the roots of the tallgrass grew so thick, no white settler would try to plow the land. "The Heavy Eyebrows," as Wah-Ti-An-Ka called the whites, "couldn't put the iron thing into the ground here." The Osage warrior's prediction was correct, and the prairie wasn't plowed. The bluestem grass, however, provided some of the best cattle grazing in the region, and huge supplies of oil lay underneath the prairie. It's a great irony that the ground the tribe chose so they could have a little peace proved to be so desirable. Oil was discovered in the county in the 1920s, giving each enrolled member of the Osage tribe an income of approximately $15,000 a year, a small fortune in those days. For a time the Osage Nation was, in the words of a local lawyer, "the Kuwait of the United States."

In **Pawhuska,** www.pawhuska.com, headquarters for the Osage Nation, nearly ninety downtown buildings are listed on the National Register of Historic Places, including City Hall, which was built in 1894 for the Osage Tribal Council, and the Constantine Theater, a restored opera house.

Cafe Society

The **Bluestem Cafe** (114 East Main, 918–287–2308) in Pawhuska is a near-perfect example of a vanishing American institution, the small-town cafe. Among the Bluestem's virtues: (1) It has big picture windows and sits right on Main Street. (2) The waitresses here are serving biscuits and gravy for breakfast before most city dwellers have even hit the snooze button on the alarm for the first time. And (3) diners aren't territorial about their conversations. Go ahead and eavesdrop—the morning coffee drinkers seem to appreciate an audience. With its rotating daily specials and wisecracking waitresses, a cafe like the Bluestem offers travelers something that franchise restaurants can't offer: the possibility of surprise.

Some of the sandstone buildings on Agency Hill, where the modern Osage Nation tribal complex is located, date back to the 1920s. Among them is the building that houses the *Osage Tribal Museum and Gift Shop,* (918) 287–5442, where Osage beadwork and treaties, along with family mementos, are on display. The museum was established in 1938 and is the oldest continually operating tribal museum in the country. A few years ago, stacks of photographs and faded newspaper clippings threatened to overtake the building. Recently, curators have made a concerted effort not only to share traditional Osage culture and the Osage view of the cosmology, but also to preserve them for younger members of the tribe. Classes in Osage language and moccasin making are held at the museum, as are classes in ribbonwork and fingerweaving, two traditional arts used to make clothing and regalia for Osage dances. Examples of fine ribbonwork and fingerweaving are on display at the museum, and some items are for sale. Museum staff can point out where the Million Dollar Elm once stood. In the 1920s an auctioneer stood under the elm (now just a stump) each year to auction off Osage oil leases. In 1924 $11 million in leases were auctioned off. The tribal complex museum is located at 600 North Grandview Avenue; it is open Monday through Saturday from 8:30 A.M. to 5:00 P.M. Free admission. Call (918) 287–5441 or visit www.osagetribe.com to learn more.

The *Osage County Historical Museum,* at 700 North Lynn, holds souvenirs of those years of oil wealth, including a rhinestone-and-feather-bedecked ball gown worn by an Osage debutante in 1929. The museum, housed in the former Santa Fe train depot, also holds dance regalia, old saddles, and historical photographs that depict one hundred years of local history. A statue outside marks the town as the site of the first Boy Scout troop in America. The troop was organized in 1909 by a missionary priest to St. Thomas Episcopal Church in Pawhuska. The museum is open Monday through Saturday from 9:00 A.M. to 5:00 P.M.; (918) 287–9119 or visit www.osagecohistorical museum.com.

Two sisters, Nancy Woodyard and Carol Maupin, run *The Inn at Woodyard Farms.* Built in 1988 by the Pawhuska High School carpentry class, this pale gray, 1880s-style farmhouse has a wide front porch. (Nancy Woodyard is a local school administrator.) Maupin worked in the Zodiac Room at Neiman Marcus in Dallas before coming back to her hometown. Before her return, *Texas Monthly* magazine named her the best biscuit maker in Texas. The inn has four bedrooms with private bathrooms and phones. Reserve your rooms early. Call (918) 287–2699 for reservations and information.

Today, the 37,000-acre *Tallgrass Prairie Preserve,* www.okprairie.com, 17 miles north of Pawhuska, has been established on what is one of the largest remaining unbroken swaths of bluestem prairie in the nation. The preserve is owned by the Nature Conservancy, which purchased the historic Barnard-Chapman cattle ranch in the 1980s after efforts to create a national park fizzled. The landscape is much the same as the one that greeted settlers heading west in the 1800s, made more authentic with the reintroduction of a herd of bison onto the prairies. Along with bison, the preserve is home to more than 79 species of mammals, 250 species of birds, including prairie chickens, bald eagles, and short-eared owls, and a sea of big bluestem grass. In some places the grass sends down roots 10 feet deep and grows as high as a man on horseback. The Nature Conservancy has strictly limited cattle grazing on the preserve, which is creating an extravagant increase in the number of wildflowers seen on the prairies.

The Nature Conservancy headquarters is in a restored bunkhouse on the ranch, and board meetings are held in the same room where ranch cowboys used to play poker. The entire bunkhouse isn't open to the public, but there's a gift shop at its east end. A literature rack holds brochures that explain the landscape from various points along the preserve's nearly 3 miles of hiking trails, which are open from dawn to dusk. A lone gravel road loops through the preserve, with 7 miles designated as the Bison Loop. The preserve, (918) 287–4803, is 17 miles north of Pawhuska on Tallgrass Prairie Drive, marked as Osage Avenue in downtown Pawhuska. The visitor's center is open from mid-March to late November from 10:00 A.M. to 4:00 P.M. The preserve itself is open from dawn to dusk.

A west entrance to the preserve is found at the intersection of Highways 11 and 18 at Shidler (chamber of commerce, 918–793–4171). A quarter mile west of Shidler is *The Bivin Garden,* www.thebivingarden.com, a cultivated contrast to the wild prairie. Mollie Bivin, a transplanted Englishwoman, has created six acres of English gardens where peacocks and exotic pheasants stroll. The gardens and a gift shop featuring plants and gifts are open to the public on weekends from 10:00 A.M. to dusk from May to September. Admission is $2.00. Call (918) 793–4011 for information.

Hominy, another little half-cowboy, half-Indian town, was established in 1874 as a subagency for the Osage Tribe and named after a chief called Ho-Mo-I, which translates to "Walks in the Night." Downtown Hominy is brightened considerably by the presence of about forty murals painted on the exteriors of buildings, which, considering the size of the town, works out to a pretty good concentration of art. Most were painted by Chá Tullis, a native who left town as Charles David and returned with a new name and a degree in jewelry making. Tullis's theme is often the juxtaposition of contemporary Native Americans with traditional symbols. One of Tullis's most striking projects is *New Territory,* a 200-foot-long series of fifteen sheet-metal sculptures, which sits on top of Sandpipe Hill, along Highway 20 west of Hominy. The sculptures are silhouettes of Native Americans with lances on horseback. Pick up a map to the murals at Chá Tullis Designs, 108 West Main, Hominy, where Tullis sells jewelry, beadwork, and other art, both his own and that of other artists; open Monday through Saturday from 10:00 A.M. to 5:00 P.M. Call (918) 885–4717 for information or visit their Web site at www.chatullis.com.

Just off Main Street is the **Drummond Home,** a 1905 Victorian home that was built by merchant Fred Drummond for his wife and five children. The house, given to the Oklahoma Historical Society in 1980 by the Drummond family, was a curator's dream because Mrs. Drummond never seemed to throw anything away: not check stubs, not her 1917 calendar, not even half-empty bottles of cuticle cream or corn plasters. The result is a pretty complete picture of early twentieth-century life on the plains, from the Pendleton blanket on a college-age son's bed to the parlor furniture, purchased in Kansas City in 1908. The house and gardens are open for tours Wednesday through Saturday from 9:00 A.M. to 5:00 P.M. and Sunday from 1:00 to 5:00 P.M.; (918) 885–2374.

When the Osage Tribe settled on the **Osage Reservation** in the 1870s, it settled in three traditional groups. The Dwellers in the Thorny Thicket settled at Pawhuska Village (farther east than where the town of Pawhuska is today), the Dwellers on the Hilltop settled at Gray Horse, and the Dwellers in the Upland Forest settled in Hominy. The villages were centers for ceremonial dances, performed in circular community buildings called "roundhouses."

The only remaining **Osage Roundhouse** in the county is one built in 1919, southeast of the junction of Highways 99 and 20 east of Hominy. Osage from all over the nation come home for *I-Ion-shka* dances held in June, both in the

Drummond Home, Hominy

roundhouse and under a brush arbor built outside. For four days men and women perform these traditional Osage dances to the beat of a drum. Non–tribal members are welcome, but tribal members emphasize that the dances are not intended as tourist fare. No photographs are allowed. For more information about the reservation or roundhouse, contact the White Hair Memorial Osage Resource Center at (918) 538–2417 or by e-mail at whitehair@ok-history.mus .ok.us; open Monday through Friday from 8:00 A.M.to 5:00 P.M.

Land of the Ponca

Ponca City's well-mannered downtown, filled with Art Deco–era architecture and public gardens, conceals a boisterous beginning. Ponca City, www.ponca city.com, was settled during the opening of the Cherokee Outlet in 1893, which was essentially a horse race: Would-be settlers lined up at the boundary lines and stampeded in to stake their claims.

The land opening was the biggest, rowdiest—and the last—land run in Oklahoma. (After the dust from 100,000 settlers competing for 50,000 allot-ments settled, the government figured maybe a horse race wasn't the best method of apportioning homesteads.)

Ponca City was a typical pioneer community until after statehood, when oil was discovered under Ponca land. The discovery didn't help the tribe as a whole, because tribal members already had been allotted homesteads, and, unlike the Osage, didn't hold the mineral rights collectively. To learn more about Ponca City, call (866) 763–8092 or visit www.poncacitytourism.com.

One person who did understand the fine print was E.W. Marland. A Pennsylvania-born lawyer who came to Oklahoma in 1908 and drilled his first well in 1911, Marland's fortune peaked in the 1920s at $30 million. The oil man built his first showplace home on Ponca City's main thoroughfare, a structure that is now the **Marland Grand Home,** 1000 East Grand. Among the museum's exhibits is the best existing collection of memorabilia about the fabled 101 Ranch (pronounced "Hundred and One," not "One-oh-One"), which at one time covered 101,000 acres in the Cherokee Outlet. The ranch was started in the 1870s, and its owners, Colonel George W. Miller and his sons, farmed, raised cattle, and drilled for gas and oil. They gained fame, however, as the originators of the Miller Brothers 101 Ranch Wild West Show. The show toured the coun-try from the 1880s to the 1930s and counted among its former employees Will Rogers, Tom Mix, and Bill Pickett, a black cowboy who invented bulldogging. (Bulldogging is a rodeo event in which cowboys wrestle steers to the ground, then subdue them by biting the steer's upper lip, a trick Pickett picked up from watching a bulldog trained to work cattle.) In addition to the 101 exhibits, the home holds an Indian museum, exhibits of the local Daughters of the American Revolution, and sculptor Bryant Baker's studio, purchased at an auction a few decades ago. The museum is open Tuesday through Saturday from 10:00 A.M. to 5:00 P.M.; closed Sunday and Monday. Admission is $3.00. Call (580) 767–0427 for information or visit www.marlandgrandhome.com.

Marland and Baker were responsible for one of Ponca City's defining landmarks, the *Pioneer Woman Statue.* In 1926 Marland reportedly looked around the room at a party and declared, "The Indian is not the vanishing American, it's the pioneer woman." Marland asked twelve leading sculptors to each submit a bronze of an archetypal pioneer woman. The winning entry chosen by a majority vote by three-quarters of a million Americans during a national tour—and (probably most importantly) by Marland—was one by sculptor Bryant Baker. The sculpture depicted a determined-looking woman with a Bible tucked under her arm, wearing a bonnet and leading a little boy. Critics were more impressed with some of the other models (which are now on display at Woolaroc, purchased by Frank Phillips when Marland was in need of cash) and sniffed that the winning sculpture was merely "a pretty lady leading a little boy in his Eton suit." The 17-foot-high bronze statue now stands on Monument Avenue, near the intersection of U.S. Highway 77 and Lake Road (turn north on US 77 from US 60) in Ponca City.

Adjacent to the statue is the *Pioneer Woman Museum,* www.pioneer womanmuseum.com, which includes exhibits about how women lived on the Oklahoma prairie in the nineteenth century, as well as exhibits about pioneering female Oklahomans like astronaut Shannon Lucid. Admission is $3.00 for

The Saga of Standing Bear

It would be hard to find a North American tribe more ill-treated than the Poncas were in the nineteenth century. In 1865 the tribe ceded part of its lands in Nebraska to the federal government but was to retain 96,000 acres. Three years later, the government gave that same land to the Sioux, who soon overran the Ponca. In 1876 Congress passed an act relocating the tribe to Indian Territory, a piece of legislation the tribe knew nothing about until a federal agent arrived to oversee their move south. Some of the tribe refused to leave; the ones who did eventually moved to Oklahoma. Many tribal members died during the first year, including the son of Chief Standing Bear. Today a 22-foot-high statue of Standing Bear has been erected at the intersection of US 60 and 77. The statue is in *Standing Bear Native American Memorial Park,* where plaques tell Standing Bear's story and pay tribute to eight traditional Poncan clans. Free admission. Call (580) 762–1514 for more information.

adults, $2.50 for seniors (sixty-five and above), $1.00 for students (6–18), and free for children under six. The museum is open Tuesday through Saturday from 9:00 A.M. to 5:00 P.M. and Sunday from 1:00 to 5:00 P.M. It is located at 701 Monument Road; (580) 765–6108.

Marland's biggest legacy, however, is 8 blocks north, at 901 Monument Road. The **Marland Estate Mansion,** www.marlandmansion.com, is an Italian Renaissance–style villa, modeled after the Davanzati Palace in Florence. Marland imported oak from the forest of King George V in England, Waterford chandeliers from Ireland, and a wooden throne from Germany, and brought craftsmen from Italy to paint gold leaf on the ballroom ceiling of the fifty-five-room house. He built polo grounds, a golf course, and an artist's studio. He

oklahoma
atlantis

East of Ponca City, visitors will find **Kaw Lake.** The lake is over 25 miles long and 90 feet deep in areas. Campsites are abundant. On its western side sits **Kaw City,** the new township. In 1976, the old township went underwater to make way for the lake. Kaw is a little town with big heart. The Kaw City Museum and Kanza Museum celebrate their unique heritage and Tom's Old Town Café is the place to find awesome hamburgers and curly fries. In January, the town welcomes visitors to experience an Eagle Watch and in August, the Kaw Pow Wow. For more information call (580) 762–9494 or visit www.kawlake.com.

and his family moved into the house in the late 1920s. Marland and his wife, Mary Virginia Collins, had adopted Mrs. Marland's niece, Lydie, and nephew, George, when they were children. In 1926 Mrs. Marland died. Two years later Marland shocked the conservative town by annulling Lydie's adoption and marrying her.

By the early 1930s Marland had lost most of his fortune on Wall Street. The Marlands moved into the artist's studio and opened the house only for parties. Marland still was influential enough to be elected to Congress in the mid-1930s and served a term as governor of Oklahoma. He returned to Ponca City in 1939 but never was able to regain his financial footing. He died in 1941 after selling the villa to an order of Carmelite nuns.

Lydie stayed on in Ponca City but was shunned by polite society. She disappeared from Ponca City for twenty-two years, and when she returned in the 1970s, she was destitute. She kept very much to herself but did write what amounted to a love letter to the local newspaper when townspeople were trying to pass a sales tax to buy the mansion and restore it: "I would like to say this much," she wrote. "To me it is a place of rare beauty and artistic integrity. A structure that is an expression from mind into substance of the quality, the strength, and the heart of a man."

stillentertaining

In 1927 when the **Poncan Theatre** opened, she was unique. Catering to both live entertainment and films, she gave the people of Ponca City and visitors alike somewhere to be seen and entertained. The building was designed by the Boller Brothers, who were known across Middle America for atmospheric theaters. Vaudeville was at its peak and entertainers like Bo Jangles, Sally Rand, and Ethel Barrymore, and other vaudevillians performed on the theater's stage. Comedians, singers, hoofers, jugglers, animal acts, and more brought their talent to the area. When Al Jolson made film history with the first talkie that year, the Poncan was converted to sound and many more years of entertainment followed.

Through the years, the Poncan has had its ups and downs. The theater needed refurbishing and on September 17, 1994, Ponca Citians were proud to celebrate its complete restoration. The Poncan Theater is listed on the National Register of Historic Places and is home to the Arts and Humanities Council, Ponca Playhouse, Ponca Area Chamber Orchestra, and the Poncan Theatre Company Presentations. The Poncan is a not-for-profit business, so all proceeds are put back into operation costs.

The theater is located at First and Grand Streets in Ponca City. Call (580) 765–0943 or visit www.poncan theatre.org for more information.

After Ponca Citians bought the house in 1975, Lydie moved back into the studio. Some said she stood on the lawn and danced during the parties that were once again held in the house, though others dismissed the reports as sentimental imaginings. After her death in 1987, a statue of Lydie commissioned by Marland was found smashed and buried behind a barn. The statue has been put back together and is on display in the mansion's entrance.

There are fifty-five rooms plus outbuildings included on the estate. The **Marland Oil Museum** is included, as is the John Duncan Forsyth Room and the Marland Family Exhibit. Open daily from 10:00 A.M. to 5:00 P.M. and Sunday from 1:00 to 5:00 P.M. Guided tours are given on weekdays at 1:30 P.M. and weekends at 1:30 and 3:00 P.M. Visit www.marlandmansion.com or call (800) 422–8340 for more information. Admission is $7.00 for adults, $5.00 for senior citizens (sixty-five and above), $5.00 for students age twelve to seventeen, and $4.00 for students six to eleven.

The **Rose Stone Inn** was once a downtown savings and loan; now each of its twenty-five rooms has been decorated in honor of an Oklahoman. Rooms have private baths, and guests have access to an exercise room and video library. Rates are $49 to $99 a night. A continental breakfast is served. Call (580) 765–5699 or go online to www.poncacitylodging.com.

Leave your worries behind and come spend some time at the **Hidden Garden Bed and Breakfast,** also in Ponca City. A quiet three-room Frank-

Lloyd-Wrightian suite offers a bedroom filled with antiques and unique art. Enjoy your private bath with Amazon shower, then relax in the garden featuring annual and perennial plants, an arbor, and chimera just steps away. In the morning, start your day with a breakfast of homemade quiche, fresh fruits, or select homemade pastries, which can be served in the dining room or delivered to your door. Reservations are required as this B&B is in high demand. Call and talk to Shirley at (580) 765–9922 or visit www.poncacitylodging.com.

On hot summer days, travelers follow Lake Road from its intersection with US 77 to Kygar Road and drive north for about 150 yards, then turn east onto L. A. Cann Drive. At the end of the road is ***Lew Wentz Pool***, built for Ponca City in the 1920s by oilman Lew Wentz and named one of the top five pools in the country. The pool caused quite a splash when it opened with its elaborate diving towers and wide stone-and-marble seats rising on one side, and it's still considered the prettiest swimming pool in Oklahoma. The pool opens at 1:00 P.M. and closes at 7:00 P.M. Tuesday through Sunday from Memorial Day through Labor Day. Adults are charged $2.00; children under twelve are charged $1.00. Call (580) 767–0432 for information.

The Wilder West

First a trading post on Bear Creek, the ***Pawnee Agency*** was established in 1876 when the tribe was removed to Indian Territory from Nebraska. The original stone Pawnee Agency, standing ½ mile east of the town of Pawnee, is a cluster of sandstone buildings built on wooded grounds. A man named Gordon Lillie, who came to teach at the government school, transformed the town (and himself) by creating ***Pawnee Bill's Wild West Circus***. Lillie hired the local Pawnee to perform in the show, which traveled the country from the 1880s to 1918, staging depictions of the West that were, according to his own advertisements, "Surpassing All Truthfulness." Lillie opened a trading post where he sold Pawnee beadwork and souvenirs and built a ranch on Blue Hawk Peak, just west of town. The ranch, now owned by the state, is operated as a museum and holds costumes, programs, and other artifacts from the Wild West show, including a billboard advertising the show, found in 1980 when an old store a county away was being remodeled. Also open to the public is the rambling house built by Lillie and his wife, Mae, a crack shot who appeared in the circus. Constructed of stone with wide porches, the house is furnished as you might expect from a man of means who traveled the world with a Western circus; stuffed alligators are lit by imported chandeliers. A herd of about fifty bison graze the ranch.

For a little town of scarcely more than 2,000 people, Pawnee offers tons of entertainment. During the first weekend in May, the town hosts the Oklahoma Steam Threshing and Gas Engine Show at **Steam Engine Park** near the fairgrounds, north of town on Highway 18. Exhibitors and visitors come from all over the United States to celebrate steam power. (The gas engines are used mainly to run the antique cars that are part of the show.) Pawnee boasts the second largest steam turbine in the country—last used to power up the generators at a local hospital—and it supplies the energy to run a sawmill. There are demonstrations of baling and threshing, as well as corn grinding, and visitors can buy stone-ground cornmeal. A parade of steam-powered vehicles and antique cars is held daily.

On the last three Saturdays in June, a reenactment of Pawnee Bill's historic Wild West show is performed at **Pawnee Bill Buffalo Ranch.** Townspeople have put the show together with the help of the Oklahoma Historical Society, resurrecting old scripts and working to make it as close to the original as possible. Actors stage wagon-train attacks, gunfights, and even the mock hanging of horse thieves; a barbecue dinner is available for an extra charge. Admission to the museum is free; admission to the Wild West show is $12.00 for adults, $6.00 for ages seven to twelve, and free for children six and under. The museum, home, and buffalo ranch are open year-round. Closed Monday and Tuesday. Open Wednesday through Saturday 10:00 A.M. to 5:00 P.M. and Sunday 1:00 to 4:00 P.M. The last tour starts forty-five minutes before closing. For information call (918) 762–2513.

Since townspeople began to participate as actors in the Wild West show, it seems they never miss a chance to put on their chaps, haul out the buggies, and play cowboy. Their once three-day rodeo now spans ten days and begins with a cattle-drive reenactment. Fourth of July festivities start on horseback, too, with a Cowboy Ride-In Breakfast at the Pawnee Bill Buffalo Ranch. For a full schedule of events, contact the Pawnee Chamber of Commerce, www.cityofpawnee.com, at 608 West Harrison, Pawnee 74058; or call (918) 762–2108.

Every Fourth of July, tribal members return from all over the country to take part in the **Pawnee Homecoming Powwow.** The powwow began fifty years ago as a way to honor the returning veterans of World War II and is now the largest free powwow in the United States. Native American families set up camp at the fairgrounds in RVs, tents, and tepees, and on the first or second day, the local Pawnee Tribe distributes rations of beef, coffee, and flour to the campers. Dances are scheduled nightly from 8:00 to 11:00 P.M., but the dancing usually doesn't end until much later. In addition to the dances, the tribe holds a softball tournament in honor of major-league baseball player Moses Yellowhorse. Non–Native American visitors are welcome at the tournament and powwow. For more information visit www.pawneenation.org or call (918) 762–3621.

Lake Pawnee Park, a city-owned recreation area north of the city, is wooded and peaceful and offers RV campsites, with electricity and water, for $11.00, or tent camping sites for only $6.00 a night. There's a nine-hole golf course nearby, a swimming beach and two boat docks, and the native stone *Pawnee Bathhouse,* built in 1939 by Works Progress Administration stonemasons. The bathhouse had fallen into disuse over the last few decades; today the Pawnee Tribe, a local branch of the state conservation office, and the local chamber of commerce have restored the water gardens and the old bathhouse to something residents are proud to use. For more information, call (918) 762–2110.

Downtown Pawnee is centered around a courthouse square; Harrison Street on the south side is the main drag. At 502 Harrison, the world's largest Dick Tracy cartoon is painted on the side of a building; Dick Tracy creator Chester Gould was from Pawnee.

For a great time, good eats, and some little white lies, check out *Honest John Fibber's.* Serving breakfast, lunch, and dinner, the cooks make their own hash browns, the "best steaks in the state," and homemade desserts like pecan pie, coconut cream pie, and Milky Way Cake, to name a few. Friday night you can enjoy live music, and everyday you can experience tall tales spread throughout the restaurant. Be sure to check out Pandora's Box and bring a friend to help spread the word about the place where "they fib about everything". . . except the food. The restaurant is located at 620 Harrison, Pawnee. Open Monday through Thursday 7:00 A.M. to 2:00 P.M. and Friday and Saturday 7:00 A.M. to 8:00 P.M. Closed Sunday. Call (918) 762–2414.

At one time, Indian Territory was truly the Wild West—a haven for outlaws because the nearest federal judges were posted in Arkansas and Kansas. Travelers can visit the hideout of the notorious Dalton Gang in the caves nestled in the rocky bluffs along the Cimarron River. *Horsethief Canyon,* with views in three directions, feels like a sandstone sky box—all the better to keep an eye out for the marshal. From Perkins, at the intersection of U.S. Highway 177 and Highway 33, drive 1 mile south and 8 miles west. (There's a sign on the highway and signs marking each of the turns.) A hiking trail leads visitors to the canyon and down to the river; primitive camping sites and a picnic pavilion are available. The park is open every weekend from April to October, 9:00 A.M. until sunset. Weekdays and off-season are by appointment; (405) 547–5757.

In *Perkins,* www.cityofperkins.net, stop by the *Prairie's Edge.* Established in an early twentieth-century building on Main Street, the restaurant now serves homemade cinnamon rolls, cobblers, and other country fare from the city's sales barn. Call (405) 547–8383.

Stay on Highway 33, take US 177 north to **Stillwater,** www.visitstill water.org. Located at 405 West Hall of Fame, next to Gallagher-Iba Arena, wrestling fans will not want to miss the **National Wrestling Hall of Fame and Museum.** Besides giving a historical view of the sport, this museum show-cases the stars of wrestling today. The museum is open Monday through Fri-day 9:00 A.M. to 4:00 P.M. Admission is $5.00 for adults and $2.00 for children. For more information visit their Web site at www.wrestlinghalloffame.org or call (405) 377–5243.

stillchugging

Tracing its origins back to 1907 when Oklahoma became a state, the Tulsa–Sapulpa Union Railway is one of the oldest operating shortline railroads in the state. In its early years, the company operated an interurban streetcar line using trolley cars around Sapulpa. Today visitors can learn more about the railroad and the trolley cars by visiting the **Sapulpa Trolley and Rail Museum** located at 701 East Dewey. The museum is open year-round Monday through Saturday 8:00 A.M. to 5:00 P.M. For more information visit www.sapulpatrolley.org or call (918) 224–1515.

The **Dancing Deer Lodge** is the place to rest after attending an Oklahoma State University sporting event in Stillwa-ter. The lodge has been open since 1998, and Carlene Slater and Doug Groesbeck, the owners, show visitors hospitality the way it's meant to be experienced. All rooms have private baths and range in price from $65 to $155. Breakfast is deliv-ered every morning in a basket. Lodge quiche or southwest enchiladas are only a few delicacies you may be served. Visit www.dancingdeerlodge.com or call (800) 675–5684 to make your reservations. From Stillwater, travel east on Highway 51 for 6 miles. There's a sign to the **Washington Irving Trail Museum** on Mehan Road. It's 3 miles south to the museum. The museum is on a site near the route traveled in 1824 by writer Washington Irving, accompanied by dra-goons from Fort Gibson, a French trap-per as a guide, and a Swiss count. Along with exhibits about that expedition, the museum offers assorted stories and artifacts about such topics as outlaws and gun battles in Indian Territory; the Battle of Round Mountain, the first Civil War battle fought in Indian Territory; and the Indian Territory recruits into Teddy Roosevelt's Rough Riders. Museum officials can give interested parties directions to Ingalls, a ghost town where the members of the Doolin and Dalton gangs had a gun battle with federal marshals. The museum is open Wednesday through Saturday from 10:00 A.M. to 5:00 P.M. and on Sunday from 1:00 to 5:00 P.M. Free admission. For information call (405) 624–9130.

Highway 33 roughly parallels the track of the Cimarron River and takes travelers east, to **Sapulpa,** www.sapulpachamber.com. Many of Sapulpa's downtown buildings date from 1898 to 1922, and antiques and gift shops along Main Street make window-shopping a treat. Six old advertisements painted on the sides of brick buildings have been restored to their original, colorful glory; local elementary-school students raised the funds for the project.

Then if you are looking to learn more about "The Crossroads of America," visit the **Sapulpa Historical Society Museum.** Located in a three-story brick building at 100 East Lee, this museum has displays of the area's local history, such as the railroad, oil, American Indians, and the glass and pottery industries. The museum also offers assistance for those researching their family genealogy, and is open Monday through Thursday from 10:00 A.M. to 3:00 P.M. Admission is free. Call (918) 224–4871.

Travel east along Route 66 to the outskirts of Sapulpa and **Frankoma Pottery.** The Frank family has been mining Oklahoma clay from Sugar Loaf Mountain since the 1930s and creating pottery with a decidedly Western flavor. The pottery—particularly pieces made before a fire destroyed some of the molds a few decades ago—was a hot collectible even before Martha Stewart gave it the nod in a magazine spread. Today, Chef Paula Deen uses Frankoma's Mountain Air Dinnerware and Bakeware for her Food Network television program, *Paula's Home Cooking.* Factory tours are conducted Monday through Friday from 10:00 A.M. to 2:00 P.M. The tours last about twenty minutes. There is a gift shop with shelves filled with seconds, where shoppers can find real bargains. Note to collectors: Some of the antiques stores downtown specialize in Frankoma pottery. The factory is at 9549 Frankoma Road, Sapulpa. Call (800) 331–3650 or visit www.frankoma.com.

thegoldendriller

Tulsa likes to think of itself as a discriminating town, and some residents are a little embarrassed about the no-holds-barred boosterism of the *Golden Driller,* a statue found in front of the Tulsa Exposition Center on Twenty-first Street, just west of South Yale Avenue. But there's no ignoring him. The statue, a 76-foot-high helmeted oil driller, towers over an oil derrick and wears a 48-foot-long belt with a buckle emblazoned with the word TULSA. His shoe size is a 393-DDD and his helmet is a size 112. The big guy was put on the spot to celebrate the 1966 International Petroleum Exposition.

Tulsey Town

Continue east on Route 66 to *Tulsa,* Oklahoma's second-largest city. The town began as Tulsey Town, a little Creek community built along the banks of the Arkansas River. Travelers can actually see Tulsa's roots with a visit to the *Creek Council Oak,* at Eighteenth and South Cheyenne. From 1836 to 1898, the tree was the traditional meeting place for the heads of the Creek families that formed the Tallassee Town. (Tallassee should really be spelled Tullahasee, which is made up of two Creek words: *Tulla* means "town" and *hassee* means "old." The name got shortened to Tulsey and then ultimately Tulsa.) The town's chief called meetings by sending messengers out with bundles of sticks to give to the heads of all the families that made up the council. Each day, the head family member took a stick from his bundle and broke it, counting down the days until the meeting. When only one stick was left, he took it to the chief for roll call at the meeting.

Tulsey Town remained a little Creek crossroads until after the turn of the twentieth century, when the Mid-Continent oil field was discovered nearby. Tulsa, which became known as "The Oil Capital of the World," was at its wealthiest when the popularity of Art Deco architecture was at its peak; as a result, only New York City and Miami have better collections of Art Deco buildings. Tulsa's chamber of commerce, www.visittulsa.com or (800) 558–3311, 616 South Boston

Boston Avenue Methodist
Church, Tulsa

Avenue, distributes "An Art Deco Walking Tour" brochure that directs visitors to such downtown jewels as the *Philcade Building,* 511 South Boston Avenue, with a marbled, gilded lobby built in the shape of a T for Tulsa and filled with zigzag motifs. Six blocks south is the soaring *Boston Avenue Methodist Church,* 1301 South Boston Avenue, built with a 255-foot pleated tower embellished with terra-cotta sculptures. The church is open Monday through Friday from 9:00 A.M. to 5:00 P.M. and Sunday morning for church services. Call (918) 583–5181 or go to www.bostonavenue .org for information.

The old zigzag-style *Warehouse Market Building,* at 401 East Eleventh, boasts a brilliantly hued tower and has a history to match. It served Tulsa as a farmers' market, was home to a blues club, and currently houses *Lyon's Indian Store,* www.lyonsindianstore.com. Ray Lyon moved to Oklahoma in the 1930s to work for Pawnee Bill at his trading post in Pawnee, and his son Frank began a store in Tulsa by the downtown train station. The Warehouse Market location is the store's third in Tulsa. The store sells contemporary Native American beadwork and prints; many of the items displayed date back to the Pawnee Bill days and are not for sale. The store has had many famous customers over the years, including Johnny Cash and Cher. Hours are Monday through Friday 10:00 A.M. to 6:00 P.M. and Saturday, 10:00 A.M. to 5:00 P.M. Call (918) 582–6372.

Another community flourished in Tulsa during the oil-boom years: *Greenwood.* The largest and wealthiest of Oklahoma's black communities, the neighborhood was a hotbed of jazz and blues during the 1920s. William "Count" Basie was discovered playing at a club in Greenwood and recruited by the Oklahoma City Blue Devils, a band that included jazz legends Little Jimmy Rushing, fiddler Claude Williams, and saxophonist Lester Young, all from Oklahoma.

On May 30, 1921, a riot began when a white female elevator operator accused a black passenger of attempted rape. A mob of 1,500 to 2,000 armed whites marched on Greenwood, looting, burning buildings, and opening fire on Greenwood residents. Thirty-six people were reported killed before the National Guard quelled the mob. The riot was designated as the worst race riot in U.S. history.

Greenwood was one of the most prosperous black communities in the nation and earned the nickname "America's Black Wall Street" in the 1930s and 1940s. As time passed, however, the neighborhood began to decline; today two blocks are restored as the *Greenwood Historical District.* At 322 North Greenwood is the *Greenwood Cultural Center and Mabel B. Little Heritage House and Museum,* www.greenwoodculturalcenter.com or (918) 596–1020, where a 1915 house burned during the Greenwood riot but was

reachingforthe stars

Interested in air flight? Head on down to the *Tulsa Air and Space Museum.* Located at 3624 North Seventy-fourth East Avenue, this museum features full-size aircraft, exhibits that present the history of air travel in and around Tulsa, and interactive exhibits like the F-16 Wind Tunnel. The ESky Theater Planetarium is also housed here. For more information, visit www.tulsaairandspacemuseum.com or call (918) 834–9900. Hours are Tuesday through Saturday 10:00 A.M. to 5:00 P.M. and Sunday 1:00 to 5:00 P.M. Closed Monday.

rebuilt exactly as it was, only in fireproof brick. The museum holds photographs and memorabilia about Greenwood and the riot. Behind the museum is the **Oklahoma Jazz Hall of Fame,** featuring blues and jazz memorabilia, along with portraits of musicians inducted into the hall since its inception in 1989; they include Jay Mc-Shann, Lowell Fulsom, and Charlie Christian. The museum and hall of fame are open Monday through Friday 9:00 A.M. to 5:00 P.M. and Saturday 10:00 A.M. to 1:00 P.M. (918) 582–1001.

Music festivals are held throughout the year. Visit www.okjazz.org and click on Calendar of Events. Juneteenth on Greenwood is celebrated the third weekend in June, marking the celebration of the day that word reached the area about the Emancipation Proclamation. (Though the proclamation was signed on January 1, 1863, the news took six months to reach rural communities.) Call (800) 348–9336 for information.

A shrine to another musical tradition sits a few short blocks away. Between 1934 and 1943, Bob Wills and the Texas Playboys performed a live radio show at noon each day from **Cain's Ballroom,** 423 West Main, and held dances on Friday and Saturday nights. The ballroom's curly-maple dance floor is mounted on springs from 1926 Dodge pickup trucks. The original bar and ticket booth are still in place, and huge black-and-white portraits of Gene Autry, Ernest Tubb, Bob Wills, and Bob's little brother Johnnie Lee line the walls. Larry Schaeffer, the ballroom's owner, a baby boomer who grew up idolizing the Playboys' steel-guitar player, books diverse acts into the old ballroom, from alternative rock to country. Schaeffer welcomes visitors to the old ballroom, pulling out a pair of Wills's Nicoma boots and a white Stetson for loyal fans. He also holds the Bob Wills Birthday Party and Festival the first weekend in March, gathering together as many of Wills's original Playboys as he can. Call (918) 584–2306 or visit www.cainsballroom.com for information.

funwithfives

Every year, the Tulsa Artists' Coalition holds their 5 x 5 event. Artists are invited to submit a piece of art on a 5" x 5" canvas. These requested art pieces are received and hung in the gallery. Pieces are sold for $55. The event is held May 5 and the gallery opens at 5:55 P.M. Public admission is $5.00. For more information, visit www.tacgallery.org or call (918) 592–0041.

The **Brady Arts District** is a growing arts community just west of downtown, with galleries centered around Brady and Main. The **Tulsa Artists' Coalition Gallery,** 9 East Brady, www.tacgallery.org, is run by a local artists' group and hosts about a dozen shows of local and regional work every year. Other galleries in the area include **Living Arts,** 19 East Brady; **Ceramics Gallery and Studio,** 23 East Brady; and **Mother Tongue,** 212 West Main. Artists meet at the friendly *Caz's Bar,* a cute little bar that's also the hangout of Sam, the neighborhood "art dog," or at *The Bower* for a pint of Guinness and a sandwich. Galleries have limited hours: Tuesday through Friday 11:00 A.M. to 2:00 P.M. and Thursday through Saturday 6:00 to 9:00 P.M. For a list of current shows, call the Artists' Coalition at (918) 592–0041.

Hamburger aficionados should make a point to stop in the Brookside area at *Weber's Superior Root Beer,* 3817 South Peoria. Weber's makes the bold claim of having invented the hamburger, flying in the face of Yankee tradition, which holds that the hamburger was first served in 1900 in a Yale University lunchroom. Harold and Rick Bilby, great-grandsons of Oscar Weber Bilby, claim their ancestors beat other contenders by a few years: Family records show that Oscar was grilling hamburgers and serving them on Harold and Rick's Grandmother Fanny's homemade yeast buns at Fourth of July gatherings in Indian Territory as early as 1891. Oscar opened a hamburger stand in Tulsa in 1933, serving burgers and their own root beer, made from fourteen natural root juices. A black-and-orange wooden shack that held the original Weber's has been replaced by a modern shopping center, but the old orange-and-black sign still hangs outside. More important, Oscar's century-old grill is still in use inside, where his great-grandsons cook as many as 400 hamburgers a day. Along with hamburgers, Weber's sells hand-cut French fries, onion rings, and root beer in frosted mugs or to take home by the liter. Open Monday through Saturday 11:00 A.M. to 8:00 P.M. Call (918) 742–1082 or visit www.webersoftulsa.com for information. Web site has coupons.

The *Metro Diner,* a neon-and-chrome-filled reproduction of a 1950s-era diner, makes the most of its Route 66 location. The restaurant serves milk shakes, burgers, french fries and gravy, blue-plate specials, and cream pies. The diner is at 3001 East Eleventh Street; (918) 592–2616.

Places to Stay in Black Gold and Golden Prairies

BARTLESVILLE

Hampton Inn
130 Southeast Washington
Boulevard
(918) 333–4051

Hotel Phillips
821 South Johnstone
(918) 336–5600

Weston Inn Best Western
222 Southeast Washington
Boulevard
(918) 335–7755

PAWHUSKA

**Inn at Woodyard Farms
Bed and Breakfast**
3 miles north on Lynn
(918) 287–2699

PAWNEE

Pecan Grove Motel
611 Fourth Street
(918) 762–3061

PONCA CITY

Fairfield Inn
3405 North Fourteenth
Street
(800) 228–2800

**Hidden Garden Bed
and Breakfast**
719 North Fourteenth Street
(580) 765–9922

FOR MORE INFORMATION

Bartlesville Area Convention and Visitors Bureau
201 Southwest Keeler
Bartlesville 74005
(918) 336–8708
www.bartlesville.com

Pawnee Chamber of Commerce
608 Harrison
Pawnee 74068
(918) 762–2110
www.cityofpawnee.com

Ponca City Visitor Center
Tenth and Grand
Box 1450
Ponca City 74602
(580) 763–8092
www.poncacitytourism.com

Tulsa Convention and Visitors Bureau
2 West Second Street
Tulsa 74103
(918) 585–1201
www.visittulsa.com

Holiday Inn
2215 North Fourteenth Street
(800) 465–4329

Rose Stone Inn
120 South Third Street
(800) 763–9922

TULSA

Best Western Trade Winds
3141 East Skelly Drive
(918) 749–5561

Crowne Plaza Hotel
100 East Second
(918) 582–9000

Doubletree Hotel
616 West Seventh Street
(918) 587–8000

La Quinta
35 North Sheridan
(918) 836–3931

McBirney Mansion
1414 South Galveston
(918) 585–3234

Ramada Inn Tulsa
3175 East Fifty-first Street
(918) 743–9811

Tulsa Fairfield Inn
9020 East Seventy-first Street
(918) 252–7754

Tulsa Marriott Southern Hills
1902 East Seventy-first Street
(918) 493–7000

Places to Eat in Black Gold and Golden Prairies

BARTLESVILLE

Dink's Pit Barbecue
2929 East Frank Phillips Boulevard
(918) 335–0606

Grill 66
821 South Johnstone
(918) 337–6666

ALSO WORTH SEEING

Gilcrease Museum of Art,
Tulsa, www.gilcrease.org

Jenks Antiques District,
downtown Jenks, www.jenks.com

Philbrook Museum of Art,
Tulsa, www.philbrook.org

Murphy's Steak House
1625 Southwest Frank
Phillips Boulevard
(918) 336–4789

Sterling's Grille
2905 East Frank Phillips
Boulevard
(918) 335–0707

Weeze's
328 South Dewey
(918) 337–0881

PAWHUSKA

Bad Brad's Bar-B-Q
1215 West Main
(918) 287–1212

Bluestem Restaurant
114 East Main
(918) 287–2308

Buffalo Jo's Dairyland
714 West Main
(918) 287–2356

PAWNEE

Honest John Fibber's
620 Harrison Street
(918) 762–2414

PONCA CITY

**Chick and Millie's Blue
Moon BBQ**
1418 East South Avenue
(580) 762–2425

Head Country BBQ
1217 East Prospect
(580) 767–8304

TULSA

Atlantic Sea Grill
8321 East Sixty-first Street
(918) 252–7966

Billy Sims BBQ
5213 South Sheridan Road
(918) 270–1978

**Blue Dome Diner and
Route 66 Mother
Roadhouse**
313 East Second
(918) 382–7866

Bourbon Street Cafe
1542 East Fifteenth Street
(918) 583–5555

Carrabba's Italian Grill
4848 South Yale
(918) 481–9500

Chimi's (Mexican)
1304 East Fifteenth Street
(918) 587–4411

Elephant Run
3141 East Skelly Drive
(918) 749–5561

The English Oven
3711 South Harvard
(918) 749–1296

Famous Dave's Bar-BQ
8247 East Seventy-first
Street
(918) 249–2140

Green Onion (American)
4532 East Fifty-first Street
(918) 481–3338

Hideaway II (pizza)
1419 East Fifteenth Street
(918) 582–4777

Metro Diner
3001 East Eleventh Street
(918) 592–2616

Polo Grill
2038 Utica Square
(918) 744–4269

Savoy Restaurant
(American)
6033 South Sheridan
(918) 494–5621

Spudder (American)
6536 East Fiftieth Street
(918) 665–1416

White River Fish Market
1708 North Sheridan
(918) 835–1910

Cherokee Country: Northeastern Oklahoma

Oklahoma's northeast corner has crowned itself "Green Country," a title it earns with its profusion of rolling green hills, scatterings of pine forests, and the state's largest concentration of lakes and state parks. A quarter of Oklahoma is covered by forest, almost all of it found along the eastern border, where the foothills of the Ozark Mountains spill over from Arkansas and then into the rugged Ouachita Mountains to the south.

Two major thoroughfares take travelers through northeastern Oklahoma. Interstate 44, built along the corridor established by Route 66 and shadowed by remnants of the old highway, bisects the region on a diagonal. Highway 69 takes travelers straight south, along the former path of the Texas Road, an old cattle trail.

Hands down, the prettiest stretch of road is found along Highway 10 as it follows the Spring River in the north, takes travelers into the Grand Lake area, and then drops south along the limestone bluffs and oak and hickory forests found along the Illinois River.

For travel information about the region, contact Green Country at 2805 East Skelly Drive, Tulsa 74105; call (918) 744–0588, or visit www.greencountryok.com.

CHEROKEE COUNTRY

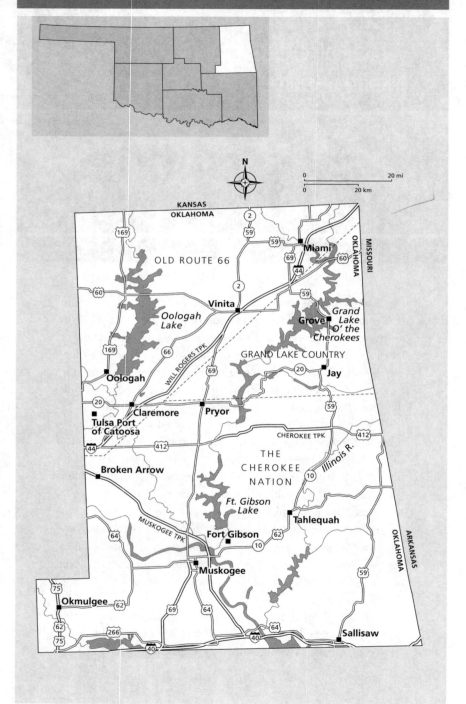

OLD ROUTE 66

KANSAS
OLAHOMA

Miami

OKLAHOMA
MISSOURI

Vinita

Oologah
Lake

Grand
Lake
O' the
Cherokees

Grove

GRAND LAKE COUNTRY

WILL ROGERS TPK

Jay

Oologah

Claremore   Pryor

Tulsa Port
of Catoosa

CHEROKEE TPK

THE
CHEROKEE
NATION

Illinois R.

Broken Arrow

Ft. Gibson
Lake

Tahlequah

OKLAHOMA
ARKANSAS

MUSKOGEE TPK

Fort Gibson

Muskogee

Okmulgee

Sallisaw

Old Route 66

Route 66, the road that once stretched from Chicago to California, just might be the quintessential American highway. For the motorists who pore over old maps, trying to piece together the fabric of the historic road from old alignments and the bones of abandoned buildings, Route 66 is a link to the past. The road was America's first transcontinental highway and is a mirror of twentieth-century growth; the oldest sections in Oklahoma were graded in the 1920s by mules dragging logs. By the time the road was supplanted by the interstate system, it was the jet age. With its neon-lit diners, shady city parks, and the few old-fashioned mom-and-pop tourist courts that remain, Route 66 appeals to motorists who are in search of a slower pace.

Travelers can easily pick up Route 66 heading northeast out of Tulsa along Interstate 244. The original highway left Tulsa along Eleventh Street, and purists may want to follow along that route. Otherwise, use I–244 until just south of Catoosa, where the toll road begins. Route 66 veers to the west. Not far along the road, one of Route 66's most beloved icons appears: the smiling, 50-foot wooden *Blue Whale,* docked in a pond that was once a water park and "Alligator Ranch." Once faded and sinking fast, it has been saved by locals who have raised thousands of dollars and secured a federal grant for restoration to make sure the whale keeps its loony grin. The Blue Whale is immediately south of a pair of twin bridges that straddle the Verdigris River. A few miles northeast of Catoosa on the Arkansas River is the *Tulsa Port of Catoosa,* the furthest inland ice-free port in the United States. The Port Authority building houses the *Arkansas River Historical Society Museum,* www.arkansasriver.org, where you can learn about the history and see pictures of the navigation system from the Mississippi River to this port. Learn about the environmental benefits of this waterway and products shipped, and see a working model of a lock and dam.

AUTHOR'S FAVORITES IN CHEROKEE COUNTRY

Arthur's Bookbinding International	Dog Iron Ranch
Ataloa Art Lodge	Elephant Rock Nature Park
The Castle of Muskogee	Har-Ber Village
Cherokee Heritage Center	Totem Pole Park
Coleman Theatre	Will Rogers Memorial Museum

Take U.S. Highway 169 north to Forty-sixth Street, then go east 5 miles. Call (918) 266–2291 for hours and tours.

From Catoosa, Route 66 rolls north into **Claremore,** www.claremore.org, a pretty town that humorist Will Rogers claimed as home. Rogers is buried at the **Will Rogers Memorial Museum,** www.willrogers.com, along with his wife and two of his three children, under an epitaph that he himself suggested: "I never met a man I didn't like."

Everyone, it seems, likes Will Rogers. Easily Oklahoma's best-loved native son, Rogers learned to rope and ride growing up on a ranch in Indian Territory. Rogers's father, Clem Rogers, was a member of the Cherokee Paint Clan, and Will was nearly one-quarter Cherokee. Of his Native American heritage, Will Rogers said: "My ancestors didn't come over on the Mayflower, but they met 'em at the boat." Rogers left home at seventeen to travel in South America and with the Oklahoma-grown Miller's 101 Ranch Wild West Show as the rope-twirling Cherokee Kid. Rogers took his roping act all the way to the Ziegfeld Follies, but it wasn't until he began to add wry political commentary and his own good-natured philosophy to his act that his popularity skyrocketed. Fans read his syndicated newspaper columns and his books. They listened to his commentary on the radio and revered him on the silver screen. Will Rogers starred in seventy-one motion pictures.

The memorial, a sandstone building on twenty hilltop acres Rogers bought and intended for a homesite, also serves as a museum and archives and is filled to the brim with examples of Rogers's warm humor. The museum features an amphitheater, which shows a documentary about Rogers's life, and a smaller theater, where some of Rogers's movies can be seen. One of the best is a silent clas-

Will Rogers Memorial Museum, Claremore

Plain Fare

A little enclave of Amish families has settled in northeastern Oklahoma near Chouteau, about 30 miles east of Catoosa along U.S. Highway 412. Several families offer visitors a taste of the Amish lifestyle and home cooking. A typical dinner features roast beef, homemade noodles and rolls, mashed potatoes and gravy, garden-grown green beans, cabbage slaw, and fruit pie for dessert, followed by a walk around the farm. Dinners are available only to groups and must be reserved in writing (Amish farms don't have telephones). Write Fannie's Country Cookin', Route 1, Box 318; Lloyd and Anna Mae Ropp, Route 1, Box 345-A; or Christie and Edna Miller, Route 1, Box 79. All addresses are in Chouteau, in the 74337 zip code area.

While it may lack the atmosphere of an Amish farm, the cooking at the **Dutch Pantry Restaurant and Bakery** in Chouteau is heavenly. A Mennonite family owns the restaurant and serves buffet-style, all-you-can-eat home cooking. The Dutch Pantry is at 10 West Main, Chouteau.

And just south of Chouteau, visitors to **Chet and Beth's Bakery** will find several kinds of pie, bread, rolls, cookies, noodles, and jams and spreads. The bakery is in a converted gas station ¼ mile south of Chouteau on U.S. Highway 69. It's open Monday through Saturday.

sic, *The Ropin' Fool,* a twenty-two-minute documentary written and produced by Rogers in 1922. In the movie Rogers performs some of his famous lariat tricks, including one with three ropes that loop a running horse's leg, its neck, and the rider at the same time. Included in the memorial's displays are the saddles Rogers collected from around the world, family photos, correspondence, and perhaps the memorial's most poignant items: Rogers's battered typewriter and smashed eyeglasses, found near Point Barrow, Alaska, after the plane crash that took Rogers's life and that of pilot Wiley Post, another Oklahoman.

In the memorial's basement, a children's museum has been added and is loaded with activities. There are video and art areas, a little library, and puppet and vaudeville stages, the latter with a well-stocked wardrobe area. The memorial is open daily from 8:00 A.M. to 5:00 P.M. and is on Will Rogers Boulevard, between Highway 88 to the east and Route 66 to the west. Call (800) 324–9455 for information.

Another worthwhile stop in Claremore is the **J. M. Davis Historical Arms Museum,** a very diverse 20,000-piece collection that will delight gun enthusiasts and pique everyone else's interest, too. The entire history of the development of firearms is addressed, with artifacts that range from a fourteenth-century "hand cannon" to dueling pistols to guns used by Pancho Villa. Davis, who once ran a downtown hotel, collected a lot more than guns: The museum holds

2,000 beer steins, saddles, and other Western memorabilia. The museum is at 313 West Lynn Riggs Boulevard. Call (918) 341–5707 or visit www.thegun museum.com for information. Admission is free.

There are numerous antiques and craft shops in Claremore; most are found along Will Rogers Boulevard and Route 66. *Hoover's Have-All Mall,* east of the Will Rogers Memorial at 714 West Will Rogers Boulevard, is as extensive as its name suggests. A few blocks east, at 524 West Will Rogers Boulevard, is the *Will Rogers Center.* Originally a six-story hotel, it was renovated into housing for senior citizens. The lobby has been restored to its 1930 splendor and displays a bronze statue of Oklahoma's favorite son. Old postcards and other memorabilia are also on display. From mid-October to mid-December, a Christmas crafts and antiques market is held at *The Belvidere,* a restored mansion owned by the Rogers County Historical Society. The historical house is at 121 North Chickasaw. The market is open Wednesday through Saturday 10:00 A.M. to 4:00 P.M. For information call (918) 342–1127.

Restaurant choices are as nostalgic as Claremore's downtown would suggest. LaNelle Hammett's Pamper-Fried Chicken and lemon pie are specialties of *The Hammett House,* www.hammetthouse.com, a family-friendly restaurant that has been a Claremore institution since the 1960s. Current owners Bill and Linda Baird prepare chicken with LaNelle's secret blend of twenty herbs and spices. The restaurant is at 1616 West Will Rogers Boulevard, and is open Tuesday through Sunday from 11:00 A.M. to 9:00 P.M. Can view full menu online. Call (918) 341–7333.

For lunch, a good bet is the *Pink House Restaurant,* 210 West Fourth, located in a big pink 1902 Victorian house. The frilly antiques-filled tearoom serves a dozen different kinds of desserts and surprisingly hearty fare, includ-

"If you don't like cowboys, don't come to Claremore." —Hurley Hughes

Peddling more cowboy commodities than the local western-wear outfitter, tack room, or feed store, *Cowboy Trade Day,* www.cowboytrader.com, in Claremore, draws cowboy craftsmen and entertainers from all over the country. According to the swap-meet architect, Hurley Hughes, they come to buy, sell, trade, and visit. Everything a cowboy needs from the tip of his hat to the tip of his boots he, or she, can find at the Roundup Club on the third Saturday in September. "I've heard of a lot of flea markets, but never an all-western flea market. We have everything from horses to hats and bits to boots, with some old-time cowboy entertainment thrown in."

Oklahoma Writer's Legacy

Rollie Lynn Riggs, poet and playwright, was born a few miles southwest of Claremore on August 31, 1899. While in France on a Guggenheim Fellowship, he wrote a play titled "Green Grow the Lilies." This play was adapted into the musical, "Oklahoma!" Today, visitors can learn more about Riggs by visiting the **Lynn Riggs Memorial.** The memorial is located in Lynn Riggs Park, in the south annex of 121 North Weenonah, Claremore. Admission is free. Open Monday through Friday 9:00 A.M. to noon and 1:00 to 4:00 P.M. Closed weekends and major holidays. Call (918) 622–7595 or visit http://members.cox.net/lynn.riggs/lrmem.htm to learn more.

ing chicken enchiladas and stuffed pork chops. The Pink House is open Monday through Saturday from 11:00 A.M. to 2:00 P.M. Call (918) 342–2544 or visit www.pinkhouseofclaremore.com for information.

Visitors to Claremore are welcome to watch the afternoon milking, courtesy of a glass-fronted dairy barn, at the **Swan Brothers Dairy.** The dairy started in Claremore in 1923 with one cow and now sells milk and cheese directly to the public. No chemical pesticides are used on the fields where the cows graze, nor does the dairy use growth-hormone injections to stimulate milk production. Milking begins at approximately 3:00 P.M. The dairy is at 938 East Fifth Street. Take Highway 20 to Maiden Lane. The dairy is at the top of the hill. Call (918) 341–2298.

There are a couple of good reasons to detour off the path of Route 66 near Claremore. Visitors can tour the white farmhouse where Will Rogers was born at **Dog Iron Ranch,** a working cattle ranch, 2 miles northeast of **Oologah.** (Take Highway 88 west from Claremore.) Rogers claimed Claremore as his home, he said, because he was afraid no one could pronounce Oologah (*OOH-la-ga*), where Rogers was born in 1879. His two-story home was originally two log cabins, which were later covered with weatherboarding. In Rogers's day, a smokehouse, a blacksmith shop, a toolhouse, sheds, a barn, and stock corrals were built around it. A reproduction of the ranch's nineteenth-century oak barn now stands on the farm, built in an old-fashioned barn raising by Amish carpenters. The barn replicates the original barn, with the exception of the addition of restrooms and of ramps to make it accessible to all visitors. Longhorn cattle, horses, donkeys, pygmy goats, sheep, geese, chickens, dogs, and cats roam around four acres. The house is a mile from Lake Oologah. The ranch is open seven days a week from 8:00 A.M. to 5:00 P.M. RV camping, $10 per night, is allowed in a pasture near the house. (There's a seven-night limit.) Call (918) 275–4201 for more information.

Oologah remembers Rogers in the town square with a statue of "The Cherokee Kid" standing with his horse Comanche. Oologah's historic district is compact—only a block and a half long—and some days visitors can spot the town's mayor out doing errands on horseback. More Rogers memorabilia can be found at the *Oolagah Historical Museum,* at the corner of Cooweescoowee and Maple, a project that is fueled by volunteers and a snow-cone stand that operates during the summer. The 3,600-square-foot museum is filled with Native American and pioneer artifacts and early twentieth-century curiosities, such as a hair perming machine and scary-looking medical equipment. The walls are hung with local photographs and old newspaper stories about Rogers and the 1935 plane crash in which he was killed. There's also a tree branch pierced by tin, a souvenir from a past tornado. The museum spells the town's name with two Os, not three—old Cherokee records show that spelling to be the original one—but an anonymous postal official or railroad employee misspelled the name before statehood, and Oologah with three Os became the official spelling. The museum is open Monday through Friday from 9:00 A.M. to 5:00 P.M., and on Saturday from 10:00 A.M. to 2:00 P.M.; (918) 443–2934.

Museum staff will give you the key to the refurbished and spiffed-up 1906 *Bank of Oolagah,* which closed permanently during the Depression, when a bank employee embezzled the deposits. The bank president and officers, all local residents, eventually paid back all the bank's depositors, though it took years. The original fixtures were sold to pay those debts, but tellers' cages and bank equipment from that period have been installed in the bank.

For a picnic you won't soon forget, detour from Route 66 north of Clare-more at Foyil and travel east 4½ miles along Highway 28A to *Totem Pole Park.* You'll know you're closing in on your destination when you spot a 60-foot-tall, brightly painted cement totem pole on the south side of the highway. The totem pole is the signature piece of a fanciful one-acre roadside park created by Tulsa shop teacher Ed Galloway just for the fun of it. Galloway built the park between 1937 and his death in 1962, creating, in addition to the five-story totem pole, an eleven-sided "Fiddle House," which he filled with 300 handmade violins; a carved and painted tree; a 12-foot-high arrowhead; and picnic tables and stools. Galloway covered the exterior of the totem pole, which is 30 feet around at the base, with carvings of flowers, animals, and profiles of Native Americans in full headdress and painted them turquoise, pink, yellow, and other bright colors. The paint had faded over the years, but in the past decade, folk-art enthusiasts have restored Galloway's creations to their original brilliance.

On down the road from Totem Pole Park, 1.3 miles north of Claremore on Route 66, pull in and visit Eddie Burkholder, owner, head baker, and pan washer at the *Old Dutchman's Bakery.* Eddie sells his homemade cinnamon rolls to early risers, fruit and cream pies to the supper crowd, and pecan logs, cookies, brownies, and warm bread to everybody in between. The bakery is open Monday through Friday, 7:00 A.M. to 5:00 P.M. and Saturday 7:00 A.M. to 3:00 P.M. Eddie's humor and good bakin' will remind you of home. Call (918) 341–7505.

From Claremore Route 66 passes through *Vinita,* www.vinita.com, notable for its annual *Calf Fry Festival,* where townsfolk celebrate a cowboy custom that dates back to roundup time and the seasonal castration of male calves. The tradition—both the harvesting and the subsequent dining on calf "fries"— is not for the faint of heart. Each fall during roundup, male calves are roped and castrated to increase their weight gain, and cowboy gourmets cook the fruits of the roundup over an open fire. Festival cooks soak them in milk, batter them in cracker crumbs or cornmeal, and deep-fry them. The festival is held each September just off Route 66 at the American Legion Rodeo Grounds in Vinita, where cowboy cooks compete to cook up the tastiest fries. Call (918) 256–7133 for information.

If you can, stop by *Clanton's Cafe,* www.clantonscafe.com, along Route 66 on the east side of town, at 319 East Illinois; (918) 256–9053. Clanton's serves the cowboys and working people of Vinita; it opens at 5:30 A.M. for breakfast and closes at 8:00 P.M. Monday through Friday. Weekend hours are Saturday 7:00 A.M. to 2:00 P.M. and Sunday 11:00 A.M. to 2:00 P.M. Fried chicken, chicken-fried steak, chicken and dressing, and pork and dressing are on the regular daily lunch menu, and specials are added to that. This cafe is the oldest family-owned restaurant on Route 66. In February 2006, Clanton's chicken-fried steak was hailed as the "Best Chicken-Fried Steak on Route 66" by *Gourmet* magazine. Stop in and try one for yourself.

Three-fourths of a mile from downtown Vinita continuing east, the *Summerside Winery* is a must stop. Besides the gift shop, bistro, and art gallery, Gary and Marsha Butler, the owners, offer free wine and grape-juice tasting and tours. Their hours are Monday through Saturday from 9:00 A.M. to 6:00 P.M. and Sunday from noon to 5:00 P.M. Call (918) 256–3000 or visit www.summer sidevineyards.com. On the edge of Vinita, check out *Little Cabin Pecan Company,* in business for more than twenty years. Locals say, "it's the best place to get pecans." When pecans are harvested in the fall, visitors can watch as shakers, picker-uppers, and other machines do their work across the fifty-acre orchard. Call (918) 256–2218 or visit www.littlecabinpecan.com for more information.

From Vinita, take U.S. Highway 59/69 to *Miami,* www.miamiokchamber .com. Continue north on Main Street to the palatial *Coleman Theatre,* which has been described as looking like a giant wedding cake dropped down on the corner of First Street and Main. The theater was built with the fortune amassed by George Coleman, who came to Indian Territory in 1895 and discovered lead and zinc deposits on his farm while digging a water well. Coleman loved vaudeville and commissioned the well-known Boller Brothers to design the elaborate Spanish Mission–style theater in the late 1920s. Construction was completed in 1929. The theater is white stucco, with a red-tiled roof slathered with hand-carved friezes, and topped by no fewer than three bell towers. The theater was as opulent inside as out, furnished with a two-ton brass-and-crystal chandelier operated by 200 light switches, red-and-gold Louis XIV furniture, and a Wurlitzer organ. Gold brocade and gilded plaster covered the walls, and five different patterns of carpets covered the floor, including one that depicted a crossed miner's pick and shovel. The Coleman hasn't been a regular movie house in decades and was deteriorating rapidly in the 1980s when local citizens raised money to restore it. (Some furnishings were scattered and had to be retrieved, including the organ, which was sold to an evangelist who used it in revivals.) First-run movies are shown on summer evenings, and tours are conducted Tuesday through Friday from 10:00 A.M. to 4:00 P.M. and Saturday from 10:00 A.M. to noon. Winter hours are Monday through Friday from 8:30 A.M. to 5:00 P.M. The theater is operated mostly by volunteers, so the schedule is a little erratic. To contact the theater, phone (918) 540–2425 or visit www.colemantheatre.org. Information is also available from city offices; call (918) 542–6685. The theater is at 103 North Main, Miami.

From Miami, take Highway 10 due east to Highway 137, then south and east to **Twin Bridges State Park,** where you can camp on the shores of the Spring River—or the shores of the Neosho River. Take your pick, since the park is situated at the confluence of the two. Even the name of the hill where the park office is found has two variations: One side of the hill is known as Echo Hollow, and the other is called Eagle's Nest. Bald eagles roost in the park

Oklahoma Junction

In the early days, Vinita was simply referred to as the "Junction." Cowboys, Indians, and railroads combined to make this territory town memorable. The *Eastern Trails Museum* brings those memories alive through its exhibits. Relics from the Civil War Battle of Big Cabin Creek, photos from Will Rogers' early days in Vinita, and a vast display of Osage, Choctaw, and Cherokee artifacts make this museum worth visiting. It is located at 125 West Illinois Avenue, at the back of the Vinita Library. Hours are daily 1:00 to 4:00 P.M. There is no charge for admission. Call (918) 256–2115 for more information.

in the winter, picnickers come to swim in the rivers in spring and summer, and fishing is good year-round—and comfortable even in January, thanks to an enclosed fishing dock. The park is at the intersection of U.S. Highway 60 and Highway 137. Call (918) 540–2545.

Grand Lake Country

From Twin Bridges, continue east along Highway 137, then pick up Highway 10 again and drive south. The straight road begins to wind itself into curves the closer you come to **Grand Lake O' the Cherokees,** (918) 588–4726 or (866) LUV–GRAND, www.grandlakefun.com, where northeastern Oklahoma residents go to unwind. Named for the Grand River, one of several rivers dammed a half century ago to give farmers relief from flooding and to provide electricity, the lake truly does have grand proportions. It boasts more than 1,300 miles of shoreline and 59,000 surface acres of water and ranges into three counties.

Nearly all of those miles of shoreline are privately owned, and dozens of resorts have sprung up on the lake, ranging from crusty fishing cabins to cushy condominiums. A quiet and affordable place to enjoy Grand Lake and its natural beauty is **Reflections Bed & Breakfast,** www.grandnorthstar.com/REF. Visitors will enjoy three and a half acres of Oklahoma peacefulness as they watch a variety of wildlife, such as deer, coons, the bald eagles, or the neighborhood fox pass through the property. Three rooms, Rose Garden, Lighthouse, and Captain's Quarters, with two overlooking the lake, ensure privacy. Owners John and Pam invite you to come and visit them for a romantic interlude or just to "turn it down a notch or two" from your hectic pace. John and Pam request advance notice, so call (918) 787–7727 for information.

Activity on the north end of the lake centers in **Grove,** (918) 786–9079 or www.groveok.org, once a little farming community but now a sprawling hub for recreation. You can find the old Grove at the **Koffee Kup Cafe,** over a slice of homemade pie and coffee. The new Grove is found at places like **Rheingarten Restaurant**, a German restaurant housed in a cozy house, with dark moldings, wooden floors, and forest-green and burgundy tablecloths. Specialties include sauerbraten baked in a clay pot, potato pancakes and dumplings, and Rheingarten Schnitzel, a breaded pork loin topped with asparagus and Hollandaise sauce. For dessert, try ice cream with raspberry sauce served with hazelnut cookies. Imported beer, wine, and brandy are available. The restaurant is at 911 South Main Street, (918) 786–8737.

Lendonwood Gardens is a botanical garden featuring Japanese-style cascading pools, a shade garden, an English terrace garden, a bonsai collection, and rare varieties of flowers and trees. The three-acre garden, surrounded by a

Getting Afloat

Grand Lake is so large, the surface of the water is almost a geographic entity unto itself—if you stay long at all, you'll feel left out if you stay on dry land. Cruising across the lake to dinner, fishing at sunrise, sailing, waterskiing, holding floating parties on pontoon boats, and zipping around on "jet skis" are all favored activities. For marina information or boat and other equipment rental, check out Lee's Grand Lake Resort, (918) 786–4289, www.leesresort.com; Martin Landing, (918) 257–4265, www.martinlanding.com; or Paradise Cove Marine Resort, (918) 782–3767, www.paradisecoveresort.com.

cedar fence and laced with footpaths, blooms with dogwoods in early spring, followed by rhododendrons in April and May and daylilies in June and early July. The site is a display garden for the American Hemerocullis (daylily) Society. Unusual trees, such as Himalayan cedar and black Japanese pine, are intriguing year-round. The garden is at 1308 West Thirteenth Street, marked as Har-Ber Road. A little cedar box collects donations; the suggested amount is $5.00 per person. The gardens are open from dawn to dusk. Call (918) 786–2938 or go to www.lendonwood.org.

If you're hankerin' for some local history and sweets, check out the *Historic Corey Hotel* located at 208 South Main. Built in 1909 by Colonel Charlie Corey, the hotel is listed on the National Register of Historic Places. While the building is no longer a hotel, it is open to the public. The lower floor is home to the Candy Kitchen, which features fudge, homemade chocolates, and more. There is no admission charge and hours are Tuesday through Sunday from 10:00 A.M. to 5:00 P.M.

A little farther down Har-Ber Road is its namesake, *Har-Ber Village,* a reconstructed early twentieth-century frontier town with more than one hundred historic cabins and buildings. Har-Ber Village was built by Harvey and Bernice Jones, founders of a very successful trucking company. The life-size bronze statues of the couple standing at the village gate show an average American couple—Harvey Jones is wearing overalls—and the couple's intention in creating the village was to preserve the heritage of the average Americans who were pioneers in Arkansas, Kansas, and Oklahoma. Tribute is paid to occupations of all stripes—there are offices outfitted for a mayor, lawyer, newspaper editor, and doctor. Local institutions are represented as well, including churches, schools, stores, a stage stop, a jail, and even a gallows. (The latter is very popular with children.) There's a water-powered gristmill, a windmill, antique cars, rows of plows and other antique farm equipment, and walking paths that lead to the lake's shore and a little chapel with a statue of Christ with outstretched arms. The village takes about three hours to tour, and the numerous signs marking paths and giving instructions grow a little tedious—STAY ON THE WALKWAY!, GUARD DOGS LOOSE AT NIGHT, and THIS IS NOT A TOY!—but the operation is obviously well intentioned. Admission is free, armies of retirees volunteer to give tours, and wheelchairs are available for the asking to those who need them. To get to the village, travel along Har-Ber Road for 3½ miles west of Grove. There's a big sign marking a turn south. Follow that road south and then back west to Har-Ber Village. Har-Ber Village is open Monday through Saturday from 9:00 A.M. to 6:00 P.M. and on Sunday from 12:30 P.M. to 6:00 P.M. from March through November. For information call (918) 786–6446 or visit www.har-bervillage.com.

Within walking distance of Har-Ber Village is the **Candlewyck Cove Resort,** a lakefront cluster of suites on a little peninsula. The inn is on a roomy estate overlooking a wooded cove with its own boat dock and swimming platform. A dozen contemporary two-room suites are quite comfortably furnished with queen-size beds and oversize bathtubs, sitting rooms with fireplaces, televisions, telephones, and private balconies or patios. Rates for the suites range from $99 to $169, depending on the season. Dogwood Cottage, furnished with two fireplaces, a whirlpool spa, and steam shower, is $225. Breakfast, served in a common room at tables for four, often features innkeeper Ken West's cheese blintzes. For reservations call (918) 786–3636 or visit www .candlewyckcove.com.

Be There!

Imagine the model car you built in the 1960s come to life, in full gleaming color. That fantasy comes true every day at the **Darryl Starbird National Rod & Custom Car Hall of Fame and Museum** on Highway 85A. Twenty of Starbird's famed custom cars, including some of the thirteen cars that the Mattel toy company copied for model kits, are on display at the museum.

Starbird, a car-customizing king in the '50s, '60s, and '70s, has re-created his 1954 Star Kustom garage at the museum and is often on hand to talk with visitors about his Moonbird, his bubble-topped Predicta, and the three-wheeled Futurista, later reborn as the Star Trek coupe. The museum is open from April to October, Wednesday through Sunday, from 11:00 A.M. to 5:00 P.M. Admission is $6.00 for adults, $5.00 for senior citizens, and $3.00 for children eight through twelve years old. Call (918) 257–4234 for information or visit www.darrylstarbird.com.

For an old-fashioned church service, take Highway 10 north 3 miles to *Cayuga Indian Mission Church.* Mathias Splitlog, owner of a local sawmill, buggy factory, and general store, began construction of the church in 1895 for his wife, Elisa. She died before it was finished, and her funeral was the first service held in the church. Limestone for the building was quarried locally, but the bell was imported from a foundry in Belgium. Today the congregation sings "Church in the Wild Wood" at every service, and the dress code is "come as you are." Kids attend services in their bathing suits, and for convenience, adults sometimes wear their fishing clothes. To learn more visit www.cayugamission .org or call (918) 786–7607.

There's a little cluster of entertainment just east of Sailboat Bridge on US 59 west of Grove. The **Cherokee Queen II** is a diesel-powered boat designed to resemble the paddle wheelers that used to steam the Mississippi River. Ninety-minute cruises depart daily from May through September. Two more cruises are added on Saturdays: a sunset tour of the lake and a moonlight dinner-dance cruise, with a disc jockey and a fried-chicken-and-barbecue buffet dinner. On the Fourth of July, there's an evening fireworks cruise. For reservations call (918) 786–4272.

berrydelicious

Four northeastern Oklahoma counties lie in the Ozark Plateau, rolling upland that is particularly well suited to growing berries. For proof, visit *Stilwell's Strawberry Festival* the second Saturday in May or blueberry-picking farms near Tahlequah. One to try: *Blueberry Acres,* 5 miles north on Highway 82, (918) 456–5407. Harvest is in June.

Be sure to check out the *Kountry Kuzins Jamboree Music Theatre* for summer music fun when you're in the area. The jamboree offers five different music shows, which range from bluegrass to country-and-western. For show information and to find out where and how to buy tickets, call (918) 791–9555 or visit www.kountrykuzins.com.

After you cross Sailboat Bridge, keep an eye out for Tomcat Corner, a little grocery store and gas station on the right; the road that turns back to the southwest is a shortcut to *Monkey Island,* long a destination for Tulsa's and Oklahoma City's oil rich. Locals says the "Monkey" in Monkey Island refers to "monkeying around." Only about 1,000 people are full-time residents of the area—the rest are vacationers or own weekend homes.

Down the road is *The Shebang,* a sprawling pink-and-gray restaurant that caters to both families and couples. Families can eat pasta and pizza in one part of the restaurant, while couples dine and dance in the Den of Iniquity on the other side. Pasta is a specialty, but the restaurant also serves ribs, prime rib, and seafood. Call (918) 257–5569.

Fourteen miles south of Grove on Highway 10 you will find quiet **Lake Eucha,** where you can rent an entire fifty-five-acre state park, with sixty picnic tables, outdoor cookers, a fishing lake, a picnic shelter, and a swimming pool for $150 a day. (If you want just the park, the rate drops to $45.)

A state visitors' information center, near the intersection of Highway 10 and the Cherokee Turnpike, is stocked with brochures (and free coffee). Travelers could take the turnpike east to **Natural Falls State Park,** but save yourself the toll and take the more scenic Highway 412; it intersects the highway ½ mile to the south. A spot known historically as **Dripping Springs** is the centerpiece of the park: Visitors hike down to where a 77-foot-high waterfall of spring water cascades over a limestone ridge after a good rain. (When it's dry, the water falls in a steady little stream; when it's really dry, it drips.) The moisture in the falls area has created an entirely different ecosystem than the one found on the rocky ridgetop above. Near the falls, maples, chinquapin, and white oak trees are found, along with sassafras, coral berry, spicebush, a dozen different ferns, and fourteen mosses. Dripping Springs was a camp spot for both Union and Confederate forces during the Civil War. Local tradition has it that Union soldiers dynamited the opening to a cave where Confederate guns and supplies were hidden and buried them, but the location has never been found. There are 44 RV sites and 30 tent-camping sites with a bathhouse in the 120-acre park. Park personnel are restoring formal gardens and hiking paths in the park and collect a $3.00 per car fee for a maintenance fund. The park phone number is (918) 422–5802.

If you are interested in Cherokee history, it will be worth your time to take a side trip to the **Saline District Courthouse.** Off Highway 10, go west on

Saline District Courthouse

Highway 412. Get off at the Leach/Oaks exit. Go north to Highway 33/Scenic 412 West to the Mayes/Delaware County line, then 1 mile south. The site is on the east side of the road. The courthouse is owned by the Cherokee Nation and played a prominent role in their history. One of the nine district court-houses through the Cherokee Nation, it is the only one still standing. The court-house was built between 1884 and 1889. It sits in fourteen acres, has a springhouse and the "Teehee Cemetery," with tombstones dating back to the 1860s. The Saline community, where the courthouse is located, had a large general store, a blacksmith shop, a church or two, a doctor, and a school at the turn of the twentieth century. On January 1, 1976, it was listed on the National Register of Historic Places and is on Preservation Oklahoma's 2004 Endangered List. The courthouse is currently being restored, but its grounds are open to the public. Call (918) 456–0671 or visit www.cherokee.org for more information.

As you drive south on Highway 10, canoe liveries begin to crop up along-side the highway, a sign that you've begun to follow the course of the Illinois River. A full 70 miles of the Illinois River, which twists through limestone bluffs and stands of oak and hickory, is protected as a Wild and Scenic River. The river, a tributary of the Arkansas, provides a tranquil, rather than heart-thumping, adventure. The Illinois is a Class II river, with easy rapids, waves up to 1 foot high, and wide, clear channels. There are about a dozen canoe liveries along the river that rent canoes and inflatable rafts or kayaks and arrange trips rang-ing from half days to full weeks. *Thunderbird Resort* offers accommodations that range from rustic log cabins without showers or commodes to cottages fur-nished with televisions. The resort operates two campgrounds: Paradise Valley and Arrowhead Camp, which has a general store complete with an antique ice-cream fountain. You can also rent a tent for $15.00 (which includes putting it up and taking it down). The basic camping rate is $6.00 a night for two peo-ple. *Hanging Rock Camp,* (918) 456–3088, offers tent campsites, a motel, and a cafe, and *War Eagle Floats,* (918) 456–6272, www.wareagleresort.com, has a motel and camping, plus a swimming pool.

There are nine public-access areas for boaters along the river, including *Round Hollow,* 15 miles north of the junction of Highways 10 and 62, and *No Head Hollow*, less than a mile north of the Oklahoma Scenic Rivers Commission office. The commission keeps tabs on river conditions and main-tains a list of canoe liveries and safety tips. Floaters can pick up a map marked with public-access areas, resorts, canoe liveries, and natural landmarks.

Elephant Rock Nature Park was established in the woods surrounding Elephant Rock, a limestone formation on a curve in the river that has reminded generations of river travelers of an elephant's head and trunk. Park visitors who hike out onto the top of the formation are treated to a spectacular view of the river below: Hawks circle at eye level and schools of fish can be spotted in the water. Bald eagles roost in oak and hickory trees in winter, making the spot truly, as owner Rod Foster says, a place to get "a bird's-eye view." Trails marked with stones and covered with soft green lichen run through the woods, to the river and past deer-feeding stations; in addition to deer, hikers have spotted bobcats and wild turkey. The Fosters lead interpretive hikes, teach environmental education and outdoor skills classes, and host sunrise breakfasts and acoustic music events on special holidays like Earth Day. Guests camp in secluded campsites with private trails or stay in 20-foot-high Native American–style tepees. Prime accommodations, however, are "yurts," modern interpretations of the circular domed tents used by Mongolian nomads. These yurts are air-conditioned and equipped with kitchenettes, showers, and televisions. The top of the dome is clear for stargazing. Reach Elephant Rock by way of a steeply graded road, on Highway 10, 2 miles north of the highway's junction with Highway 62. To make reservations call (918) 456–4215 or visit www.elephant-rock.com.

The Cherokee Nation

Tahlequah, www.tourtahlequah.com or (918) 456–3742, just around the corner, is the 160-year-old capital of the Cherokee Nation and a picture-book small town in its own right. Men in fedoras read the morning newspaper on benches in the town square, and on Main Street, the hardware store has scarred wooden floors and a pickup truck selling Vidalia onions parked out front. The presence of Northeastern State University gives the north end of town an energetic, patchouli-scented edge. The fifty-year-old *Morgan Bakery,* (918) 456–3731, on Muskogee Street, for instance, sells sugar cookies, old-fashioned pastries, and whole-wheat bagels.

Cherokee history is found everywhere downtown, where major street and some business signs are painted in both English and Cherokee. When the Cherokee were forced to move to Indian Territory in the 1830s, the infamous Trail of Tears came to an end, local legend has it, at Bear Creek in a spot at the foot of a hill leading onto the university campus.

The university itself evolved from the Cherokee Female Seminary; the state bought the land and some buildings in 1909, after the federal government abolished tribal governments at Oklahoma's statehood in 1907. The historic seminary building has recently been restored; you can identify it on campus by its tower and gleaming copper roof.

Visitors can pick up a brochure for a tour of historic sites at the Tahlequah visitors' center at the corner of Water and Delaware Streets. The intricacies of Cherokee history become apparent right across the street, at the *Old Chero-*

kee National Capitol Building, a stately redbrick building that sits in the middle of the town square. The Cherokee Council first began to meet here in 1839, first in an open shed and then in log buildings. General Stand Watie, a Cherokee and a leader of the Indian brigade that fought for the Confederacy, burned down the council houses during the Civil War.

The building that now stands in the square was built in 1867 and served as the tribal capitol until Oklahoma's statehood in 1907, when the federal government abolished tribal governments. The building served as the Cherokee County Courthouse until 1979, until it was returned to the Cherokee Nation. The Cherokee Nation maintains modern tribal offices south of Tahlequah; the old capitol houses the Judicial Appeals Tribunal.

Across the square, at the corner of Keetoowah Street and Water Avenue, is the 1845 *Cherokee Supreme Court Building,* erected in 1845. In addition to the supreme and district courts of the Cherokee Nation, the building also held the offices of the newspaper *The Cherokee Advocate.* Continue 1 block south along Water Avenue. On the southwestern corner of the intersection of Water Avenue and Choctaw Street is the *Cherokee National Prison.* It was built in 1874 and once had a gallows on the west side. The county used it as a jail until it built a new facility.

Things are a little less weighty up the street, closer to the university. The *Iguana Cafe* has the feel of a Taos ski lodge, with Mission-style benches, Southwestern art, and a menu that includes such specials as chicken fajita wraps and tortilla soup. A potbellied stove warms things up in the winter, and the patio, right on Muskogee, is great for people-watching during spring and summer. The Iguana Cafe is at 500A Muskogee, (918) 458–0044.

Down the street, the *River City Players,* a musical revue made up of Northeastern State University acting and music majors, perform during the summer in the *Shawnee Street Theatre.* Call (918) 458–2072.

While in Tahlequah, you'll want to tour its historic home, the *Thompson House* on the corner of College and Choctaw. Built in 1882, this home's architectural style is Queen Anne Carpenter Gothic with Eastlake style interior woodwork. Completely restored, it is listed on the National Register of Historic Places. The Thompson family lived in the home until the 1930s. Mrs. Thompson was a skilled weaver and her loom room has been restored to the time period. Today, local weavers demonstrate the art of weaving at special events held at the house. Admission fee is $3.00 per person. To schedule a guided tour call (918) 456–3554.

A stop at the *Cherokee Heritage Center,* www.cherokeeheritage.org or (888) 999–6007, 3 miles south of Tahlequah, is a must for anyone intrigued with the Cherokee story or interested in Native American history. The Heritage Center traces the history of the tribe from the days before European contact 500 years ago to the present. Behind the museum, in the ***Tsa-La-Gi Ancient Village,*** members of the Cherokee Tribe don clothing representative of what Cherokee wore before European contact and demonstrate bow making, flint knapping, basket weaving, pottery making, and such arts as using a Cherokee blowgun. Reproductions of Cherokee longhouses and a council house have been built on the grounds.

At the time of their removal to Indian Territory, the Cherokee were already farmers, and most lived as well as, or better than, most settlers, raising corn, hogs, cotton, and cattle and publishing a newspaper, *The Cherokee Phoenix*. After their removal, the Cherokee prospered in Indian Territory. ***Adams Rural Village,*** next to the ancient village, demonstrates Cherokee life after their arrival in Indian Territory. Some of the buildings in the collection of log homes, churches, and schools hold furniture that came over on the Cherokee Trail of Tears. Alongside the buildings, old strains of livestock like Pineywoods cattle and Cherokee ponies are tethered. The animals, smaller and hardier than modern farm animals, are almost identical to the livestock the Cherokee brought with them to Indian Territory.

Visitors can also see how well developed the Cherokee educational system was in the nineteenth century. The Cherokee Nation built seminaries for both male and female students at the site; when it opened in 1851, the Cherokee Female Seminary was the first public institution west of the Mississippi to offer a liberal-arts education to women. The school burned in 1887, but its redbrick columns still stand at the Heritage Center.

The Cherokee Heritage Center is east of Highway 62 on Willis Road. The museum is open Monday through Saturday from 10:00 A.M. to 5:00 P.M. and on Sunday from 1:00 to 5:00 P.M. Call (918) 456– 6007 for information.

Not far from the Heritage Center is the ***Murrell Home,*** the two-story, white-columned 1845 residence of Minerva Ross, the niece of Chief John Ross. The antebellum home, furnished with brocade sofas and mahogany furniture, illustrates the gracious lifestyle of prosperous Cherokee in Indian Territory before the Civil War—and holds vivid stories of life in Indian Territory during the war. Most of the wealthy Cherokee fled the territory during the war, but one stubborn woman and her young niece stuck it out. Copies of letters written to relatives during the war, hanging on a back wall, paint a vivid picture. The house was built on extensive grounds that included a springhouse and smokehouse. In June the state historical society hosts an "1858 Lawn Social" on the grounds. The mile-long Murrell Nature Trail, which starts at the home, has a paved portion that is suitable for everybody and features a bird sanctuary. The Murrell Home is 1 mile east of Highway 82 on Murrell Road. Open

Wednesday through Saturday from 10:00 A.M. to 5:00 P.M. and on Sunday from 1:00 to 5:00 P.M.; the museum closes on Tuesday during the winter. Admission is free; call (918) 456–2751 for information.

From Tahlequah, U.S. Highway 62 takes travelers to **Fort Gibson,** the site of Oklahoma's oldest frontier fort. Fort Gibson was established in 1824 in anticipation of the Cherokee's move to the territory. The Seventh Cavalry was first stationed at the fort, charged with keeping peace between the Cherokee and the Osage; at the time the Osage lived farther north but came to the plains to hunt bison. For several decades, the fort was the most important outpost in the Southwest, launching dozens of expeditions into unmapped territory. Today visitors to the fort can tour a Works Progress Administration–era stockade reconstruction, which houses historical exhibits and military artifacts, and a handful of original buildings, including the fort bakery. Admission is $3.00 for adults, $2.00 for senior citizens (sixty-five and above), $1.00 for students (six to eighteen), and free for five and under. It is 1 mile north of the town site on Highway 80. Winter hours are Thursday through Saturday 10:00 A.M. to 5:00 P.M. and in summer Tuesday through Sunday 10:00 A.M. to 5:00 P.M.; (918) 478–4088.

oklahomatartan

On May 27, 1999, the Oklahoma Tartan was adopted and became the official Tartan for the State. Jewel R. Murray created the design and it was professionally manufactured and woven by The House of Edgar, Pitlochry, Scotland. The Oklahoma Tartan is red, white, black, and gold on a field of blue and is registered by Certificate of Accreditation with the Scottish Tartan Society, Scotland.

Fort Gibson is also home to **Bozena's Polish Restaurant,** which is owned by Zbigniew and Bozena Niebieszczanskis, who fled Poland in the early 1980s. The restaurant, tucked into a little strip mall, is the only place in the state to get authentic Polish dishes such as sauerkraut soup served with Polish sausage, *placek ziemniaczany* (a potato pancake), or combination dinners such as The Old Warsaw Variety Dinner, which includes roast beef and pork fried with mushrooms and stir-fried vegetables, rice, and pan-fried potatoes. The portions are generous—as the sign says, dinner is ALMOST ALL YOU CAN EAT. The restaurant is on the main street at 1115 South Poplar, and is open Tuesday through Saturday 11:00 A.M. to 9:00 P.M. Call (918) 478–4404 for information. Next door to the restaurant, Zbigniew runs **Arthur's Bookbinding International,** www.biblerepair.com, named after his second son. Using nineteenth-century techniques and tools, Zbigniew restores old books and family Bibles. Besides twenty dollars and three English words (*please* and *excuse me*), his bookbinding skill and his wife's cooking were all they brought with them to Oklahoma.

Cherokee Medicine

Long before Saint John's wort became the "natural Prozac" for our modern times, Cherokee women were using the flowers of the herb, which they called *A-da-wo-s-gv U-s-ti*, to make a tea to calm the nerves and help depression. Cherokee herbalist Donna "Chinosa" Lenon has identified forty-nine different natural herbs and medicines used by the Cherokee Nation and is working with the tribe to identify them along a walking path through the Heritage Center grounds. Other Cherokee natural herbs and their uses include *Sa-lo-li Ga-toh-ga*, or yarrow, used to treat blood clots, hemorrhoids, urinary tract infection, fever, and insomnia, and *Gi-ge-s-di A-tsi-lv*, button snakeroot, used as a diuretic, an expectorant, and for backaches.

Today there is a waiting list at the bindery, and the restaurant is a popular weekend hangout.

Fort Gibson is a few miles northeast of **Muskogee,** www.muskogee chamber.org, a town that was once a powerful center in Indian Territory. In 1874 an agency to serve the Five Civilized Tribes—the Union Agency—was created and established on a high hill northwest of the present-day downtown. The two-story sandstone agency still stands and is now home to the **Five Civilized Tribes Museum,** (918) 683–1701 or www.fivetribes.org, which houses art and historical exhibits about the southeastern tribes that were removed to Oklahoma: the Cherokee, Chickasaw, Seminole, Choctaw, and Creek. A good time to visit the museum is during the April "Art Under the Oaks," a two-day festival of Native American culture, featuring the work of artists from the Five Tribes and demonstrations that include Cherokee basket weaving, pottery making, tribal dancing, storytelling, and a blowgun competition. There's food, too—among the offerings are Indian tacos, fry bread, and grape dumplings. Admission to the museum is adults, $3.00; senior citizens, $2.00; and students, $1.50. Open, Monday through Saturday 10:00 A.M. to 5:00 P.M. and Sunday 1:00 to 5:00 P.M.

The agency-turned-museum sits on Honor Heights Drive, which leads right into **Honor Heights Park,** renowned for its annual Azalea Festival. When the literally millions of pink, white, red, and purple azaleas are at their peak of bloom (usually in mid-April), the park is so crowded, visitors creep in their cars along the park's roadways. A better choice is to park in designated satellite parking lots and take a tram into the park. With a rose garden, a gazebo, picnic pavilions, playground, waterfalls, and fountains, the park is a great place to picnic or stroll year-round.

Muskogee's leading citizens built mansions on Sixteenth Street, locally known as "Silk Stocking Row." One of the more imposing mansions was a three-story Gothic-Victorian mansion at 501 North Sixteenth, now operating as the **Graham-Carroll House** bed-and-breakfast inn. Surrounded by English gardens, the inn has five beautifully and comfortably furnished guest rooms and suites, all with private baths. Suites have whirlpools and fireplaces, and all rooms have televisions and telephones. Lunch and dinner are available by reservation, served on a table that publishing magnate William Randolph Hearst presented to his mistress Marion Davies. Room rates are $85 to $125. For reservations call innkeeper Dale Robertson, (918) 683–0100, or visit www.bdonline.com/ok/grahamcarroll.

publicbakeday

Every spring, the big stone Civil War–era army oven at Fort Gibson is fired up, and the public is invited to bring dough to bake right on the oak-heated oven floor. Dough and baked goods can also be purchased from the post baker (a regular soldier's ration was one loaf a day) at the Fort Gibson Historic Site. A Civil War reenactment and dance lessons are also part of the fun; (918) 478–4088.

A wonderful, small, Native American museum is the **Ataloa Art Lodge,** on the campus of Bacone College. Bacone was founded in 1880 as Indian University in nearby Tahlequah and moved to Muskogee in 1885 when teacher Almon C. Bacone persuaded the Muskogee (Creek) tribal council to donate 160 acres to the school. The art lodge, built of native sandstone hauled in by students, was the project of English teacher Mary Stone McLendon. McLendon collected Native American artifacts to use as teaching tools for the arts-and-crafts classes that she also taught. Indian crafts and painting are still taught at the college, but today the art lodge is a museum, holding such treasures as a 1754 Mohawk carved ladle; thirty carved walking sticks; a water jug made of willow branches and pine tar (that once belonged to Geronimo); Apache violins made of magua cactus; and Navajo, Pueblo, Hopi, and Mayan blankets and rugs. One blanket was woven from yarn torn from army blankets by a group of imprisoned Navajo women. More poignant and rare is a beaded bonnet worn by an infant named Lost Bird, who was the lone survivor of the Battle of Wounded Knee in Dakota Territory in 1890. The Ataloa Art Lodge, www.bacone.edu/ataloa, is on the northwest corner of campus. The campus is northeast of the junction of Highways 16 and 62. The lodge and a gift shop are open Wednesday through Saturday from 8:00 A.M. to 5:00 P.M. and Sunday from 1:00 to 5:00 P.M. Admission is $3.00 for adults, $2.00 for students, and $1.00 for senior citizens. Call (918) 781–7283 for information.

Muskogee, 500 miles away from the nearest shore, is the unlikely home to the ***USS Batfish,*** www.ussbatfish.com, a World War II submarine docked at the Port of Muskogee on the Arkansas River. The 1943 submarine served in the South Pacific and once sank three enemy submarines in four days. Visitors can tour the submarine from mid-March to mid-November. Also nearby are an artillery display and picnic tables. Call (918) 682–6294.

If sightseeing leaves you hungry, look no further than ***Runt's Barbecue,*** 3003 West Okmulgee. Russell, the owner, smokes ribs, chicken, and brisket for his sliced- and chopped-beef sandwiches. He also cooks the "best catfish [grilled or fried] in the state." Runt's has daily specials, with "all you can eat ribs" Wednesday and Saturday and "all you can eat fish" on Friday. Desserts include homemade peach and blackberry cobblers and banana-split pie. Open Monday through Saturday from 11:00 A.M. to 6:00 P.M. Call (918) 681–3900.

You'll find quite a different atmosphere downtown in flowery ***Miss Addie's Tearoom.*** Lunch is served daily from 11:00 A.M. to 9:00 P.M.; dinner starts at 5:00 P.M. Closed Sunday. (For dessert, try the baked fudge.) The tearoom was built in what was once a corner drugstore and pharmacist's living quarters. Three suites, some with balconies, have been built upstairs. Call (918) 682–1506.

The Cherokee Civil War

In 1835 a minority group of Cherokee signed the Treaty of New Echota, which signed away the entire tribe's Georgia holdings in exchange for land in Indian Territory. The treaty was ratified by Congress in 1836 over the protests of Cherokee Chief John Ross and despite petitions of opposition signed by thousands of Cherokee. In 1838 soldiers forced the resisting Cherokee from their homes and burned their houses. The Cherokee set out in forced marches, beginning in the late fall of 1838. Four thousand people, which was nearly 25 percent of the tribal population, died during the journey. The treaty resulted in decades of bitter tribal politics and the midnight assassinations of four of the treaty signers. Stand Watie, a signer of the treaty and the brother of one of those assassinated, gathered an unsuccessful force to overthrow the Ross government.

When the U.S. Civil War broke out, it divided the Cherokee Nation as painfully as it did the United States. Part of the tribe remained neutral; Stand Watie recruited a regiment of Cherokee and was made a brigadier general in the Confederate Army. Under Watie, Confederate troops ransacked the homes of Ross family members and burned the Cherokee Council House. Watie was the last Confederate general to lay down his arms. He surrendered at Fort Towson, two months after Appomattox.

A local attraction you don't want to miss is *The Castle of Muskogee,* www.okcastle.com. Surrounded by sixty acres of tree-lined lakes and meadows, you'll think you just stepped back in time to merry ol' England. During the month of May, the castle holds the Oklahoma Renaissance Faire. Mingle with lords and ladies, knights and maidens, as you enjoy the thatch-roofed village and Castleton marketplace. To learn more about the castle, their yearly events, hours, and admission, call (918) 687–3625 or (800) 439-0658.

History buffs will want to take a scenic detour west and drive 45 miles along Highway 16 to *Okmulgee* to visit the historic town square. In the center is the 1878 sandstone *Creek Council House,* where the Creek legislature met until statehood. The council house has been restored as nearly as possible to its original condition, an accomplishment made easier because no major renovations had ever been made. The light fixtures installed when the city was "electrifed" were still hanging, as was the bell that rang to call the Creek Nation to council. Open as the Creek Council House Museum, 106 West Sixth, the restored building, which won an award from the National Trust for Historic Preservation, includes displays of Creek artifacts, such as a 1765 treaty made between a Creek chief and a British agent, a piece of Spanish chain mail dating from the sixteenth century and carried across the Creek Trail of Tears, and a George Washington peace medal, dated 1793. The *Red Stick Gallery,* a museum gift shop, sells high-quality crafts items, such as hand-carved flutes made by Creek elders, the turtle-shell shakers used in Creek dances, bows, and language tapes. Sixth Street is downtown Okmulgee's main street. The museum is open Tuesday through Saturday from 10:00 A.M. to 4:00 P.M. and is closed on federal holidays. Call (918) 756–2324 for information. There are numerous antiques shops and historic buildings around the town square; contact the Okmulgee Chamber of Commerce for a self-guided historic architecture tour by writing to 112 North Morton, Box 609, Okmulgee 74447.

Massey's likes a challenge and every day they put themselves to the test. Located at 200 Northwest Wood Drive, just off Highway 75, this eating establishment cooks up the best ribs, brisket, hot links, and bologna in the area. It may not be anything fancy. You won't find china here, but if you want good food and fixin's, step up to the counter. Your order will be served on Styrofoam plates along with plastic forks. You can eat your food outside in the shade or inside while watching the television tuned to a sporting or news event, or you can pick it up at the drive-through window. Massey's is open Monday through Saturday 11:00 A.M. to 8:00 P.M. Closed Sunday. Call (918) 756–8227 to order.

From Muskogee, head east and then south back into the woods along Highway 10. It's a 20-mile trip to *Greenleaf State Park,* where visitors will find one of Oklahoma's most tranquil settings. A 930-acre lake in the park is off-limits to speed boats; other park features include stone cabins (some with fireplaces), a pool, swimming beach, floating restaurant, and enclosed and heated fishing dock. Mountain bikes, canoes, kayaks, fishing boats, and even houseboats are available for rent. An 18-mile hiking trail begins and ends in the park and takes hikers through the Cherokee Wildlife Game Management Area. Call (918) 487–5196.

From the park continue along Highway 10 to the south end of *Lake Tenkiller.* The lake, formed by damming the Illinois River, is surrounded by oak and hickory trees and limestone bluffs. Cabins with fireplaces and lake views, and RV and tent-camping sites, are available at *Lake Tenkiller State Park,* 2 miles north of the junction of Highways 82 and 10A. The Tenkiller State Park Nature Center offers programs on bird-watching, tree identification, and animal habitats and is open seven days a week during the summer. Rainbow trout are stocked below the dam in the Illinois River, and the park is handy to fishing areas. Call (918) 489–5643 for park and cabin information.

The lake's limestone lining keeps the water of the *Illinois River* more clear than that in most other state lakes, making it a popular destination for scuba divers. When the Illinois River was dammed to create the lake, entire towns were submerged, making for intriguing areas for scuba divers to explore. The scuba store *Nautical Adventures,* on Highway 82 near Cookson, rents equipment and leads historical dive tours. Call (918) 457–DIVE (3483). At the south end of the lake, *Gene's Aqua Pro Shop* offers scuba certification and rents equipment. The shop is at Strayhorn Landing near Highway 10A.

MarVal Family Camping Resort, www.marvalresort.com, is south of Lake Tenkiller on the Lower Illinois and a favorite of trout fishermen. Access to the scenic Illinois is provided for fishermen, swimmers, and floaters; the resort also has horseback riding, hiking, a Laundromat, camp store, and swimming pools. Accommodations include tent-camping sites, RV sites, rustic log cabins, and cabins with decks, grills, and air conditioning. Day-use passes are also issued. For information or to make reservations, call (800) 340–4280.

One of Lake Tenkiller's liveliest recreation spots is *Barnacle Bill's Resort and Marina,* on the west side of the lake near Park Hill. The resort offers boat rentals, fishing guide services, moonlight pontoon rides, and a floating restaurant with live entertainment. Call (918) 457–5438.

One of locals' favorite haunts is the *Cookson Game Refuge,* 5 miles west of Cookson. The refuge is open to visitors from January 1 through August 31 for automobile touring, hiking, and mountain biking. Deer, turkey, and bobcat can be spotted in the refuge, and mountain bikers have found themselves pedaling alongside a herd of elk.

From Lake Tenkiller State Park, take Highway 10A to Highway 100 and travel south to Gore. Three miles west of town on Highway 64 is *Tahlonteeskee,* the capital of the first Cherokee, who arrived in Indian Territory in 1828. The original log capitol is gone; it was moved to Tahlequah after the assassinations of the signers of the New Echota treaty. In its place stands a reproduction of the old Cherokee courthouse, holding artifacts related to nineteenth-century Cherokee life. Call (918) 489–5663 for information.

Dwight Mission, www.dwightmission.org, north of Vian, was established in 1830 by Presbyterian missionaries and operated as an Indian school for the Cherokee until the 1940s. Most of the original buildings are gone, but the school administration building and sandstone dormitories are still standing, along with a reconstruction of a dogtrot-style cabin. This style is characterized by two separate buildings connected by one roof. This allows for an open-air breezeway typical of pioneer buildings in warmer climates. The mission now operates as a Presbyterian camp and retreat center, but visitors are welcome. It's best to call ahead to make sure someone is there; (918) 775–2018. Signs directing travelers to the mission appear just north of Vian.

From Vian, take U.S. Highway 64 east into Sallisaw to its junction with US 59. Travel north to Highway 101 and then east 7½ miles to *Sequoyah's Cabin,* a historic site operated by the Oklahoma Historical Society. Sequoyah, a half-Cherokee and half-white silversmith and the owner of a saltworks, invented a Cherokee alphabet, making the Cherokee the only Native American tribe with a written language. When Sequoyah began work on the syllabary, his fellow tribesmen put him on trial, suspecting him of being possessed by evil spirits. After a week of testimony, the jury had all learned to read and write and acquitted him. Sequoyah moved to Indian Territory in 1828 and built a log cabin, where he stayed with his family. That cabin is on display, enclosed in a sandstone building that was erected by Works Progress Administration workers in the 1930s, and holds artifacts from Sequoyah's life and from the Cherokee Nation. Visitors can also get a mini-lesson in the syllabary if they are interested. The museum is open Tuesday through Friday from 9:00 A.M. to 5:00 P.M. and on weekends from 2:00 to 5:00 P.M. Admission is free. Call (918) 775–2413 for information.

Along Highway 101, between US 59 and Sequoyah's Cabin, is a little country cemetery on the south side of the road. *Akins Cemetery* is notable as the resting place of Charles "Pretty Boy" Floyd, an outlaw who became a folk hero in Oklahoma during the Depression. Floyd was regarded as a kind of Okie Robin Hood, robbing banks and giving some of the spoils to the poor. Floyd's tombstone, chipped by souvenir seekers, is often covered with flowers.

Places to Stay in Cherokee Country

CLAREMORE

Best Western Will Rogers Inn
940 South Lynn Riggs Boulevard
(800) 644–9455

Claremore Motor Inn
1709 North Lynn Riggs Boulevard (Historic Route 66)
(800) 828–4540

GROVE

Best Western
Eighteenth and Broadway
(918) 786–6900

Blue Bluff Harbor Resort
63251 East 256 Road
(800) 891–5531

Stonebrook Inn
10400 US Highway 59
(918) 786–9799

MONKEY ISLAND

Cliff Dwellings Condos
(918) 521–1055

Shangri-La Resort
Highway 125 South
(800) 331–4060

MUSKOGEE

Graham-Carroll House Bed and Breakfast Inn
501 North Sixteenth Street
(918) 683–0100

Holiday Inn Express
3133 Azalea Park Drive
(918) 687–4224

Miss Addie's
Ninth and Broadway
(918) 682–1506

Whitlock Wishhouse
1113 North Country Club Road
(918) 683–3900

TAHLEQUAH

Oak Hill Motel
2600 South Muskogee
(918) 458–1200

Oak Park Motel
706 East Downing
(918) 456–2571

Places to Eat in Cherokee Country

CLAREMORE

The Hammett House
1616 West Will Rogers Boulevard
(918) 341–7333

Hugo's Restaurant
1217 West Archer
(918) 343–0063

The Pink House
210 West Fourth Street
(918) 342–2544

GROVE

Bubba's Smokehouse
2230 South Main Street
(918) 786–9599

FOR MORE INFORMATION

Grand Lake Association
9630 US Highway 59 North
Grove 74344
(918) 786–2289
www.grandlakefun.com

Muskogee Convention and Tourism Center
425 Boston Avenue
Box 2361
Muskogee 74402
(918) 684–6363
www.cityofmuskogee.com

Tahlequah Area Chamber of Commerce
123 East Delaware
Tahlequah 74464
(918) 456–3742
www.tourtahlequah.com

Cowskin Prairie Restaurant,
on Highway 10
northwest of Grove
(918) 786–6047

Lupe's Mexican Restaurant
½ mile south of Sailboat
Bridge on US 59
(918) 786–8723

Rheingarten Restaurant
911 South Main
(918) 786–8737

MUSKOGEE

Chet's Dairy Freeze
3510 West Okmulgee
(918) 687–9364

**Harmony House
and Bakery**
208 South Seventh Street
(918) 687–8653

My Place Barbecue
4322 West Okmulgee
(918) 683–5202

Okie's Restaurant
219 South Thirty-second
Street
(918) 683–1056

Runt's Barbecue
3003 West Okmulgee
(918) 681–3900

OKMULGEE

Cafe on the Square
112 South Morton
(918) 756–2223

Kirby's Cafe
219 West Sixth Street
(918) 756–8480

TAHLEQUAH

Bandy's Barbecue
441 South Muskogee
(918) 456–0711

Echota House Restaurant
14635 Highway 82 North
(918) 458–0768

Iguana Cafe
500A Muskogee
(918) 458–0044

The Porter House
2600 South Muskogee
(918) 456–0100

Ouachita Country: Southeastern Oklahoma

It's not just the pine-covered mountains running with clear streams and game-filled forests that make southeastern Oklahoma seem a world apart. For years the blue-tinged ridges and the rugged valleys of the Ouachita Mountains, the high point between the Appalachians and the Rockies, kept all but the most determined travelers away. When English botanist Thomas Nuttall made his way through the area in 1819, he wrote in his journal, "We passed and repassed several terrific ridges, over which our horses could scarcely keep their feet, and which were, besides, so overgrown with bushes and trees and half burnt with ragged limbs, that everything about us, not of leather, was lashed and torn to pieces." The first highway through the mountains wasn't built until 1919, a century later.

Modern travelers will find the going much easier. U.S. Highway 59/259 makes a north–south passage through the mountains, staying just a few miles west of the state's eastern border. U.S. Highway 271, a little farther west, is more circuitous, climbing through the Kiamichi Mountains in a slow arc. Both highways offer mountain views and access to the region's many parks and wilderness preserves. And the Talimena Scenic Byway, shown on maps as Highway 1, is arguably the most spectacular 36 miles of highway found anywhere in the state.

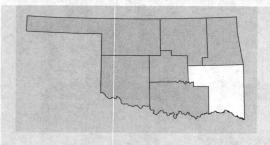

Built by the U.S.D.A. Forest Service in the 1960s purely for the view, the road follows the crest of the Kiamichi Mountains from US 271 to the Arkansas border, offering travelers numerous camping and picnic spots and scenic turnouts.

Thousands of acres of forest in southeastern Oklahoma are managed as wilderness preserves, making the area a paradise for hikers, photographers, mountain bikers, fishermen, birders, hunters, and outdoor enthusiasts of all stripes. The area's remoteness is its greatest charm, but it does make it necessary for travelers to do a little extra planning. Since so much land is off-limits to development, cabins and other accommodations are often booked up for months in advance, especially for summer weekends. Restaurant choices are limited in most places, and it can be a thirty-minute drive to the nearest well-stocked grocery store from some campgrounds.

This chapter will take travelers on a big loop through southeastern Oklahoma, first south through the Ouachita Mountains along US 59/259, then south along the Red River on U.S. Highway 70 and north along U.S. Highway 270.

Choctaw Country

Before 1800 Choctaw hunting parties came west into what's now southeastern Oklahoma to hunt deer. The Choctaw word *owa* means "hunting expedition," and the word *chito* means "big." The French spelling and pronunciation of the Choctaw phrase *owa-chito* gave the Ouachita Mountains their name.

In 1831 the Choctaw Nation, now the third-largest Native American tribe in the United States, became the first of the southeastern tribes to be removed to Indian Territory. The Choctaw owned land in common and allowed Choctaw

AUTHOR'S FAVORITES IN OUACHITA COUNTRY

Beavers Bend State Park	Overstreet-Kerr Living History Farm
Choctaw Chief's House	Peter Conser House
Choctaw Nation Museum	Robbers Cave State Park
Heavener Rune Stone State Park	Spiro Mounds Archaeological Park
Hugo Heritage Railroad and Frisco Depot Museum	Talimena Scenic Byway

Trail of Treaties

In the 1830 Treaty of Dancing Rabbit Creek, the Choctaw ceded approximately 10 million acres of land in Mississippi in exchange for all the land in what's now southern Oklahoma from east to west. The treaty promised "that no Territory or State shall ever have a right to pass laws for the government of the Choctaw Nation of Red People and their descendants; and that no part of the land granted them shall ever be embraced in any Territory or State."

Chief Pushmataha once boasted, "The Choctaws have never taken up arms against the United States. But we have accomplished more in this treaty by diplomacy than we could have done by war, had we chosen that method and been entirely victorious. For we have acquired from the United States here her best remaining territory west of the Mississippi."

But this was not for long—by 1907 the Choctaw Nation had made sixteen treaties and agreements with the United States, most of them making ever-greater concessions of land.

citizens to make their homes anywhere they wished in the new country, and they could fence all the land that they could clear, plus a ¼-mile perimeter, as long as they didn't trespass on fenced lands of another Choctaw.

In 1871 Tom Overstreet, a Missourian, and his Choctaw wife, Margaret Victor Overstreet, moved south of the Canadian River and began clearing what eventually became a 3,000-acre farm. The Overstreets grew wealthy raising cattle, hogs, horses, cotton, and potatoes, and today their fifteen-room former home, a mansion on the frontier, is the nucleus of **Overstreet-Kerr Living History Farm.** Visitors learn the household arts and farming methods that Tom and Margaret might have used, such as making lye soap and candles and weaving baskets and chair seats. In small fields around the house are demonstrations of early-day (and energy-efficient) forms of soil cultivation and pest control. Gardens are planted with medicinal plants and "heirloom" vegetable seeds, and old strains of livestock, genetically similar to those brought over on the Trail of Tears, graze in the pastures.

The farm is managed under the direction of the Kerr Center for Sustainable Agriculture, www.kerrcenter.com, a Poteau-based foundation committed to the study of alternative farming methods. During the October Historical Farm-Fest, cider- and sorghum-making are demonstrated. The living-history farm is open for tours Friday and Saturday from 10:00 A.M. to 4:00 P.M. The farm is 10 miles south of Interstate 40 on US 59 and ¼ mile west on Overstreet-Kerr Road. Call (918) 966–3282 for information; www.kerrcenter.com/overstreet/index.html.

Scullyville, www.scullyville.com, is the site of the former capital of the Choctaw northern district and site of the first Choctaw Agency. The town received its name from the Choctaw word for money, *iskuli,* because the government annuities that were part of the tribe's relocation treaty were paid there. The town, one of the first stops for the 12,000 members of the tribe who walked here from Mississippi, now consists of a cemetery filled with the names of nineteenth-century Choctaw leaders. The cemetery is shaded by ancient oaks and elms, and if you decide to visit, be sure to carry along your road map. The cemetery is a virtual "Who's Who" of the Old Choctaw Nation, and some place names of modern towns and counties—LeFlore, McCurtain, Krebbs—are the same as the names on the tombstones. The cemetery is 2 miles northeast of Spiro on Highway 9.

Ten miles west of Scullyville, at *Spiro Mounds Archaeological Park,* are the remains of a Native American culture that inhabited the area much, much earlier than the Choctaw. The mounds, packed earth covered with scraggly brush, aren't much to look at, but they once marked the religious center for a confederation of sixty tribes, which stretched from the Rocky Mountains to Virginia and from the Gulf of Mexico to the Great Lakes. The eleven earthen mounds in the 140-acre park held the homes and underground tombs of an elite group of priests who fasted and prayed to prevent disasters like floods and tornadoes and to ensure good crops. The mounds also served as a kind of huge prehistoric calendar, used to keep track of the movements of the sun in order to set planting and harvesting dates. Twice a year, on the vernal and autumnal equinoxes, site archaeologist Dennis Peterson leads guided hikes that show how the mounds were used to predict the precise time when the sun would cross the equator. Among the artifacts found at the site are vast amounts of conch shells and copper, prehistoric America's equivalents of gold and diamonds.

The site was used by the Spiro Mounds people from A.D. 600 to 1450 and was the religious and trading center of the tribal confederation between 1100 and 1450. The site's significance was discovered during the Depression when a half-dozen bounty hunters went looking for the Spanish gold rumored to be in the area. Not aware of what they had stumbled

A shell gorget on display at Spiro Mounds Archaeological Park

into at first, the men formed a mining company and secured a lease. They were soon unearthing a Tut-like array of burial treasure, including engraved shells, embossed copper plates, stone tools, textiles, stone effigy pipes, pearls, baskets, and the only known examples of prehistoric lace in the country. By 1935, when the miners' lease expired, the state legislature had passed a law barring the sale of antiquities, and a scholarly excavation began in 1936. But by then, so many of the excavated articles had disappeared that much of what could have been known about the culture is gone, including an explanation for why the Spiro people disappeared from the site abruptly in 1450. Some artifacts from the site are on display in an interpretive center at the park. A mile-long trail takes visitors near the mounds, and Peterson will act as a guide when available. (He is so knowledgeable, it's worth checking in advance to see if he will be there.) The park is open Wednesday through Saturday from 9:00 A.M. to 5:00 P.M. and on Sunday from noon to 5:00 P.M. The park is 3 miles east of Spiro on Highway 9, then 4 miles north on Spiro Mounds Road. Call (918) 962–2062 or visit www.myspiro.com for information.

Aunt Jan's Cozy Cabin, with its handmade quilts and porch swing, more than lives up to its name. This charming log cabin, a few miles west of US 59, sits on a small cattle ranch. It is equipped with a grill, hot tub, television, and VCR and is stocked with refreshments. There is a kitchen, but you can have a

TOP EVENTS IN OUACHITA COUNTRY

1830s Traders and Trappers Rendezvous,
Fort Towson, March;
(580) 873–2634

Italian Festival,
McAlester, Memorial Day;
(918) 426–2055

Kiamichi Owa Chito Festival of the Forest,
Beavers Bend State Park, June;
(580) 584–3393

Grant's Bluegrass Festival,
Hugo, August;
(580) 326–5063;
www.grantsbluegrass.com

Choctaw Nation Labor Day Festival,
Tuskahoma, September;
(918) 569–4465

Robbers Cave Fall Festival,
Wilburton, October;
(918) 465–2565

Beavers Bend Folk Festival,
Forest Heritage Center, November;
(580) 494–6497;
www.beaversbend.com

big country breakfast delivered to your door. Make reservations by calling (800) 470–3481 or visit www.bbonline.com/ok/cozycabin.

As you continue to drive south along US 59 through Poteau, be sure to look to your west at "The World's Highest Hill." *Cavanal Hill* was measured at 1,999 feet and missed being classified a mountain by only a foot. The *Kerr Conference Center,* www.kerrconferencecenter.com, a native-stone ranch house that belonged to former Oklahoma governor and U.S. Senator Robert S. Kerr, is a few miles south of Poteau and is open to the public. There are ten rooms in the house, all with private baths, some decorated with idiosyncratic charm, such as the "Ship Room," with real portholes and bunk beds suspended from the ceiling, built for the Kerr grandchildren. There's a museum next door, with some Spiro artifacts and stones that some believe are Viking rune stones. Room rates range from $60 to $80, including a continental breakfast. Follow the signs west from US 59. Call (918) 647–8221 for information.

Nearby Lake Wister was built along the Poteau River in 1948 by the U.S. Army Corps of Engineers for flood control. As the dam was built, the site, a former hunting ground for tribes, including the Choctaw and the Mound Builders, was excavated. A nice collection of arrowheads and other finds is on display in the park office on Quarry Island. The island, actually a fifty-acre peninsula, has five cabins; there are ten more cabins on the heavily wooded west side of the lake, along with 115 picnic sites, 97 campsites with utilities, and 100 more campsites with water and electricity. The 4,000-acre reservoir is a favorite of fishermen for its abundance of northern bluegill and sand bass. *Lake Wister State Park* is 2 miles south of Wister off US 270. Call (918) 655–7756 for information.

Another intriguing artifact is found in *Heavener,* formerly called Choctaw City, 7 miles south of Poteau and home to *Heavener Rune Stone State Park,* 2 miles east of town. To get there, turn to the east at the town's only stoplight, then north right across the railroad tracks on Main Street for 2½ blocks. Turn east on Avenue A for 6 blocks, then north again on Morris Creek Road for 2 more blocks. Turn east at the sign and follow the road up the side of the mountain. On display at the park is a slab of sandstone measuring 12 feet high, 10 feet wide, and 2 feet thick and carved with eight runic letters. The first recorded descriptions of the rock were made after the arrival of the Choctaw in the 1830s, and the stone became known as Indian Rock, a marker, some thought, for buried treasure. When a 1923 analysis done by the Smithsonian Institution identified the markings as runelike, some became convinced it was an inland version of the Kensington rune stone. An early reading of the stone translated it as a date, "November 11, 1011," but a more recent, more convincing translation is "Glome Dal," which has been interpreted as a claim on the valley ("dal" is valley) by a Norseman named Glome. There's still plenty of debate about whether or not the markings were actually made by Vikings, who theoretically sailed around Florida, into the Gulf of Mexico, on to the Mississippi River, then up the Poteau River by way of the Arkansas. (A local amateur historian, Gloria Farrell, devoted most of her life to trying to prove the Viking origin of the stone, and her book—something of a slab itself—is on display at the visitors' center.)

Viking artifact or not, the stone, still in its original spot, now is shielded from the elements and vandals by a pretty wooden structure, under Plexiglas and surveillance by a security camera. Sandstone steps and a bridge make the steep incline more manageable and lead to a nature trail into the forest and along a mountainside cliff. Overnight camping isn't allowed in the park, but there are a number of picnic tables with panoramic views. The park is open daily. Call (918) 653–2241 for information.

The Ouachita Forest

Four miles south of Heavener is the historic site the **Peter Conser House,** former residence of a prominent Choctaw politician and businessman. During the 1880s Conser was captain of the Choctaw Lighthorsemen, an elite law-enforcement corps of eighteen members that patrolled the Choctaw Nation during territorial days and possessed the combined powers of sheriff, judge, jury, and executioner. There were no jails in the Choctaw nation. The punishment for a first offense was usually whipping, and a second offense was punishable by death. Those sentenced to die were released to make arrangements for their families and were honor bound to show up for punishment—and virtually all of them did. Conser, who served in the Choctaw equivalent of Congress, owned a blacksmith shop, gristmill, sawmill, and general store on his 660-acre spread. The house, built in 1894, is largely in its original condition, furnished with some of the family's furniture and period pieces. It is open Wednesday through Saturday from 10:00 A.M. to 5:00 P.M. and on Sunday from 1:00 to 5:00 P.M. A sign along US 59 near Hodgen directs travelers west 3½ miles. Call (918) 653–2493 for information.

Conser's house is just a few miles north of the boundary of the 26,445-acre **Winding Stair Recreation Area** in the **Ouachita National Forest,** the oldest national forest in the South. It's heaven for campers—overnight camping is permitted anywhere within the recreation area—while others will want to plan day trips into the forest since there are no motels, cabins, or restaurants within the recreation-area boundaries.

Cedar Lake Campground is a good camping base from which to explore the forest. A peaceful ninety-acre lake has a boat ramp and a ban against boat motors bigger than seven horsepower. There are water and electric hookups, sanitary stations, picnic shelters, showers, and a hiking path all around the lake. Campers with horses head to *Cedar Lake Equestrian Camp,* a base from which more than 200 miles of horse trails fan out across Holson Valley. Trails range from gentle, hour-long rides, like the switchbacks up nearby Snake Mountain, to two-day treks that take riders from mountain peak to mountain peak. There are RV and tent sites, a group shelter with grill, hot showers for humans and horses, wash stations, a corral, and hitching posts. The camp is 5 miles south of Hodgen, 3 miles west on Holson Valley Road, and then 1 mile north along forest service roads.

Cedar Lake Campground is a trailhead for the *Ouachita Trail,* pieced together from old buffalo trails, logging roads, and footpaths by a cadre of senior citizens, forest service employees, and Civilian Conservation Corps youth, who worked on the trail for more than a decade. The workers aimed for an average 8 percent grade along the trail's 46 miles in Oklahoma; elevations, however, reach 1,500 to 2,000 feet near the Oklahoma–Arkansas border.

Maps to the trail are available at the *Ouachita National Forest West End Information Center,* (918) 567–2046, in *Talihina,* also the gateway to the Talimena Scenic Byway. The highway, Highway 1, was built in the 1960s purely for the spectacular scenery afforded along the ridges of the Ouachita Mountains. The road links Talihina, Oklahoma, in the west to Mena, Arkansas, in the east; Talihina is Choctaw for "iron road" and dates back to 1888, when the Frisco railroad went through. Locals called the mountains the "Winding Stair Mountains" for the way the mountain ridges forced travelers to loop back and forth.

The *Talimena Scenic Byway,* www.talimenascenicdrive.com, (see map on following page) still does plenty of looping, affording sweeping views of the blue-green mountains and valleys at the numerous scenic turnouts and picnic and camping areas found along the byway. The Ouachita Mountains once extended to the Appalachian Mountains, before the Mississippi River separated the ranges. Fault lines, where the sandstone and shale were folded and faulted, are still visible along the drive. There's plenty of more-recent history to be found along the road, such as *Horse Thief Springs,* where nineteenth-century horse thieves stopped to rest their horses. *Emerald Vista* is one of the prettiest spots along the drive and has one primitive campsite with a prime view. Hikers can picnic along the old road at *Old Military Road Historical Site* where there are small picnic tables and rest rooms, and then follow a 3-mile stretch of the old Military Road that once linked Fort Towson near the Red River to Fort Smith, in Arkansas.

On summer evenings black bears lumber along the roads in southeastern Oklahoma, especially on the Talimena Scenic Byway, looking for food. They

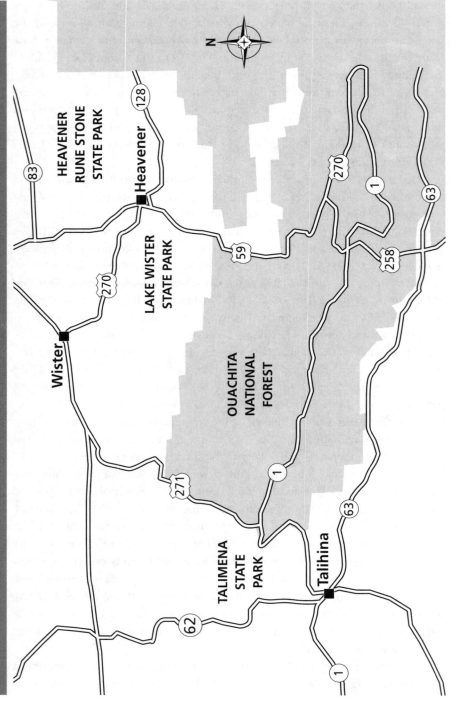

TALIMENA SCENIC BYWAY (HIGHWAY 1)

eat ripe poke- and blackberries, acorns, and persimmons. When their natural food supply is low, they forage a little closer to home. Camping out in fruit trees and nibbling dog kibble, they become a nuisance in residential areas.

The **Robert S. Kerr Nature Center Arboretum,** 2 miles west of the junction of Talimena Drive and US 259, was created in an 8,000-acre natural botanical area between the Winding Stair Mountains and the Rich Mountains and gives visitors a chance to learn how different tree species are affected by various weather and soil conditions. For example, the east–west orientation of the forest has created separate plant communities on either side of the slopes. Post oak, pine, and blackjack grow on the southern slopes, while white oak, hickory, dogwood, and pawpaw grow on the north. Markers along a tree-identification trail explain such things as why the vistas have a blue cast (short leaf pine needles have a bluish tinge) and which trees were used by Native Americans to make rope (basswood). There are three trails of differing degrees of length and difficulty; a little visitors' kiosk near the road holds trail information.

There are eleven campsites and a natural pool on Billy Creek at **Billy Creek Campground,** northeast of Muse. Farther south and east, travelers find one of only two beech tree stands in the state at **Beech Creek National Scenic Area and Botanical Area.** The Beech Creek Trail is south of Talimena Drive, between Blue Bouncer and Walnut Mountains.

A to Z Guest Ranch, www.atozguestranch.com, is nestled in a little valley adjacent to the 215,000-acre **Honobia Creek Wildlife Management Area.** Travelers drive down along a steep gravel road and climb back up into miles of trails cut into the mountains. Most of the camp's guests bring their own mounts. Three cabins are available, including two log cabins that sit on a creek bank and have their own corrals. Tent campers, hikers, and mountain bikers are welcome. Call (580) 244–3729 for information.

A mile north on Octavia Road, **Eagle Creek Guest Cottages** offer luxurious yet rustic accommodations. The dozen log cabins sprinkled over forty acres on the backside of a mountain were built with native stone fireplaces and full kitchens and are furnished with such amenities as Jacuzzis, microwave ovens, VCRs, cable television, and back porches overlooking Big Eagle Creek. The creek is a popular spot for bass fishing and canoeing, and a spring-fed lake is stocked with channel catfish, Florida-strain largemouth bass, and bluegills. Rates range from $125 to $190 a night, with a minimum two-night stay. No pets or children under sixteen are allowed. Call (580) 244–7597 or visit www.guest cottages.com for information.

Guided trail rides are available through **Wild Horse Trail Ride,** 8 miles east of Honobia (Ho-NUB-ee), which offers three-day-long rides on Memorial Day and Labor Day and seven one-day rides in the spring and fall. Base camp has electrical hookups and showers and a log cookhouse where cooks turn out fare such as turkey and dressing, chicken and dumplings, and chicken-fried steak. All-day and half-day rides available. The daily rides pass historic areas that seem untouched by time, such as a crossing where white oak trees were laid in the riverbed a century ago and Noali Trail, once the main thoroughfare into Arkansas. Prices range from $195 for a three-day ride to $295 for a week. For information call (918) 755–4570 or (580) 244–3232.

The Mountain Fork River flows into the 14,000 acres that make up the **McCurtain County Wilderness Area,** www.mccurtaincountygetaways.com. The pine forest was set aside by the Oklahoma legislature in 1918 and is the last refuge in the state for the red-cockaded woodpecker. Flying squirrels, bobcats, red and gray foxes, and one hundred species of birds have been spotted in the wilderness area. There is a 1-mile self-guided walking trail west of the river, with markers designating prime wildlife viewing stops. To go east of the river, you'll need to get a day-use permit from the Oklahoma Department of Wildlife Conservation, P.O. Box 53465, Oklahoma City, 73105. The wilderness area is 18 miles south of Smithville; a gravel road points travelers to the east. Stay right and follow signs for 7½ miles.

If you never outgrew loving treehouses, you'll love staying in the **Tree Top View Cabins,** near Battiest (pronounced *Bah-TEEST*). The eight cabins, built on piers on the banks of the Glover River, are nestled in the sycamores and pines, each hidden from the view of the others by leafy branches. The Glover is distinguished as the only undammed river in the state, and it is far more mercurial than most. The river is too unpredictable to attract canoe outfitters, but Tree Top owners Billy and Charlotte Parsons keep a flat-bottomed johnboat and canoes that guests are welcome to borrow. Billy Parsons logged and cut all the lumber for the cabins, built the road, and laid the water lines. Five different kinds of wood were used to finish out the cabins: yellow pine, red oak, white oak, birch, and sycamore. Cabins are equipped with full kitchens, including microwaves, grills, linens, and basic cookware. There are no televisions or telephones—but there is a porch swing in the living room. Charlotte Parsons says cabin guests sometimes load up in the car and travel to area attractions, but most fish, walk, loaf, read, and enjoy the Glover River nightlife: star watching. "They drive out in the middle of the pasture to where there are no trees," she says. "They say they've never been anywhere so dark or seen stars so bright." Cabins sleep six; rates range from $100 to $150 a night, depending on the number of people. Battiest, a tiny town with a post office, store, and arcade, is north of US 259 along Highway 144. The Tree Top Cabins are west of Battiest: The last mile is along a gravel road. Call (580)

A Work of Art

History has it that Oklahoma's first flag was not impressive. It consisted of the numerals "46," in blue, placed in the center of a white star upon a red field. The Daughters of the American Revolution took it upon themselves to change it and an invitation for designs was sent. Many submitted artwork for the competition, but one in particular, designed by Mrs. George Fluke Jr., stood out. The committee who made the selection felt her original work of art, the hand-painted flag, "was beautiful, of appropriate symbolism, and with the individuality which would serve to attract attention." Mrs. Fluke's flag was approved by the Tenth Legislature and became the official emblem of Oklahoma on April 2, 1925.

While the state flag flies proudly over Oklahoma government buildings and educational institutions, the flag has seen its share of travel. Back in 1963, a piece of the flag was scheduled to be sent into space tucked away in Gordon Cooper's flight suit. All systems were "go" until someone in the chain of command nixed the idea, ruling that the flag must be chemically analyzed and there wasn't time to do the procedure. Seven years later, on August 5, 1970, Ed Wise, a graduate of Tecumseh High School who was serving on the USS *Queenfish,* displayed the Oklahoma flag at the North Pole.

241–5599. You can find photographs of the river and the cabins at their Web site: www.treetopviewcabins.com.

Hochatown State Park and Beavers Bend State Park, both on Broken Bow Lake, are surrounded on three sides by undeveloped land. Of the cabins and resorts clustered west of the lake along US 259, one of the best is **Whip-Poor-Will Resort,** www.okresort.com, a friendly, family-oriented resort. The seventeen cabins here range from one room just big enough for a brass bed, patchwork quilt, and a fireplace, to two-bedroom cabins that sleep eight to ten and are furnished with full kitchens complete with microwave ovens, wood-burning stoves, and porch swings. Attached to the Resort Office is the **Fudge Shop**. Stop in and try some of their 15 to 20 varieties of fudge including butter pecan and coconut cream. The gift shop area features Made in Oklahoma products. Call (580) 494–6476.

Just across the road is the entrance to Hochatown State Park, where the **Cedar Creek Golf Course** was carved out of the piney woods; the first fairways were cleared in the 1970s with chainsaws and machetes. A mountain stream winds through the eighteen-hole course, and golfers may spot wild turkey, deer, fox, or even the occasional wild hog or a bald eagle fishing at nearby Broken Bow Lake. The golf course clubhouse is 3½ miles east of US 259. Call (580) 494–6456 for information.

Nearby *Lakeview Inn Lodge* perches on the edge of a peninsula. Each of the thirty-six rooms and four suites has a balcony view of Broken Bow Lake, overlooking a little island. There is no restaurant or bar in the lodge; breakfast is served in a great room each morning, and you are on your own for lunch and dinner. Rooms range from $80 to $175. Call (580) 494–6179 for reservations.

quartzhound

Cephis Hall's uncanny ability to locate quartz crystals is one thing, but when the self-taught paleontologist found and excavated one of the rarest dinosaurs in the world, the 120-million-year-old *Acrocanthosaurus,* the scientific community sat up and took notice. That was in the late '70s, and Hall is still unearthing treasure in the Beavers Bend area, arranging crystal-digging tours from his West Slope Rock Shop near Hochatown. Hall's second sense for finding the purest, clearest quartz crystals and his access to digging spots on private land make his guide service popular. (The dinosaur fossils are at a university, but Hall keeps plaster casts of the bones at his shop.) Note: Taking quartz crystals from the state park isn't permitted.

Stevens' Gap Restaurant, right near the park entrance, offers regional specialties such as catfish fillets served with hush puppies and baked sweet potatoes, Southern fried chicken, fried okra, and brown beans. Steaks, cheeseburgers, and hand-cut onion rings are on the menu, and you can get breakfast (biscuits, gravy, and the works) all day long. Call (580) 494–6350.

Driving 7 miles south down US 259 takes travelers to *Beavers Bend State Park,* www.beaversbend.com, (580) 494–6300, which encompasses 3,500 densely forested acres. Beavers Bend is the most remote of all of Oklahoma's state parks and is the most popular—the park's forty-seven wood-and-stone cabins stay at nearly full occupancy year-round. In addition to cabins, there are fifteen primitive camping areas and eight areas for RVs. Mountain Fork River runs through the heart of the park, collecting mist in the early mornings and spilling into Broken Bow Lake. The lake is a draw for land-locked scuba divers: The rocky shores of the lake's numerous islands are strewn with crystals, which act as filters and clarify the water. Wildlife also abounds on the islands, especially deer, which can sometimes be spotted swimming out from shore. Trout aren't native to the area, but the Oklahoma Wildlife Department regularly stocks the lake with rainbow and brown trout. (The area below the dam is a favorite spot for fly fishermen.)

Visitors to the park can swim in a natural pool, visit the park's nature center, hike along 24 miles of trails, ride horseback, rent canoes, play tennis or miniature golf, or take a train ride through the park. *Beavers Bend Restaurant,* in the middle of the park, serves breakfast, lunch, and dinner. Next to the park office is the *Forest Heritage Center,* which traces the history of the area back to prehistoric times with painted murals and artifacts. The center is built around an atrium that holds a hundred-year-old oak log cabin moved to the park from the Kiamichi Mountains. In November, the Heritage Center is the stage for the Beavers Bend Folk Life Festival, a three-day demonstration of vanishing everyday arts, such as basket weaving and broom, rope, and lye-soap making. The festival also includes contemporary arts and crafts, traditional music, and regional food.

Every third weekend in June, the center hosts the *Owa-Chito Festival of the Forest,* where a "Bull of the Woods" top lumberjack is named and old-time logging skills are tested. There are also canoe races, turkey calling, and country music. A special treat: The Choctaw Nation sets up a Choctaw cafe featuring Indian fry bread, hominy pork stew, and *bahaha*, dumplings made from cornmeal, sweet potatoes, and pinto beans, wrapped in corn shucks and boiled. For information call the Forest Heritage Center, (580) 494–6497.

The path of early Choctaw history can be traced along US 70, which parallels the Red River. Six miles west of the state's border with Arkansas is *Eagletown,* a mostly vanished community named for the bald eagles that nested in local cypress trees. Still standing is the 1884 home of Jefferson Gardner, chief of the tribe from 1894 to 1896. The house is 6 miles east of Broken Bow, then ¼ mile north of the highway. (There's a sign.) For $2.00, Lewis and Frances Stiles, the current owners, will give you a tour of the two-story wood-frame house, show you their collection of fossils and Native American and pioneer artifacts, and escort you to a cypress tree that was measured at 90 feet tall and

Refuge on Little River

Extraordinary trees grow in the bottomlands along the Little River: Eight of Oklahoma's biggest trees are found within the boundaries of the 13,000-acre *Little River National Wildlife Refuge.* A decade ago, the U.S. Fish and Wildlife Service bought the parcel of old-growth forest from a logging company and established the refuge in order to preserve the plants and animals in one of Oklahoma's last remaining examples of bottomland hardwood habitat. The preserve, dotted with sloughs, swamps, and oxbow lakes, is home to wintering mallards and wood ducks, beaver, river otter, mink, and bobcat and some species found only in this area, including the bird-voiced tree frog, the mole salamander, western pygmy rattlesnake, and red buckeye and horse sugar bushes. The refuge also shelters the only known population of nesting warblers and nesting anhingas known in Oklahoma. You'll find the refuge 4 miles south of Broken Bow on US 70. For information and maps, stop by the USFWS refuge headquarters at 635 South Park, Broken Bow; (580) 584–6211.

estimated to be 2,000 years old when it was struck by lightning in 1982 (despite the lightning rod attached to its branches). Part of the path to the tree follows an old military road, and the Stileses can also point visitors to ruts made by Choctaw wagons. (A closer look at the ruts is for the very determined, because it involves going into a well-used cow pasture, according to Mrs. Stiles.) Call (580) 584–6588 for information.

At the intersection of US 259 and US 70 in *Broken Bow* is the *Memorial Indian Museum.* Archaeologist LaMarr Smith opened it in 1962, when his collection of artifacts became too big for his house. He began treasure hunting as a kid in a region long populated by native cultures. The Caddo Indian civilization settled the southeastern part of Oklahoma along with parts of Arkansas, Louisiana, and Texas around the time of the Spanish exploration in the mid-1500s. Before that, Archaic peoples (6000–200 B.C.) and Paleo-Indians (9000–6000 B.C.) hunted game there. Arrowheads, spear points, and "bird stones" (small arrowheads that look like birds) found on a neighbor's farm are now part of a collection of primitive artifacts representing 20,000 years. Most were found within 75 miles of Smith's home. The museum is located on the south side of Second Street. It is open Monday, Thursday, Friday, and Saturday 9:00 A.M. to 5:00 P.M.; no charge. If you get lost, stop and ask for directions. Almost everyone in town knows where to find LaMarr Smith, but if you need the museum's number, it's (580) 584–6531.

The Red River Valley

In *Idabel,* www.idabelchamber.com, the small *Museum of the Red River* holds examples of locally excavated Caddoan pottery, which date from A.D. 700 to 1200, and local Indian artifacts furnish a log cabin that illustrates life in the Choctaw Nation circa 1890. The nucleus of the museum is the personal collection of Quintus and Mary Herron, a local couple who are passionate about archaeology. The Herrons created the museum and a foundation in 1975 as a way to showcase local history as well as Native American artifacts they and others had collected from North, South, and Central America. The museum is at 812 East Lincoln Road, on the South Highway 70 Bypass. The museum is open Tuesday through Saturday from 10:00 A.M. to 5:00 P.M. and Sundays 11:00 A.M. to 4:00 P.M. Most days, Mary Herron herself will be on hand. Call (580) 286–3616 or visit www.museumoftheredriver.org for information.

Birdwatchers will want to visit the *Red Slough Wetland Reserve Project.* Located 13 miles east of Idabel on Mudline Road, this 5,814 acres of land offers unique bird viewing experiences. Visitors will enjoy one of the top bird-watching areas in Oklahoma, with more than 230 species documented. Besides waterfowl, the reserve has wading birds, shorebirds, and neotropical migrants. Some of the unusual species include white ibis, roseate spoonbills, wood storks, and black-bellied whistling ducks. The refuge area is closed to the public October 31 to January 31 to provide a resting area for waterfowl. For more information contact the Ouachita National Forest at (301) 321–5202 or the Oklahoma Ranger District, (580) 286–6564. Open daily twenty-four hours.

About 20 miles west of Idabel on US 70, near Millerton, an old iron archway announces **Wheelock Academy.** In 1832 missionaries to the Choctaw Tribe established the academy as a day school, and in 1842 the Choctaw Tribal Council turned it into a boarding school for Choctaw girls. Eight buildings are all that remain of an educational institution that served the tribe for more than one hundred years. In the old administration building are a small museum and gift shop. The Choctaw Tribe is renovating the remaining buildings, including the old heating plant. The largest is Pushmataha Hall, the main dormitory building. Inscribed on the bell in the old tower is the phrase DEFEND THE POOR AND THE FATHERLESS. There is no admission fee, but donations are appreciated. Call (580) 746–2139 for hours.

From Idabel, Highway 3 stairsteps down into the national forest to the little town of **Tom,** population 250, which sits at the highway's final turn. The first record of settlement in the area dates to 1719, when French trader Bernard de la Harpe built a fort and post just north of the Red River. The French surrendered title after the Louisiana Purchase and the removal of the Choctaws west. Chief Samuel Garland brought his family and slaves to the area and built a sawmill and cotton plantation. About 90 percent of Tom's population are direct descendants of slaves brought to Indian Territory along the Trail of Tears.

Logging trucks may slow progress west along US 70, particularly as you near Valliant, site of a huge cardboard-container manufacturing plant owned by Weyerhauser. For decades, the timber company, which owns or leases about 80,000 acres of pine forests in southeastern Oklahoma, has allowed hunters, mountain bikers, off-road-vehicle drivers, and hikers to use its logging roads (and has even furnished maps). The company is contemplating charging an access fee. Call (580) 981–2211 for information.

At Swink, turn north at the Swink Grocery and Feed Store and travel for ½ mile to the Y in the road. Turn east and travel 1 mile to the **Choctaw Chief's House,** which some claim is the oldest home in Oklahoma still standing on its original site. The 1830s dogtrot-style log cabin was touted for years by the Oklahoma Historical Society as having been built as part of treaty negotiations for one of three Choctaw district chiefs who moved to Indian Territory in 1837. (The exact dimensions of the home are even spelled out in the 1830 Treaty of Dancing Rabbit Creek.) In recent years, the historical society has dropped the house from its official roster of historic sites because of its many reconstructions, but Swink residents have stuck by the story. The house was home to district chief Thomas LeFlore, who made the house the center of his Thousand Acre Farm cotton plantation. Whatever its provenance, the lonely log cabin in the quiet clearing brings home how remote the area was in the 1830s. The town raised money to restore the building, and today it is open daily from 10:00 A.M. to 4:00 P.M. Guided and group tours are conducted by appointment. Call (580) 873–2301 for information.

Fort Towson, Oklahoma's second-oldest frontier post, was founded in 1824 to protect settlers traveling to Texas, guard the Spanish border, and protect the residents of what was then Arkansas Territory. (On at least one occasion, the local population was called out to defend the fort.) Abandoned in 1829, the fort was reopened after the signing of the Treaty of Dancing Rabbit Creek in 1830 in order to protect the Choctaws from Arkansas settlers and the Plains Indians in the west. The fort was an active military installation until 1854, when it became headquarters for the federal agent assigned to the Choctaws. In 1863 the commander of Confederate forces in Indian Territory made the fort headquarters, and on June 23, 1865, when Stand Watie, a Cherokee general, surrendered his troops, he became the last Confederate military leader to lay down arms at the end of the Civil War.

Today *Fort Towson Military Park,* 1 mile northeast of the Fort Towson town site, is both an interpretive and archaeological site. The limestone foundations of officers' quarters and other post buildings have been excavated, revealing their layout. The park also has a reproduction of *Sutler's Store,* which is outfitted with old barrels, gourds, iron pots, and other frontier household goods. Every June, the fort is the site of an annual "homecoming" town picnic, along with an 1830s and 1840s rendezvous, with historical reenactors representing traders, pioneers, craftsmen, and soldiers. Events such as Pony Express horseback relay races, black-powder rifle and pistol demonstrations, and axe throwing are featured, along with tours of the site of the first Choctaw capital, in the now-vanished Doaksville. The abandoned town, a 2-mile hike from the fort, is currently under excavation. The fort, operated by the Oklahoma Historical Society, is open Monday through Friday from 9:00 A.M. to 5:00 P.M. and Saturday and Sunday from 1:00 to 5:00 P.M.; (580) 873–2634.

Eight miles farther west is *Hugo,* www.hugochamber.org, a town notable for the number of circuses and rail lines that came through it. The town was a railroad hub at the turn of the twentieth century, when seven daily passenger trains and numerous freight trains hauling out cotton and timber kept the two-story Frisco depot humming. At one time a dozen circuses wintered near Hugo, to take advantage of the moderate climate and the easy access to rail trans-

Choctaw Chief's House, Swink

portation. Hugo is down to three circuses now, including the ***Carson-Barnes Circus,*** a three-ring traveling tent show, the largest of its kind left in the United States. The circus animals from all three circuses spend the winter at the Carson-Barnes circus grounds. Carson-Barnes also runs the ***Endangered Ark Foundation.*** This nonprofit organization runs an elephant retirement home and has a breeding program. Contributions are accepted. Visitors to the elephant home are allowed, but there are no regular visiting hours. Call to arrange a visit. Visitors can also make an appointment to visit the circus from December through March for a behind-the-scenes peek at the animals. (You might catch a trapeze artist at practice, as well.) The circus is west of Hugo, on Kirk Road, which is about a mile north on Highway 93. Call (580) 326–3173 or visit www.carson-barnescircus.com for information.

Angie's specialty is hand-tenderized chicken-fried steak, and her homemade pies and cobblers are also delicious, but the decor really makes the meal at ***Angie's Circus City Diner,*** at 1312 East Jackson, Hugo. Pictures of circus performers, promotional posters, old tickets, and a collection of circus letterheads decorate the walls and tabletops. Call (580) 326–2027 for more information.

While passenger rail service has also disappeared from Hugo, it has not been forgotten, thanks to the ***Hugo Heritage Railroad and Frisco Depot Museum.*** The old brick, two-story depot is filled with a hodgepodge of local memorabilia and artifacts, including railroad models, a handmade miniature replica of each and every act performed by the Carson-Barnes circus, and most—but not all—of a moonshine liquor still that was seized by the federal government in the nearby Kiamichi Mountains. The museum is open Tuesday through Saturday 10:00 A.M. to 4:00 P.M. Call (580) 326–6630.

The original marble counter and fixtures are still in place at **Dawna's Diner,** formerly known as the Harvey House Restaurant. It was established by early twentieth-century entrepreneur Fred Harvey as part of what was America's first restaurant chain, famed for its white-aproned "Harvey Girls." Harvey recruited girls from eastern cities to work in his restaurants, requiring them to live under strict supervision. Today, supervision isn't quite as strict for the girls who work at Dawna's, but visitors will still find the same good food they've come to expect here. The diner's specialties are barbecue and catfish, and the staff is always ready to fill orders to go. Open Monday through Saturday from 11:00 A.M. to 9:00 P.M. Call (580) 317–9000 to place your order or find out about booking your party here.

undergod'sbigtop

Circus performers who considered Hugo home are buried at Mt. Olivet Cemetery at Showmen's Rest, where tombstones are shaped like circus tents and ticket booths and engraved with dancing elephants. A marker at the entrance is inscribed, IN TRIBUTE TO ALL SHOWMEN UNDER GOD'S BIG TOP. The cemetery is at Eighth Street and Trice. (Go south on Eighth from Highway 70.) Showmen's Rest is at the east end of the cemetery, to the south side of the entrance road.

Most of the furnishings, right down to the rockers on the wraparound front porch and the books on the bookshelves, are original to the **Old Johnson House Inn Bed and Breakfast,** www.oldjohnsonhouse.com, in Hugo, owned by Metra Christoffers. The 1910 house was built by Dr. Edward Johnson. Cabbage-rose wallpaper and bird's-eye maple decorate the six upstairs bedrooms, and there is a guest cottage out back where daylilies and peonies bloom. Metra's guests indulge in her Tropical Fruit Parfait, scones, and fruit cobblers. The inn is at 1101 East Kirk Street. Call (580) 326–8111 for reservations and to check room availability.

The Kiamichis

From Hugo the Indian Nation Turnpike will speed travelers back up toward the mountains; take scenic US 271 from **Antlers,** a little town that got its name from a Native American custom of fastening deer antlers to a tree to mark a spring. Local history and artifacts are on display at the **Old Frisco Depot,** the headquarters for the Pushmataha County Historical Society. Hours are irregular. Call (580) 298–2488.

The fact that US 271 is so sparsely settled, with only a sprinkling of houses between Antlers and Clayton, makes the lights at the **Clayton Country Inn,** www.claytoninn.bizland.com, seem that much more welcoming. The stone-

OTHER ATTRACTIONS IN OUACHITA COUNTRY

Barnes-Stevenson Home,
Idabel

Raymond Gary State Park,
Fort Towson

Fountainhead State Park,
Eufaula

and-wood inn, with eleven guest rooms and two cottages, sits atop a hill 1½ miles south of Clayton on the east side of US 271. The inn was formerly a hunting lodge, and an aesthetic of practical comfort still operates: Colorful quilts and afghans clash merrily with the carpeting. The inn's great room invites conversation, with its sofas and easy chairs, a log-beamed ceiling, stone fireplace, and view of the Kiamichi Mountains. The dining room, paneled in knotty pine, serves steak, chicken, catfish, and fudgy chocolate cake with ice cream. For reservations call (918) 569–4165.

Outdoorsy guests predominate because the inn is adjacent to two lakes, the Kiamichi Mountains, public hunting areas, and two wildlife management areas. Clayton Lake State Park, 3 miles south of the inn and on the west side of the highway, is a quiet gem, with RV campsites and a fishing dock. The 14,000-acre Sardis Lake is 3 miles north of Clayton. Call (918) 569–7981 for information.

Just south of the inn is the road leading to *Indian Mounds Camp,* an equestrian campground with access to 100 miles of logging roads and marked horse trails. The rustic camp (hot showers, ice, and lots of shade trees are the primary amenities) rents RV hookups and tent campsites for $5.00 to $10.00 a night, plus $1.00 per person. Owner Jess Johnson organizes about seven guided rides into the mountains each year from March through November. The rides include meals and a Saturday-night dance for $25 a day. Call (918) 569–4761 or visit www.indianmoundshorsecamp.com for information.

Every Thanksgiving weekend, about 200 Jeep and other four-wheel-drive-vehicle owners descend—and ascend—on the mountains for the Turkey Day Run, a three-day scramble over logging trails. The event was started by four-wheel-drive-club members from northern Texas in 1989, and some trails now bear nicknames such as "Rollover." (Club members pack pulleys and winches.) The group hosts potluck cookouts in Clayton Lake State Park on Friday and Saturday nights and eats Thanksgiving dinner at the K-Country Motor Lodge Restaurant in Clayton.

The **Choctaw Nation Museum,** 2 miles west of Tuskahoma, is housed in the tribe's 1884 brick-and-sandstone national capitol building. The tribe's very first Indian Territory capitol was a log structure built 2½ miles to the southwest, where a military road crossed the Kiamichi River. The capitol was called *Nanih Wayay,* after a sacred mound in Mississippi. The capitol moved to three different spots in the Choctaw nation before being established at *Tuska Homma,* Choctaw for "red warriors." The tribal business offices are now headquartered in Durant, but the courtrooms at the historic capitol are still in use, with the only remaining lighthorseman in the nation acting as bailiff. The first-floor museum holds Choctaw heirlooms such as Chief Pushmataha's hunting bow, spinning wheels, iron pots carried over the Trail of Tears, bone spoons, arrowheads, and pottery. During Labor Day weekend, the Nation hosts a Choctaw Nation Labor Day Festival at the site, with a parade, traditional food, and Native American arts and crafts. Year-round, bison, longhorn cattle, and wild horses graze near the museum grounds. The museum is open Monday through Friday from 8:00 A.M. to 4:30 P.M.; (918) 569–4465.

Coal Miners' Valley

The roomy sandstone caves at **Robbers Cave State Park** were a handy place for the outlaws who rode in the area during Indian Territory days to spend a few days, and the park's canyons and pine-covered hills still make a fine place to hang out. The park, originally a Boy Scout camp turned Civilian Conservation Corps (CCC) work camp in 1935, is in the heart of the San Bois Mountains, built around the canyons and gorges cut by Fourche Maline Creek. The creek has been dammed to form Lake Carlton, where visitors can fish, rent paddleboats, and swim. (There's also a pool.) The CCC built the park's sandstone bridges and retaining walls as well as a wood-and-stone bathhouse that has been restored and now houses a nature center and museum overlooking Carlton Lake.

The workers also carved steps into the 100-foot-high sandstone cliffs near the park's namesake cave, making it more easily accessible to hikers. The climb requires a little stamina. The main cave is in a 100-foot-tall sandstone formation that holds a 20-foot by 20-foot rock room. The French explorers who came through the area in the eighteenth century stashed provisions in the cave. Stories about the Dalton and Doolin gangs hiding out in the caves to escape federal marshals are hazy. The main cave was connected to two separate passageways, one leading directly to a three-sided canyon that would have been perfect for hiding horses. On top of the formation, Lookout Point offers a panoramic view of the valley—and advance warning of approaching lawmen. A stash of gold rings that was found in the caves fuels the legends about the outlaw hideout.

A park naturalist who leads tours of the formation tells visitors the best local stories: You can sign up for a tour at the park's nature center. The hike through the formation takes about an hour.

Robbers Cave has an equestrian camp, with facilities for horses and miles of horse trails. Horseless guests can hire a horse and guide at *C Spur Trails* in the park; (918) 465–5200, www.cspurtrails.com. There are numerous RV and tent campsites, and thirty utilitarian cabins with fully equipped kitchens, bedding, and fireplaces. Guests can also stay at the *Belle Starr View Lodge*, a twenty-room inn. Call (918) 465–2565 for information about rooms and tours given by C Spur Trails. Robbers Cave State Park is 5 miles north of Wilburton on Highway 2.

Hopscotch to the northwest along Highways 2, 31, 71, and 9 to *Eufaula,* which sits on the banks of Lake Eufaula, Oklahoma's largest, most placid lake. Eufaula's 20-block downtown, listed on the National Register of Historic Places, is a good place to stroll along brick sidewalks and window-shop. Call (918) 689–2791 or visit www.eufaulachamberofcommerce.com to learn more about the area.

Travel 6 miles west of Eufaula on Highway 9, turn north for 7 miles, and you will find *Big River Crossing,* home of Rockin L H Asparagus Farm, Big River Emporium, Cast Iron Kettle Cookout, and the Stagecoach Inn Bed and Breakfast. Lee and Sharon Harvey started building their western town some years ago when growing and selling their asparagus and cooking for family and friends went from part-time to full-time. Today their Old West enterprise

When Coal Was King

Coal was discovered in Indian Territory by European sportsmen who were hunting wild turkey in the Choctaw Nation and noticed coal residue on the ground. The hunters returned home to raise capital, then opened a coal mine in 1871 on land leased from the Choctaw Nation. Coal company owners brought over their own labor force at first, bringing in miners from England, Scotland, and Wales; Italian workers began immigrating to the mine in 1874. Since the land still belonged to the Choctaw Nation until statehood, mining companies were required to pay a tax to the Choctaw Nation for each miner they employed. When one of the companies stopped paying the tax in 1894, when its miners went on strike, the Choctaw Nation asked that the workers, who were mostly Italian nationals, be deported. Three companies of infantrymen and two cavalry units arrested the miners, loaded them into railroad boxcars, and took them away—to Arkansas. By 1905 forty-eight mining companies were in operation in the Krebs area, with a labor force made up of members of twenty-six different ethnic groups. The ascendancy of oil in Oklahoma—and the Depression—closed the mines in the 1930s.

has expanded to include a showroom where they sell their gourmet products, a place for visitors to stay and rest a spell, an amphitheater where country-and-western music is performed, and an authentic chuck-wagon cookout. Food served from the back of the chuck-wagon can range from brisket to chicken, chili beans to boiled potatoes and corn. Sharon says her husband should have been a cowboy. He continues to build their town, with a cantina in the works. So if you need some peace and quiet from all the "city livin'," come to the rustic, quiet country. Call (918) 689–5086 or visit the Big River Web site at www .bigriverbedandbreakfast.com.

Housed in a 1901 mining company house, *Lutie Coal Miners' Museum,* at US 270 and Museum Road, 2½ miles east of Wilburton, holds artifacts from a nearly forgotten age. From 1880 to 1930, coal mining was the area's biggest industry. The museum is open by appointment only; call (918) 465–2216 to make the arrangements.

Though the coal mines closed in the 1930s, many of the miners' families settled in Oklahoma for good. The tiny community of *Krebs* (population 1,950),

Belle's Serenade

There are old stories of an eerie, lonesome sound heard near the mouth of Robbers Cave during the harvest moon. The sound, it's been said, is a pitiful song of the ghost of "Fiddlin' Jim," who was killed by a jealous rival as he serenaded Belle Starr, the notorious "Bandit Queen of Indian Territory."

According to the many legends that swirled around "The Petticoat Terror of the Plains," as she was known in dime novels, Belle was the alluring captain of multiple outlaw bands who ran whiskey, robbed banks, and stole horses throughout Indian Territory. Belle supposedly eloped with a desperado, was married on horseback by another member of the outlaw gang, bore Cole Younger's illegitimate child, cleaned out poker games with a pair of six-shooters, and rode down the sidewalks of city streets with her guns blazing.

The truth about Belle, born Myra Maybelle Shirley, appears to be far more prosaic. Myra Maybelle was born in 1858 to wealthy and respectable parents whose fortunes were ruined by the Civil War. Myra's first husband, Jim Reed, worked first as a saddle salesman and farmer, but he later fell in with Sam Starr, who ran whiskey and rustled horses in Indian Territory. After Reed was killed by a deputy, Belle married Sam, and the couple's farm on the banks of the Canadian River became a rendezvous for horse thieves and fugitives. Belle and her husband served nine months in prison for stealing horses, and Belle was tried for robbery but was acquitted. Portrayed on the silver screen as a glamorous heartbreaker, in real life Belle was bony and dowdy, with a severe face. She was killed by a shotgun blast while riding her horse home from a neighbor's farm in 1889; the most likely suspect was a disgruntled man to whom Belle had agreed to rent land and then changed her mind. (She backed out when she learned he was wanted for murder.) Belle's grave is southeast of Porum.

with four Italian restaurants and a specialty grocery and bakery, has become a sort of culinary Little Italy. Sausage and cheese hang from the ceiling at *Lovera's Grocery and Meat Market,* www.iloveitalian.com. The fifty-year-old family-run Italian grocery sells bread, caciocavallo cheese, and Italian sausage all made on the premises, as well as the largest selection of imported Italian specialties found in the state. The grocery's cluttered, fragrant shelves sit in a 1910 sandstone build-ing with red, white, and green awnings. If you can't take your goodies with you, Lovera's will mail them to your home. The store is open Monday through Satur-day, 6:00 A.M. to 6:00 P.M.; closed Sunday. The grocery is at 95 West Sixth Street, 2 blocks north of Highway 31. Call (918) 423–2842 for information.

Italian bread, made from a century-old recipe, comes out of the oven at *Snell's Bakery,* at 610 East Washington. Bread from Snell's is served at all four of the well-known Italian restaurants in the area. *Pete's Place,* www.petes.org, an eastern Oklahoma institution, was started by one-time miner Pete Prichard, who began to sell "Choc" beer—the local home brew—out of his home in 1925 after breaking his leg in the mine. (It was risky business. Not only was alcohol prohibited in Indian Territory, but Prohibition lasted until 1957 in Oklahoma.) Prichard started selling sandwiches and homemade wine along with the beer. Thanks to micro-brewery legislation, Pete's grandson Joe Prichard sells the Choc beer legally now, brewing it not in secret, but in gleaming silver vats. The restaurant has grown far beyond sandwiches: It is now famous for its veal parmesan, lamb fries, and generous portions. Entrees are served with pasta, bread, salad, spaghetti, ravioli, and meatballs. Pete's Place is between US 270 and Highway 31, just east of U.S. Highway 69 in Krebs. The restaurant is open for dinner Monday through Saturday and for lunch on Sunday. Call (918) 423–2042 for information.

Relatives of Pete Prichard, and relatives of his relatives, run the three other Italian restaurants nearby: *Isle of Capri,* 150 Southwest Seventh Street, (918) 423–3062, www.isleofcapriofkrebs.com; *Roseanna's Italian Food,* 205 East Washington, (918) 423–2055; and *Giacomo's Italian Cuisine,* US 69 and Comanche in nearby McAlester, (918) 423–2662.

On Third Street in *McAlester* is *Chadick Park.* Dogwood blossoms dip and hover there in the spring, and the larger shade trees make it perfect for picnics during summer. Residents planted the dogwood trees as a memorial to the children who died in the bombing of the federal building in Oklahoma City. Coal Miners Memorial Plaza pays tribute to the town's heritage with a bronze statue of a coal miner and a wall inscribed with the names of thousands who lost their lives in local mines. The *J. G. Puterbaugh House* on Fifth and Adams is another vestige of the coal mining industry. Residents refer to J. G. as the founding father of the coal mining industry in McAlester. Visit www.mcalester.org or call (918) 423–2550 to learn more about the area.

Places to Stay in Ouachita Country

BATTIEST

Tree Top View Cabins
1 mile west of Battiest
(580) 241–5599

BROKEN BOW

Cedar Creek Cabins
US 259
Choate Road
(888) 932–2246

Charles Wesley Motel
302 North Park
(580) 584–3303

Lakeview Lodge
U.S. Highway 259A
(580) 494–6179

Whip-Poor-Will Resort
US 259 North
(580) 494–6476

CLAYTON

Clayton Country Inn Bed and Breakfast
on Highway 271 South
(1½ miles from Clayton)
(918) 569–4165

EUFAULA

Arrowhead Resort
Arrowhead State Park
US 69
(918) 339–2204

Cabins on the Cove
Belle Starr Park Road
(918) 689-2141
www.cabinsonthe
cove-ok.com

Days Inn
US 69 and Highway 150
(918) 689–3999

Lakeview Landing Motel & RV Park
3 miles east of Eufaula on Highway 9
(918) 452–2736
www.lakeviewlanding.com

HUGO

Old Johnson House Inn Bed and Breakfast
1101 East Kirk
(580) 326–8111

MCALESTER

Best Western
1215 South George Nigh Expressway
(918) 426–0115

Days Inn
1217 South George Nigh Expressway
(918) 426–5050

Hydrangea Bed & Breakfast
349 East Washington
(918) 423–5050

Super 8 Hotel McAlester
2400 South Main
(918) 426–5400

OCTAVIA

Eagle Creek Guest Cottages
1 mile west on
US 259
(580) 244–7597

POTEAU

Best Western Trader's Inn
US 271 and US 59 North
(918) 647–4001

Kerr Conference Center
6 miles southwest
on US 259
(918) 647–8221

SPIRO

Aunt Jan's Cozy Cabin Bed and Breakfast
south of Spiro
(800) 470–3481

WILBURTON

Belle Starr View Lodge
Robbers Cave State Park
4 miles north on
Highway 2
(918) 465–2565

Places to Eat in Ouachita Country

ANTLERS

Able's Western Barbecue
600 East Main
(580) 298–2573

Bearcat Burger
Highway 3
(580) 298–3515

Burger Barn
407 West Main
(580) 245–1164

High Street Pizza
216 North High Street
(580) 298–5511

CLAYTON

Clayton Country Inn
on Highway 271 South
(1½ miles from Clayton)
(918) 569–4165

Corner Cafe
US 271
(918) 569–7845

EUFAULA

Adelita's Mexican Food
207 North Main
(918) 618–4553

Green Arch Tea Room
116 South Main
(918) 689–2883

JM's Restaurant
115 Selmon Road
(918) 689–9474

HOCHATOWN

Stevens Gap Restaurant
US 259 North
(580) 494–6350

HUGO

Angie's Circus City Diner
1312 East Jackson
(580) 326–2027

Cedar Shed (barbecue)
1300 South F Street
(580) 326–7282

IDABEL

Gemini Coffee Shop
421 South Central Avenue
(580) 286–2900

The Rib Joint (barbecue)
2015 Southeast Washington
(580) 286–7334

KREBS

Isle of Capri
150 Southwest
Seventh Street
(918) 423–3062

Pete's Place
Eighth and Monroe
(918) 423–2042

Roseanna's Italian Food
205 East Washington
(918) 423–2055

MCALESTER

Ball's Bar-B-Q
319 North Shawnee
(918) 423–4430

Giacomo's Italian Cuisine
US 69 and Comanche
(918) 423–2662

Harbor Mountain Coffee House
224 Southeast Third Street
(918) 426–9600

TALIHINA

Kiamichi Kitchen
505 Second Street
(918) 567–2772

FOR MORE INFORMATION

Antlers Chamber of Commerce
212 North High Street
Antlers 74523
(580) 298–2488
www.antlerschamber.com

Eufaula Chamber of Commerce
321 North Main Street
Eufaula 74432
(918) 689–2791
www.eufaulachamberofcommerce.com

Kiamichi Country, Inc.
P.O. Box 638
Wilburton 74578
(918) 465–2367
www.kiamichicountry.com

For maps and information about the
Ouachita National Forest, write
Choctaw Ranger District
HC 64, Box 3467
Heavener 74937
(918) 653–2991

River Country: South Central Oklahoma

There's not a lot of drama in the landscape in south central Oklahoma, an area of rolling prairies and languid rivers sandwiched between eastern forests and western prairies. Travelers looking to relax, however, are in luck. Parts of the region seem like a natural spa, filled with bubbling mineral springs and peaceful vistas. Fishermen are in luck, too: Giant Lake Texoma, which spills into three counties, is one of the best places in the world to fish for ocean striped bass.

Interstate 35 cuts the region in half, north to south, and is paralleled along the way with its more scenic predecessor, U.S. Highway 77. Two scenic loops that branch out from that highway are highly recommended. Highway 77D twists around the Arbuckle Mountains, and Highway 77S, near Ardmore, makes a tree-lined loop around Lake Murray.

The Two Boggies

U.S. Highway 69 angles through Atoka County, roughly following the path of the Old Texas Road, a major cattle trail that carried longhorns from Texas to Kansas in the days following the Civil War. The area, formerly the Choctaw Nation, was traversed

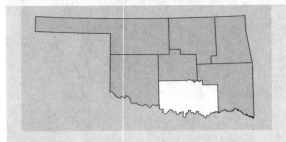

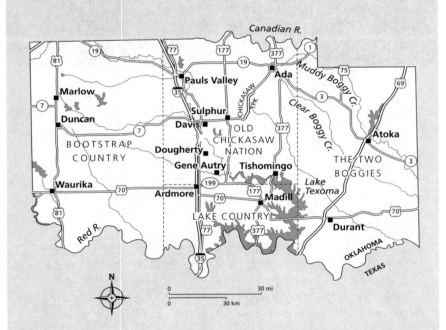

by two rivers: the Muddy Boggy, formerly known as the Middle Boggy, and the Clear Boggy. Along US 69, ½ mile north of its junction with U.S. Highway 75, is the *Confederate Memorial Museum and Information Center,* www.civil waralbum.com/atoka. Behind the museum is the only Confederate cemetery in the state. The Confederate soldiers who are buried in the cemetery behind the museum were Arkansas infantry troops and died of measles, not of battle wounds.

The museum stands near a Confederate camp established to guard the Butterfield Road Overland Mail stagecoach route, an important supply line during the war. The largest Civil War confrontation in the area was the Battle of Middle Boggy, which was actually more of a skirmish, according to the museum curator. On February 13, 1864, Union soldiers from Fort Gibson surprised the First Choctaw and Chickasaw Cavalry, a detachment of the Twentieth Texas Cavalry, which was stationed at Boggy Depot, a now-vanished Choctaw agency 15 miles to the west. The fighting lasted only thirty minutes, with forty-seven Confederate casualties and no Union losses. The history of the skirmish and the war in Indian Territory can be found at the museum, along with a re-creation of a Civil War encampment, complete with an officer's campaign table, Civil War–era photographs, sabers, and a collection of bullets, uniform buttons, and blanket buckles found in the area. There are picnic tables in a little grove behind the museum, with a view of the cemetery, a log cabin that belonged to one of the earliest settlers in the area, and the old stagecoach roadbed. Every three years, reenactors replay the Battle of Middle Boggy; the next reenactment will be in 2009. The museum is open Monday through Friday from 9:00 A.M. to 4:00 P.M. Call (580) 889–7192 for more information.

Boggy Depot State Park (580–889–5625), 15 miles to the south, is established on the site of a once-prominent Indian Territory settlement and former Confederate supply camp. There are several historic markers and the traces of

AUTHOR'S FAVORITES IN RIVER COUNTRY

Chickasaw Council House Museum	Lake Murray State Park
Chickasaw National Recreation Area	McGee Creek Wildlife Management Area and State Park
Fort Washita Historic Site	
Gene Autry Oklahoma Museum	Murray-Lindsay Mansion
Greater Southwest Historical Museum	Price Falls
	Stephens County Historical Museum

TOP EVENTS IN RIVER COUNTRY

Fur Traders' Rendezvous,
Fort Washita, April;
(580) 924–6502

Chisholm Trail Stampede,
Duncan, first weekend in May;
(800) 782–7167

National Sand Bass Festival,
Madill, June;
(580) 795–2431

Noodling Festival,
Tishomingo, June;
(580) 371–2175

Oklahoma Shakespearean Festival,
Durant, June;
(580) 924–0848;
www.osfonline.com

Chickasaw Festival,
Tishomingo, September;
(580) 371–2040

Striper Festival,
Kingston, September;
(580) 564–3910

Bigfoot Festival,
Honobia, October;
(580) 244–3292

old roads in the park, along with an old cemetery. The 630-acre park has a little fishing lake and nature trail and campsites with RV hookups. The park is on Highway 7.

From Atoka, Highway 3 heads southeast back toward the Kiamichi Mountains and *McGee Creek Wildlife Management Area and State Park,* (580) 889–5822. In Farris, turn north on a county highway and travel 3 miles to the park and recreation area. The nine-year-old lake, filled with largemouth and smallmouth bass, crappie, catfish, and bluegill, is rimmed with pine and oak trees. Two campgrounds offer tent campsites and hot showers, plus electricity and water for RVs.

West of the park is the wilderness of the 9,000-acre *McGee Creek National Scenic Recreation Area,* where 34 miles of trails wind through the forest. White-tailed deer, wild turkeys, and the occasional mountain lion live in the area, and river otters sometimes are sighted in streams. The most popular hike is the South Rim Trail, which goes around Little Bugaboo Canyon. The name has been around so long no one knows for certain how it originated, but park officials say it's fairly obvious to anyone who climbs down into the canyon and has to scramble out again that it's a real "bugaboo." (Big Bugaboo Canyon is even tougher.) Ferndale Bog is noted for its botanical diversity. A third campground has been established just within the bounds of the scenic recreation area. Though camping is not forbidden deeper in the woods, park officials discourage it because the area is so large and remote. Nonmotorized boats, horses, and mountain bikes are allowed in the area, but everyone entering must have a permit. Half of the available camping and day-use permits can be reserved; others are issued on a first-come basis. To reserve a permit, or to see if daily permits have been exhausted, call (580) 889–5822. To reach the wilderness area, go back to Farris and travel 3 miles east. Turn north (a sign marks the turn) and travel north for 11 miles.

South of Farris, on Highway 109A, aka Crystal Road, is the **Boehler Seeps and Sandhills Nature Preserve.** The site, owned by the Nature Conservancy, is the only place in Oklahoma where the bluejack oak sandhill and the acid hillside seep communities occur in tandem. Visitors will find small-headed pipewort, a rare and tiny wild-flower, growing in the preserve along with twenty-six other rare plants.

Back on US 69, between Atoka and Durant, is the **Cimarron Cellars Winery.** It was established in 1978 by Dwayne and Suze Pool, who moved to southeast Oklahoma from the Napa Valley to start their wine-making oper-ation. The Pools grow twenty-five acres of grapes and bottle approxi-mately eleven wines. They are enthu-siastic vintners and take groups of almost any size on tours, but they need advance notice; call (580) 889–5997. To reach the winery, travel 12 miles south of Atoka beyond the Caney exit and watch for a blue highway sign directing travelers east. The winery is about 4 miles east on a dirt road. To reach the winery's tasting room and shop, turn back north on the highway for about ³⁄₁₀ mile. The shop is open Monday through Saturday from noon to 5:00 P.M.

theamishauction

Early birds are rewarded at the annual auction held by an Amish community near Clarita—a pancake-and-sausage breakfast begins before daybreak, and by 8:00 A.M. there's a big dent in the mountains of homemade goodies such as wheat bread, maple-nut chiffon cakes, and apricot pies.

An auction of handmade quilts and buggies begins at 9:00 A.M. The proceeds benefit an Amish school established for children in the approximately twenty Amish families who live near Clarita in an 8-mile-long, 4-mile-wide swath of farms. The auction is held in September on a farm just east of Highway 48, between Tupelo and Wapanucka. For information contact **The Little Country Store** at (580) 428–3403. If you miss the auction, the store sells Amish baked goods year-round. Open Monday through Saturday 8:00 A.M. to 6:00 P.M. Closed Sunday.

Travel back east on Highway 22 to its intersection with Highway 78. As you drive, you'll pass the boundary line of the old Chickasaw Nation. Unlike the clear lines on a map, however, the histories of the Chickasaw and Choctaw Nations blur together at several points over the centuries. The Chickasaw are believed to have split from the Choctaw before Hernando de Soto made contact with the Chickasaws in Mississippi in 1540, but the very name *Chikasha* is from a Choctaw phrase that has been translated, "They left as a tribe not a very great while ago."

Like the Choctaw, the Chickasaw signed a treaty after Andrew Jackson declared his Indian removal policy, ceding land east of the Mississippi. By 1836, however, when no suitable land had been found for the tribe, the government drew up an agreement between the Choctaw and the Chickasaw Tribes, designating a tract of grassland in the western portion of the Choctaw Nation as "the Chickasaw District." The Chickasaw paid the Choctaw half a million dollars for a long-term lease. The Chickasaw were reluctant to settle in that area, however, since Comanche bands had been stealing livestock and terrorizing anyone who attempted to settle in the Washita Valley. In 1842 the federal government established Fort Washita to protect the Chickasaw and the Choctaw from the Plains Indians.

Still remote, **Fort Washita Historic Site** sits on a hilltop 3 miles west of the junction of Highways 78 and 199. It was occupied for only twenty years; after federal troops abandoned the fort at the start of the Civil War, it was never reoccupied by the U.S. government. Confederate troops seized the fort and

Civil War in Indian Territory

Oklahoma's Civil War history is unique, since the area was still Indian Territory in the 1860s, occupied by the Five Civilized Tribes in the east, Plains tribes who hunted buffalo in the west, and a handful of frontier forts—Fort Arbuckle, Fort Washita, and Fort Towson in the south—established to protect the eastern tribes. At the onset of the Civil War, U.S. soldiers were immediately called out of the territory's forts because of their proximity to Arkansas and Texas, which were both part of the Confederacy. The tribes in Indian Territory felt betrayed by the Army's departure, because their protection on the plains had been guaranteed by treaty. When Albert Pike, the Confederate commissioner to the Indian nations, visited Indian Territory and urged tribal councils to support the war against the United States, he found a ready audience. The leaders of all five tribes signed treaties of alliance with the Confederate States. (The Chickasaw legislature actually adopted a formal declaration of independence from the United States on May 25, 1861.) The Chickasaw and Choctaw Mounted Rifles, organized in July of 1861, garrisoned the three southern forts and guarded a Confederate supply depot at Boggy Depot. At the end of the war, the tribal alliances with the Confederacy carried a heavy price. The federal government considered old treaties null and negotiated new ones, which weakened the borders of the Indian nations. The new treaties required tribes to cede land to tribes from "Kansas and elsewhere" and negotiated railroad rights-of-way.

made it the base for the Choctaw-Chickasaw Mounted Rifles. A hundred buildings once stood on the grounds, and, of those, only a handful remain. The log
cabin where the Chickasaw agent lived still stands, along with the limestone
skeleton of a two-story-tall barracks and scattered foundations of an officers'
quarters, a bakery, and other buildings. One two-story barracks, the South Barracks, was reconstructed two decades ago, finished with a wide second-story
veranda and modern plumbing. The plumbing may not pass muster with current preservation standards, but hot running water and bunk beds have made
the fort wildly popular with historical
reenactors. Living-history events are
staged virtually every month at the
fort. The largest is the April Fur
Traders' Rendezvous, when hundreds
of civilian and military reenactors
gather to buy, sell, and barter lye
soap, knives, clothing, and other tools
and items essential to nineteenth-
century life. A visitors' center holds
exhibits devoted to the history of the
fort. At the center, pick up a map to a
nature trail that winds around fort
grounds to an old cemetery. Along the

shellshocked

Peanuts are the major cash crop in
Bryan County and inspired the 3-
foot-long aluminum *"World's Largest
Peanut"* monument that sat on a
square in downtown Durant for years.
The peanut, however, proved to be
too tempting a prize for rival high
school football teams and college
students and now is on display inside
City Hall.

way, points where eleven different medicinal plants grow are marked. The
brochure identifies each plant and explains how the difficulty of obtaining supplies, including medicine, on the frontier made it likely that troops might rely
on tribal remedies, such as the boiled roots of butterfly weed and blackberry
brambles. Fort Washita soldiers had amazingly good health compared with
their contemporaries: One winter only one soldier died due to illness. The fort
is open to visitors seven days a week except legal holidays from 9:00 A.M. to
4:30 P.M. and on Sunday from 1:00 to 4:30 P.M. Information about living-history
events is available at the fort, (580) 924–6502, or at the Oklahoma Historical
Society in Oklahoma City, (405) 521–2491.

South on Highway 78 is ***Durant,*** an agricultural center since the railroad
went through in 1882, thanks to the rich soil of the Washita and Red River Valleys. Peanuts have replaced cotton as the county's major crop.

Durant has been headquarters for the Choctaw Nation since 1951. With
70,000 members, the Choctaw Nation is the third-largest tribe in the United
States. (The Cherokee Nation is the largest.) The tribe's offices are housed in
the redbrick Oklahoma Presbyterian College for Girls, established in 1909. Ten
blocks east, at the corner of Fourth and Main, is the ***Three Valley Museum.***

The museum, named for the Blue, Washita, and Red River Valleys, is located in three renovated historic downtown Durant buildings. The 1,300-square-foot structures feature early automobiles, an early-day blacksmith shop, exhibits of turn-of-the-century Durant, and Native American displays. A small gift shop is also on the premises. The museum is open Monday through Friday, from 1:00 to 5:00 P.M.; no charge. For more information call (580) 920–1907.

Lake Country

From Durant, US 70 heads straight west to **Lake Texoma,** created in 1944 as a flood control project on the Red River just below the headwaters of the Washita River. The huge lake has 530 miles of shoreline in Texas and Oklahoma and is a mecca for fishermen interested in hooking striped bass (or "stripers" to fishermen). An anadromous species, striped bass were stocked in southern lakes after they were accidentally corralled into freshwater impoundments during reservoir projects built during the 1930s. To the surprise of conservationists, the stripers not only survived but spawned, and nowhere did they do better than in Lake Texoma. Biologists disagree as to whether it is due to the high salt content of the lake or whether the two rivers that flow into the lake offer better spawning grounds. (The fishermen don't argue, though; they just haul them in.) The daily limit is ten fish, twice that of most lakes.

Texoma is a big lake, so striper guide services flourish. You can pick up a list of guides at the Lake Texoma Association, (580) 564–2334 or www.laketexoma online.com, offices at Lake Texoma State Park, 10 miles east of Kingston. There's very little nightlife to be found in the no-frills lodge, but the restaurant is full at 7:00 A.M. on weekends with eager fishermen heading for the lake or golfers heading for the new eighteen-hole Chickasaw Point Golf Course. (Designed to compete with some of the country's championship courses, the new golf course offers panoramic views of Lake Texoma from every hole. Behind hole 13 is the famous Council Tree. According to Chickasaw legend, their chiefs held councils under the limbs of this 200-year-old oak tree.) In the winter, the park naturalist conducts waterfowl tours on a pontoon boat every Saturday. During most outings, the group spots between six and ten bald eagles, along with cormorants, pelicans, and Canada geese. There's a $10 fee for the tour, which includes lunch. It gets cold on the lake, so participants are advised to bundle up.

Fish lovers should detour across I–35 and follow Highway 32 along the Red River. About 4 miles west, signs direct travelers down a zagging series of gravel roads to **McGeehee's Catfish Restaurant,** a rustic restaurant established on a family farm right on the river. Rudy and Enid McGeehee's family-

B-I-N-G-O

A modern symbol of the tribe is the **Choctaw Indian High Stakes Bingo Palace and Casino** on US 69 south of downtown Durant. State laws regulating the amount of money paid out during bingo games don't apply on Indian land, so the size of pots rises to $25,000 and even $50,000 at the 1,800-seat bingo hall. The parking lot outside is nearly always filled with tour buses that bring players in from neighboring states to play high-stakes bingo, buy pull tabs, and try to win a minute or two in the Money Machine, where players clutch at swirling currency. Matinee and evening sessions are held daily, with the highest payouts on weekends. Along with free food buffets, players who buy a bingo card "pack" for two consecutive weekend days are reimbursed for their lodging. Call (800) 788–2464 for information.

style catfish dinners draw customers from so wide an area, an airstrip has been installed. Their recipe for success is simple: Platters of farm-raised catfish, dipped in yellow cornmeal and fried in peanut oil, are served with bowls of french fries, coleslaw, hush puppies, spicy coleslaw, sliced onions, green-tomato relish, and iced tea. Taking seconds, and even thirds, is encouraged. Steaks are also available. The restaurant is open weekdays from 5:00 to 9:00 P.M. and on weekends from 1:00 to 9:00 P.M. and is closed Wednesday. Call (580) 276–2751 for information.

Ardmore is a pretty little town near I–35, just the kind of place where you might expect to find a doll museum at the local library. Named for its original patron, the ***Eliza Cruce Hall Doll Collection*** was given to the city by a niece of one of Oklahoma's governors, Lee Cruce. Mrs. Hall was born in 1891 and collected more than 300 dolls throughout her lifetime. Along with Kewpie dolls, fashion dolls, baby dolls, elaborate porcelain dolls, and dolls dressed like George and Martha Washington, there are some rare prizes, such as a pair of carved wood French dolls that date to 1778. (Mrs. Hall maintained that Marie Antoinette played with the dolls, but the staff has been unable to document the claim.) The library has printed a booklet identifying the dolls and their histories. The doll museum is at 320 East Street Northwest, 3½ blocks north of Main Street. Hours vary. Call (580) 223–8290 for information.

Ardmore residents are justifiably proud of the ***Greater Southwest Historical Museum,*** www.gshm.org, housed in what was once a National Guard Armory. The name sounds grandiose until you discover that the museum displays artifacts from twenty states, beginning with weapons that date to the Spanish in the territory in the 1500s and continuing through the history of Indian Territory and early statehood. Themes of cowboys, Native Americans, cattle ranching, cotton, oil, farming and manufacturing, and daily life are illustrated with photographs and artifacts. There is oil-field equipment on the lawn, and a military annex holds memorabilia from the Civil War through the Persian Gulf War. Located at 35 Sunset Drive, which is 3 blocks east of I–35, the museum is open Tuesday through Saturday from 10:00 A.M. to 5:00 P.M., Sunday from 1:00 to 5:00 P.M. Call (580) 226–3857 for more information.

Situated on seventy-three acres of land northeast of town is a bed-and-breakfast. The charming and modern **Shiloh Morning Inn** has five guest rooms and two cottages. Guests can take a stroll through an orchard of cherry and plum trees or sit on one of the many porches. Dinner is available upon request. Call Bob or Linda Humphrey at (888) 554–7674 or visit www.shiloh morning.com for directions and reservations. The Humphreys also keep menus of some of Ardmore's best restaurants.

nutsaboutpecans

An 1824 law made it illegal to cut down a pecan tree in the Choctaw Nation, and pecan groves and orchards are still found throughout the Red River Valley. Some of the prettiest orchards are found at **Landgraf Farms,** where visitors buy whole, cracked, and shelled papershell pecans in November and December. Travelers drive through 75 acres of orchards to get to a little pecan store. The Landgrafs sell five varieties of pecans; the most popular are Choctaw pecans. Landgraf Farms is 4 miles west of Madill on Highway 70. Call (580) 795–7644.

On Friday and Saturday nights, live blues and jazz at the **Two Frogs Grill,** at 2646 West Broadway, (580) 226–3764, www.twofrogsgrill.com, attract fans of good music and good food. Jack Massey once played piano for B. B. King; now he sings about life's hardships and love's conditions and plays blues and jazz piano while the waitstaff serves up steak and frogs' legs to the crowd.

Two miles east of I–35 (exit 24) on the south side of US 77 sits **Fireside Dining.** Gary Jackson, who has owned the restaurant since 1981, says people come for the casual dining in an intimate atmosphere. The building, patterned after a ski lodge, offers guests lots of wood and windows. Known for their prime rib, the Fireside also offers a variety of steaks, seafood, pasta dishes, and appetizers like fried dill pickles, fried green tomatoes, and baked artichoke hearts. Desserts include peanut butter pie and their own Fireside Delight, made with homemade chocolate cake, fudge, whipped cream, and vanilla ice cream. Hours are Tuesday through Saturday from 5:00 to 9:00 P.M. Call (580) 226–4070. Jackson also owns **Cafe Alley,** located in an alley in downtown Ardmore. Open Tuesday through Friday from 11:00 A.M. to 2:00 P.M., the cafe serves a specialty lunch menu. Both restaurants have ample parking. The cafe number is (580) 223–6413.

East of Ardmore along US 70 is **Lake Murray State Park,** built in the foothills of the Arbuckle Mountains by the federal Civilian Conservation Corps as part of the New Deal in the 1930s. Before the lake was built, the area was called "The Devil's Kitchen" because of all the moonshine stills that operated back in the hills. CCC crews hewed the timber and quarried the stone for the original park cabins, shelters, and walls right on park property. The most distinctive structure at the park, however, is **Tucker Tower Nature Center,** a limestone castle reportedly built as a summer home for Oklahoma governors. The 75-foot tower was constructed with 3-foot-thick walls and offers a view of the lake from a parapet. The interior is finished with native walnut, cut from trees logged to make way for Lake Murray. Tucker Tower is now home to a geological museum and nature center and holds dinosaur bones, fossils, arrowheads, and half of a huge meteorite. The meteorite is a type called "granular hexahedrite"; it measures 16 by 23 inches and weighs 560 pounds. The other half of the meteorite is in New Mexico; it took 312 hours to saw the meteorite in half. Tours of Tucker Tower are conducted through the museum and nature center. Programs on astronomy, geology, and wildlife are offered from February through November. The tower is open daily from 9:00 A.M. to 7:00 P.M. in the summer; it is open Wednesday through Sunday from 9:00 A.M. to 5:00 P.M. from Labor Day through December 1 and from February 1 through Memorial Day weekend. It is closed during December and January. Admission is 50 cents. Call (580) 223–2109.

Bigfoot in Southeastern Oklahoma

Sightings of Bigfoot have been reported for years in and around the Kiamichi Mountains of southeastern Oklahoma. Several years ago however, this area gained media attention when one man reported being harassed by the beasts. "People started coming from all over the country to hear his story," Katie Cogburn, the man's neighbor, said. "Since they were already coming, we decided to hold a festival where others could tell their stories, too."

The festival is held the first weekend of October at the Honobia Community Center Grounds on the banks of the Little River, and includes live music, art shows, wagon rides and more. Over fifty vendors sell handmade arts and crafts and Indian jewelry, but the highlight of the festival is the Bigfoot stories told by those who have encountered the animals.

For more information, contact Katie Cogburn at (580) 244–3292 or visit www.honobiabigfootfestival.com.

Lake Murray is halfway between Dallas and Oklahoma City and far enough away from the lights of Ardmore to make it the perfect setting for the *Okie-Tex Star Party,* a week-long astronomy fest held every October at a group camp in the park. Along with stargazing, which continues almost twenty-four hours a day, the astronomy gathering also includes an equipment swap meet.

Old Chickasaw Nation

Scenic Highway 77 loops around all of Lake Murray and then continues north toward ranch country and the rolling land south of the Arbuckle Mountains. One of the more famous ranchers in this area was Gene Autry. From I–35 North, Highway 53 will take you to *Gene Autry,* the town; the little burg renamed itself in honor of the singing cowboy in the 1940s in hopes that it might attract new residents. It was the fourth name change for the town: First called Lou, the town moved and dubbed itself New Lou and then Dresden. The town moved a second time, to the railroad tracks, and called itself Berwyn, which stuck until Gene Autry bought a ranch in the vicinity. Now the town is home to ninety-seven residents and the *Gene Autry Oklahoma Museum,* subtitled "Dedicated to the Singing Cowboys of the B-Western Movie." The museum is at 601 Prairie Street, which isn't important to know since there are no street signs. Just follow the sign downtown pointing visitors up the hill to the museum, which was established in an eight-room school built in 1937. Elvin Sweeten, creator and curator of the museum, built showcases where the school lockers once stood and filled them with "cowboy stuff": movie posters, black-and-white stills, and guns and other toys endorsed by celluloid cowboys including Autry, Tex Ritter, Roy Rogers, Hopalong Cassidy, and their sidekicks. One room is filled with local history and outfitted like the old—now van-ished—post office. Sweeten doesn't charge admission to the museum, but he does accept donations. The museum is open Monday through Saturday from 10:00 A.M. to 4:00 P.M. Call (580) 294–3047 or go to www.cow-boy.com for information.

East of Gene Autry on Highway 199 is *Tishomingo,* named for the last warrior king of the Chickasaw, who died at age 102 on a journey to Indian Territory from Mississippi. Unlike the other tribes who made similar journeys from their homelands, the Chickasaw made the journey to Indian Territory in relative comfort, because the tribe financed the trip itself. Instead of swapping land in Mississippi for land in Indian Territory, the Chickasaw auctioned their farms and invested the proceeds. A trader named Pitman Colbert, of mixed European and Chickasaw ancestry, traveled to Indian Territory with six mules hauling a wagon filled with gold.

Chickasaw Capitol, Tishomingo

Only a few grand old buildings remain in Tishomingo; the modern tribal headquarters has moved to Ada. The Chickasaw wrote their first constitution in 1856 in a log council house, which is still standing today inside the *Chickasaw Council House Museum.* The museum, built around the log structure, holds maps outlining the tribe's former homeland, models of brush arbors that sheltered the first legislative houses, and artifacts from Chickasaw boarding schools and academies that were built throughout the district. The museum is open Monday through Friday 8:00 A.M. to 4:30 P.M. and Saturday 10:30 A.M. to 4:00 P.M. (580) 371–3351. West of the museum is the turreted three-story *Chickasaw Capitol,* completed in 1896. The tribe used the structure only until statehood in 1907, when the tribal government was abolished. The tribe sold the granite building to Johnston County administrators in 1910 for $7,500. Elections of chiefs were revived in the 1960s, and in 1992 the Chickasaw Nation bought the granite capitol building back from the county for more than a half million dollars. The capitol is now being restored and eventually will be used as a museum and ceremonial capitol. Visit www.chickasaw.net to learn more.

Down the hill, the Romanesque-style granite *Johnston County Historical Society Museum* was built in 1902 by a former governor of the Chickasaw Nation. The bank was open for business for less than a decade: A cashier embezzled the bank's deposits, so it closed in 1911. Local preservationists have painstakingly restored the building and plan to open it as a museum. For now the chamber of commerce will unlock the building by request; (580) 371–2175.

Southeast of Tishomingo along Highway 22 is the 16,500-acre *Tishomingo National Wildlife Refuge,* home to 250 species of birds and mammals. There are picnic and camping facilities, boat ramps on Lake Texoma, hiking trails, and an observation tower. The refuge is also home to the *Tishomingo*

National Fish Hatchery, one of the world's largest warmwater fish hatcheries. The hatchery is open Monday through Friday from 7:30 A.M. to 4:00 P.M. For details call (580) 384–5463.

Highway 1 northwest from Tishomingo connects with Highway 7, which meanders north and west to Sulphur and into the *Chickasaw National Recreation Area,* a geological curiosity tucked into the prairies. Filled with shadowy glades and a swimming hole with a waterfall dubbed "Little Niagara" and laced with freshwater and mineral springs and creeks, the area has been a favored picnic spot since before the turn of the twentieth century. Fearful that it would be overrun by commercial establishments, the Chickasaw deeded it to the U.S. government in 1902, and it was known for years as *Platt National Park.* In the 1970s, the park was combined with the nearby Arbuckle Recreation Area and renamed for the Chickasaw Tribe. The springs are found in the Travertine District in the east end of the park; most are accessible by car or by trails following Travertine and Rock Creeks. The largest are Buffalo and Antelope Springs, which produce a combined average flow of five million gallons of water a day. Displays inside the *Travertine Nature Center* explain nature's "recipe" for mineral water: Springs are formed when water passes through underground rock formations, pools, and then is forced to the surface through fissures. Water that percolates through layers of rock containing sulphur and bromine creates mineral springs.

During the first three decades of the twentieth century, mineral baths and mud wraps were touted as relief from the "nervous jars, jolts and strains of business life," according to an old brochure. *Sulphur* was a prosperous resort town, with two railroads, a half dozen stately hotels, and scores of tourist cabins. During the 1930s, Works Progress Administration crews built sandstone pavilions around the major springs, including Bromide and Pavilion Springs. You can taste the water at *Vendome Well* in Flower Park on the north end of the park on Broadway Street, where there is both a drinking fountain and spigot. (Be warned: The water has a high sodium content.)

The output of mineral water has slowed considerably since the resort town's heyday—and so has Sulphur. One place redolent of a gracious, leisurely past is the *Sulphur Springs Inn.* Across the street from the Chickasaw National Recreation Area, the inn is in a position to partner nature and nurture. It is the only original bathhouse still standing in Oklahoma. Paint that proclaimed it the CAYLOR BATH HOUSE in 1925 is still visible on a wall near the patio. During their stay, guests can get a massage, relax in the sauna, or soak in hot and cool pools on the ground floor. At night moonflowers bloom in beds around the inn. There are no strenuous exercise programs, but innkeepers Cheri

Alfalfa Bill Murray

Oklahoma's most colorful political figure was William "Alfalfa Bill" Murray. He was a Tishomingo lawyer who took part in the 1905 Sequoyah Convention (which aimed for separate statehood for the eastern half of the state), presided over Oklahoma's Constitutional Convention, and, after a failed attempt to start a colony in Bolivia, was elected governor in 1930.

Murray, who got his nickname for proselytizing the virtues of planting alfalfa, was no less active as governor. A tireless defender of the common man, he grew vegetables and grazed cattle on the state capitol lawn. He called out the National Guard thirty-two times while he was in office; once to shut down Oklahoma oil wells to drive up the price of oil and once to stop the county-sponsored sales of farms that belonged to farmers who couldn't pay their property taxes.

His bluntness extended to everyone. Once, following a Supreme Court decision that he opposed, he sent a telegram to the chief justice that read: "My compliments to the Court. Tell them to go to Hell."

Murray announced his candidacy for president in 1932 but failed to get the nomination. He died in poverty in 1956—four years after he swore in his son Johnston T. Murray as governor of Oklahoma. He is buried in a Tishomingo cemetery.

and Charlie suggest long walks in the woods or short naps in the hammock. The old bathhouse is located at 1102 West Lindsay, Sulphur; (580) 622–5930; www.sulfurspringsinn.com.

After your massage, walk on over to the ***Secret Garden Tea Room,*** 218 West Muskogee, (580) 622–3005. The historic 1906 building where the tearoom is located was restored in 1997. Today it is decorated like a garden with an archway, flowers, and a gate painted by a local artist. Serving quiche, soups, and desserts like Cinnamon Praline Carrot Cake, owner Janet Carter invites you to come in and order the Reuben sandwich, one of the sandwiches the locals order and rave about. In 1998 Oklahoma Main Street awarded the Secret Garden Tea Room the Best Interior Award, and in 1999, Best Façade. It is open Thursday, Friday, and Saturday from 11:00 A.M. to 2:00 P.M. Carter also owns the ***Arbuckle Emporium,*** a gift shop, located next door. Gourmet foods, many "made in Oklahoma," some antiques, artwork, and crafts are a few of the treasures you'll discover here. Arbuckle Emporium is open Tuesday through Saturday from 10:00 A.M. to 6:00 P.M. Ample parking is available.

On the east side of town, you'll find ***Echo Canyon Manor,*** www .echocanyonmanor.com. Owners Carol Ann and Joe Van Horn say their bed-

and-breakfast is "a place where you feel like you've escaped the rest of the world." Guests can enjoy four different options when staying here. The Admiral's Suite offers two rooms, a sitting area, full bath, and a private deck overlooking Echo Canyon Vineyards and forest. In the Captain's Suite, decorated with American antiques, guests will enjoy the king-size bed and Jacuzzi bath. The Commander's Quarters and First Mate's Quarters offer queen beds and full baths. A mineral bath is also available. Located on twenty-five acres, besides the orchard and vineyard, the property also has a creek and a canyon. Prices average from $109 per night to $169. To reserve your escape call (580) 421–5076.

Down the road from Echo Canyon is **Cedar Creek Cabins,** www.cabins atcedarcreek.com. Owners Ray and Linda Haynes saw the need for non-RV enthusiasts to have a place to stay, so they built four log cabins 3 miles from Arbuckle Lake. Each cabin has a fireplace, full kitchen, television, and VCR. A playground and fishing pond are available as well. Call (580) 622–8897.

Three miles farther west is **Quail Hollow Steakhouse,** a renovated Santa Fe Railroad depot that was moved to its present location from Dougherty, a little town 10 miles south. The depot was owned and operated by three generations of the Haines family. Patriarch Joe Haines bought the depot after watching it deteriorate when passenger service to Dougherty was discontinued and the depot was closed. Haines had the depot cut in half and hauled to a piece of land along Highway 7, where it has been painstakingly restored. Today, owners Bill and Julia Mayo serve patrons steak, catfish, chicken, and prime ribs. Voted #1 Steakhouse in the southern hills, the Mayos also own another restaurant, Bill's, in Duncan. Quail Hollow is open Thursday through Saturday 5:00 to 9:00 P.M. and Sunday 11:00 A.M. to 2:00 P.M. Call (580) 622–4080.

Davis, 1½ miles west, is home to yet another refurbished Santa Fe depot, the **Arbuckle Historical Museum,** on Main Street. The museum has a wonderfully local sense of what's important: a row of battered cowboy hats, for example, in the entrance, donated by the owners of historic area ranches, old high-school band uniforms mixed in with priceless Indian beadwork, and a scale model of Fort Arbuckle. The museum is open daily from 10:00 A.M. to 4:00 P.M. Donation of $1.00 is requested. Call (580) 369–2518 for more information.

Down the street, at the **Main Street Diner,** visitors can sit at a long, old-fashioned counter or at cheery tables. The diner serves fried ice cream, fried green tomatoes, pecan cobbler, buttermilk pie, hand-battered chicken fry, and has a large salad bar. The specialty is chicken-fried steak with cream gravy. The diner is at 202 North Third; (580) 369–2311.

A unique place to stay is the **Gingerbread House,** www.the-gingerbread house.com. Located in downtown Davis, the bed-and-breakfast offers an antiques and collectible shop on the first floor, while the third floor holds the guest rooms. The four rooms are cozy, decorated with antique furniture. Each room has wood floors, a queen-sized bed, its own Jacuzzi, and cable television. A home-cooked breakfast is served on English china each morning in the eating area. A "Romance" package is available. Prices range from $75 to $95, depending on season. Call (580) 369–7862.

Davis's claim to fame is nearby ***Turner Falls Park,*** (580) 369–2988, where a 77-foot waterfall splashes into a natural swimming pool along Honey Creek. The creek gets its name from the honeycomb-like formations caused by the deposit of crystallized calcium carbonate, or travertine. Turner Falls and the stretch of Honey Creek between the falls and another swimming hole at the east end of the park are usually jam-packed during the summer, with cars lining the roads up into the hillsides. If you continue driving upward, however, you'll come to ***Bridal Veil Falls,*** a far less dramatic but uncongested stretch of Honey Creek. Hiking trails through the Arbuckles here are generally uncrowded, too. Admission to the park is $5.00 per person.

The falls are in the very heart of the ***Arbuckle Mountains,*** which run east and west. They were created at the same time as the Appalachians and were once higher than the Rockies. Geological forces have reduced them now to a series of intriguing rocky, rolling hills that serve as a virtual textbook of the Paleozoic period.

Watch for scenic turnouts on either side of I–35, where markers identify layers of rock and link them with the geological time periods that created them. For a thorough tour of the geology of the area, you can hire the expert services of ***Arbuckle Geosciences.*** Dr. Bob Neman, the chairman of the chemistry department in a nearby university and an ardent rockhound, guides groups of almost any size for $20 per person, with a two-person minimum. Neman unravels the natural history of the area and steers clients to the fossils that are fair game for collectors. Arbuckle Geosciences is based in Ada; Neman guides groups from late May to November. Call (580) 436–1459 for information.

A recommended loop through the Arbuckles follows Highway 77D, which heads south from Highway 7 between Davis and Turner Falls Park. The first mile or so takes travelers through six distinct geological time zones, the earliest of which began about 400 million years ago. The highway winds around the top of a mountain to Falls Creek, a church campground. Stay to the left at Falls Creek; at the bottom of the hill is ***Price Falls,*** a little waterfall and swimming hole. Price Falls Camp rents cabins, tent campsites, and RV hookups on Price's Creek, where there's a reconstructed 1882 water mill. The road continues east and takes a scenic, canopied course along the Washita River.

Four miles east of the falls is **Dougherty,** a tiny crossroads with two claims to fame. The town is the birthplace of country-music singer Kay Starr; Dale Evans and Roy Rogers were married there in the 1940s.

From Dougherty, Highway 110 takes travelers back to Davis, where US 77 North makes a nostalgic trip through small-town America. The highway was once the only direct route between Dallas and Oklahoma City, and the 1907 three-story **Eskridge Hotel** in Wynnewood was the best-known hotel along the route. Now a museum, the hotel is remarkably undisturbed. The tin ceiling is in place in the lobby, and the original guest keys hang over the desk. The hotel is the official repository of local Daughters of the Confederacy memorabilia, and Wynnewood civic groups have undertaken the creation of exhibits in various guest rooms, including an early-day funeral parlor with early twentieth-century embalming kits and wicker baskets that temporarily held corpses. The museum is ½ block east of the highway at 114 South Robert Kerr Boulevard and is open by appointment only. Admission is $2.00 for adults, $1.00 for children. Call (405) 665–5221 for more information.

It's worth driving another 7 miles to **Pauls Valley,** (405) 238–2555 or www.paulsvalley.com, an agricultural community where loaded hay trucks and American flags are common sights on the brick streets downtown. (Pauls Valley officials claim their town has more brick streets than any other town in the United States.) Follow Ash Street north to **Bob's Pig Shop,** (405) 238–2332, an establishment started in 1933. Inside, the walls are decorated with photographs of JFK, rodeo queens, and historic front pages of the *Oklahoma City Times*. Wasp nests and rifles hang from the ceiling. The restaurant serves brisket and ribs with brown beans and coleslaw and a chicken-fried-steak sandwich dubbed the "Washita Valley Lobster." The restaurant made its reputation, however, with its "Pig Sandwich," barbecued pork roast served with a tangy relish and barbecue sauce.

A couple of attractions to visit here are the **Santa Fe Depot Museum** and the **Toy and Action Figure Museum.** The Santa Fe Depot Museum is located at 204 East Paul. Inside this restored 1905 depot, visitors will find old photos, school memorabilia, and pioneer collectibles. Outside, a vintage red caboose, steam locomotive, and coal tender await exploration. Open Monday and Tuesday 10:00 A.M. to 4:00 P.M., Wednesday through Saturday 11:00 A.M. to 4:00 P.M., and Sunday 1:30 to 4:00 P.M. For more information call (405) 238–2244. Those who love toys, be sure to check out the Toy and Action Figure Museum. Visitors will find comics and superheroes aplenty. The museum is located at 111 South Chickasaw Street in Pauls Valley and is open Tuesday through Saturday 10:00 A.M. to 5:00 P.M. and Sunday 1:00 to 5:00 P.M. Admission is $6.00 for adults and children over two (two and under free) and $4.00 for senior citizens. Call (405) 238–6300 or visit www.actionfiguremuseum.com for more information.

Bootstrap Country

Oklahoma's history is filled with tales of penniless immigrants who built empires through vision, hard work—and a little luck. Highway 19 from Pauls Valley takes travelers west to Lindsay and the nearby white-columned *Murray-Lindsay Mansion,* built by Frank and Alzira Murray. Frank Murray was a young Irish immigrant who came to New Orleans in the 1850s, drifted to Fort Gibson, where he married a young Choctaw woman, then settled in the Chickasaw Nation. Eventually the Murrays owned 20,000 head of cattle and 20,000 acres of land—one cornfield was reportedly 3 miles wide and 5 miles long. The area was so remote that a circuit judge held court on the lawn. The three-story house now belongs to the Oklahoma Historical Society, which every June hosts an old-fashioned county fair, complete with horse-drawn carriage rides, homemade ice cream, churned butter on homemade bread, horseshoes, and dominoes on the back porch. The mansion, 2 miles south and 1 mile west of Lindsay, is open by appointment only. Call (405) 756–2121.

There's good fishing to be found south of Lindsay; continue south on Highway 76 and then west on Highway 29 to *Lake Fuqua, Lake Humphries,* and *Clear Creek Lake.* The lakes have been stocked over the years with Florida-strain largemouth bass and routinely provide trophy fish to happy anglers. Crappies and catfish are also abundant. Clear Creek is the most developed lake, although all three have restaurants and fishing docks.

The three lakes, plus Duncan Lake (which is accessible by driving south on Highway 81), are owned by the city of *Duncan.* Duncan was founded when the Rock Island Railroad went through the area and tailor and merchant William Duncan moved his store over from a nearby stream called Cow Creek. It grew as a retail center along the railroad and as oil was discovered in the area. Its fortunes were secured in the 1920s, though, when an enterprising resident named Earl Haliburton invented a cementing process to cap off oil rigs that became the industry standard. Such was Haliburton's impact on the community that his original office furniture is on display at *Stephens County Historical Museum* in the old stone National Guard Armory in Fuqua Park, on Highway 81 and Beech Street, north of downtown. The museum also holds a replica of an early oil well, Plains Indians artifacts, old tractors, vintage clothing, school photographs, and such prizes as an 1860 velocipede, a children's toy that was the forerunner to the modern tricycle. The museum is open Tuesday, Thursday, Friday, and Saturday from 1:00 to 5:00 P.M.; for more information call (580) 252–0717.

Drive farther south to Main Street, where citizens have worked for a decade to revitalize downtown. Their efforts have paid off, because the sidewalks bustle as they did in the 1950s. The Palace Theater boasts a restored balcony, Saturday afternoon matinees, and old 1950s placards over the concession stand. Eight antiques stores are clustered around Main Street; you can pick up a list at the ***Antique Marketplace and Tea Room,*** (580) 255–2499, which has thirty-five booths and a tearoom that serves lunch every day except Saturday and Sunday. ***The Loft,*** (580) 252–3942, www.theloftduncan.com, at 916 West Main, Duncan, an interior-decorating service and home-furnishing store ensconced in a refurbished hardware store, is so successful that it draws big-city clients from Oklahoma City and Dallas.

Cement stepping stones on Main Street's wide sidewalks are engraved with events that shaped Duncan: A tornado destroyed half the town in 1898, the first automobile appeared in 1908, and Pretty Boy Floyd hid out there in the 1930s.

Before the oilmen came to town, William Duncan had a store that sold supplies to cowboys along the Chisholm Trail, a path once used to move longhorn cattle from Texas to railheads in Kansas. Outside the ***Chisholm Trail Heritage Center,*** www.onthechisholmtrail.com, on North Twenty-ninth, is a bronze depiction of this great cattle drive. The sculpture shows a chuck wagon followed by longhorn cattle moving north. A trail dog trots alongside cowboys, intent on the herd. The museum displays artifacts used on the trail and offers interactive exhibits including clips from movies and television shows about the trail. The center is open Monday through Saturday from 10:00 A.M. to 5:00 P.M. and after May 1 on Sunday from 1:00 to 5:00 P.M. Call (580) 252–6692.

The ***Lindley House Bed and Breakfast,*** www.lindleyhouse.com, north of downtown is established in a 1939 English Country–style house on two acres surrounded by flower gardens. There are two rooms in the house and three private cottages, each with a king-size bed and private bath. (An upstairs suite has its own balcony.) The owners call themselves "masters of Southern hospitality" and promise that guests will find genuine rest and relaxation at their home. A continental breakfast is served on weekdays; dishes like blueberry pancakes and French toast appear on weekends. Rates range in price from $69 per night to $149. For reservations call (580) 255–6700. The Lindley House is at 1211 North Tenth Street, Duncan.

Places to Stay in River Country

ARDMORE

Best Western Ardmore Inn
6 Holiday Drive
(580) 223–7525

**Blackberry Farm
Bed & Breakfast**
2715 Hedges Road
(580) 223–8958

Hampton Inn
410 Railway Express
(580) 223–6394

Lake Murray Lodge
2 miles east of I–35
(580) 223–6600

DAVIS

Cedarvale Cabins
Highway 77 South
(580) 369–3224

DUNCAN

Holiday Inn
1015 North U.S. Highway 81
(580) 252–1500

Lindley House
1211 North Tenth Street
(580) 255–6700

DURANT

Holiday Inn Express
2112 West Main
(580) 924–8881

PAULS VALLEY

Days Inn
Highway 19 and I–35
(405) 238–7548

SULPHUR

Secret Cove Retreat
2 Nunsuch Lane
(580) 622–6125

Sulphur Springs Inn
1102 West Lindsay
(877) 622–5930

Places to Eat in River Country

ARDMORE

Budro's Rib Joint
1606 McLish
(580) 223–2272

Cafe Alley
107 East Main
(580) 223–6413

Fireside Dining (eclectic)
2½ miles east of Ardmore on
Highway 77
(580) 226–4070

Polo's of Ardmore
1717 West Broadway
(580) 226–7656

DAVIS

Babe's Hot Tamales
115 West Main
(580) 369–5373

Dougherty Diner
207 North Third Street
(580) 369–5119

Main Street Diner
215 East Main
(580) 369–2311

DUNCAN

**Antique Market Place
Tea Room**
726 West Main
(580) 255–2499

Cedar Street Grill
1001 West Cedar
(580) 252–6540

**Eduardo's Mexican
Restaurant**
1306 North Highway 81
(580) 255–0781

**Wright's Steak and
Lobster House**
905 East Bois D'Arc
(580) 252–4363

LINDSAY

**Teran's Mexican
Restaurant**
1301 West Cherokee Street
(405) 756–1673

MARIETTA

Denim's
I–35 and Highway 32 West
(580) 276–3222

La Roca
101 North US 77
(580) 276–4167

McGeehee's Catfish
3 miles west on
Highway 32,
then 3 miles south
(580) 276–2751

Robertson's Hams
(sandwiches)
I–35, exit 15
(580) 276–3395

Sunshine Restaurant
I–35 and Highway 32
(580) 276–3760

MARLOW

Giuseppe's
201 West Main
(580) 658–2148

PAULS VALLEY

Bob's Pig Shop
829 North Ash
(405) 238–2332

Punkin's Bar-B-Que
Highway 19 and I–35
(405) 238–2320

Tio's
½ mile east of I–32 on
Highway 19
(405) 238–3535

SULPHUR

Country Cafe
905 West Broadway Avenue
(580) 622–2822

Poor Girl's Cafe
925 West Twelfth Street
(580) 622–3785

FOR MORE INFORMATION

Ardmore Tourism Authority
410 West Main Street
Ardmore 73401
(580) 221–5118
www.ardmore.org

Davis Chamber of Commerce
100 East Main Street
Davis 73030
(580) 369–2402
www.davisok.org

Cross Timbers: Central Oklahoma

Travelers driving through the short-grass prairies into central Oklahoma have to work to conjure up a mental picture of the Cross Timbers, a band of shrubby trees that once stretched in a diagonal across the region. A century and a half ago, the underbrush was so dense, it unnerved a party of Comanche traveling to Fort Gibson for their first official meeting with the U.S. government in 1834. Accustomed to wide, open spaces, the Comanches turned around and went back home.

But today, with the Cross Timbers cleared away and mile upon mile of pasture in its place, central Oklahoma unnerves travelers in quite a different way. Lacking both the forests of the eastern part of the state and the grandeur of the prairie landscapes to the west, central Oklahoma can seem mind-numbingly bland.

But travelers who simply hightail it through central Oklahoma miss some real treasures. The landscape that can look so blank holds an intriguing blend of American Indian, western, and other cultural landmarks.

Three major interstates (Interstates 35, 40, and 44) intersect in Oklahoma City and are useful for traveling in the area. The advantage of staying off the interstates in this region lies more

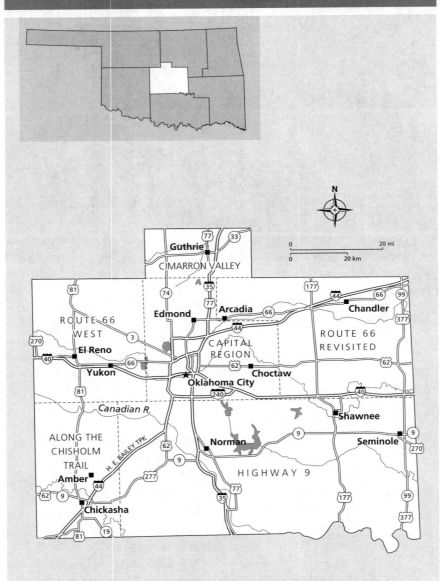

N

0   20 mi
0   20 km

Guthrie
77   33
CIMARRON VALLEY
74
35
77
ROUTE 66
WEST   Edmond   Arcadia   66   Chandler   99
81   44   66   377
270   ROUTE 66
3   REVISITED
El Reno   CAPITAL
40   66   REGION
Yukon   62   Choctaw   62
81   Oklahoma City
240   40
Canadian R.
Shawnee
ALONG THE   9   9
CHISHOLM   62   Norman   9   Seminole   270
TRAIL   9
Amber   44   HIGHWAY 9   177   99
62   9   277
Chickasha   77   35   377
81   19
177
H.E. BAILEY TPK

in a slower pace than in scenic charm. One exception is Highway 9, which runs along the southern half of the region.

Along the Chisholm Trail

U.S. Highway 81 runs north and south about 30 miles west of Oklahoma City and follows almost precisely the trail first blazed by a Cherokee trader named Jesse Chisholm before the Civil War. Chisholm began trading with the Southern Plains tribes during the 1830s, bringing wagon freighters full of goods down from Kansas. After the Civil War, cattlemen drove Texas longhorns along "Chisholm's trail." Chisholm wasn't a cattleman, but his name became forever linked with the old cattle trail. Travelers can tell for certain that they're on top of the old trail if they spot a square concrete pillar along the highway. In 1997, historians erected markers along the trail to celebrate its 130th anniversary.

Many of the towns that took root along US 81 have one thing in common: They were built near springs large enough to supply water to the enormous herds of cattle that traveled along the Chisholm Trail. The town of **Chickasha,** www.chickashachamber.com, was built northeast of a large artesian spring called **Shannon Springs.** The spring is now the centerpiece of a pretty little park, rimmed in sandstone put in place by Works Progress Administration workers, with picnic tables, a pedestrian bridge over the spring, and a swimming pool. From just after Thanksgiving to New Year's Day, the park is illuminated by the Festival of Lights, an eye-popping extravaganza of lighted holiday decorations, the biggest such display in the state. The park is at the intersection of Ninth and Grand Streets, southwest of downtown.

It's probably no coincidence that some of the best restaurants to be found in a town built along an old cattle trail serve beef. **Jake's Rib** serves up

AUTHOR'S FAVORITES IN CROSS TIMBERS

Byron Berline's Double Stop Music Hall

Fred Jones Jr. Art Museum

Guthrie Historic District

Harn Homestead Museum

Mabee-Gerrer Museum of Art

Museum of Pioneer History

The Paseo Arts District

Round Barn

Scottish Rite Temple

State Capital Publishing Museum

smoked ribs, brisket, pork, and sausage—and absolutely huge servings of French fries—in a setting made cozy with wooden paneling. The restaurant is so popular with locals that diners who arrive after 5:00 P.M. on Friday or Saturday afternoons may find not only the restaurant filled, but the waiting area as well. Knots of waiting diners sit on their cars, waiting for a call through the front door. Weeknights aren't as hectic. Jake's Rib is east of US 81, which is marked as Fourth Street through Chickasha; turn east on Almar Drive and follow it as it curves north. The restaurant's address is 100 Ponderosa; (405) 222–2825.

Downtown, travelers meet up with a specialty that makes a frequent appearance in central Oklahoma: onion-fried burgers. For decades, cooks have tossed handfuls of chopped onions onto hot, ancient grills and seared them for a minute or two before adding a half pound or so of ground beef and cooking the onions right into it. Fast-food chains have put most of the grills out of business in cities, but places like the narrow, friendly *J&W Grill,* (405) 224–9912, at 501 West Choctaw, still thrive in small towns. J&W's serves breakfast and "coneys" (hot dogs) too. It's open Monday through Thursday from 6:00 A.M. to 2:00 P.M. and on Friday and Saturday from 6:00 A.M. until 8:45 P.M.

You can continue on the trail of serious barbecue to *Amber,* which is on Highway 92, 8 miles north of its junction with Highway 9. Amber is a mere dab of a town, mostly a school and a few churches. It's a good bet on the weekends that more than half of the cars in town are at *Ken's Restaurant.* Keep an eye on your watch, because Ken's gravel parking lot is filled by 5:15 P.M. on Saturday. In the two decades that it's been in operation, the restaurant has made its way onto the short list of barbecue joints worth driving for; the guest book is

The Muscle Car Ranch

Cattle graze next to a half-buried 1969 Camaro, upended next to a stock pond, and vintage gas station signs hang from the branches of elm trees at the Muscle Car Ranch, the brainchild of Curtis Hart. Hart started a "Car Corral and Cruise In" swap meet as a way to raise the money to buy a piece of his family ranch, and his passion for restoring "muscle cars" built between the late 1950s and early 1970s, motorcycles, and old gas station, motel, and diner signs has created a kind of open-air museum of life on the road. Hart built a stage from salvaged bridge boards on a rise and hires 1960s- and 1970s-era bands to play at his August meet. Campers are welcome year-round, and there are electrical RV hookups, showers, and bathrooms. To get to the ranch from US 81 south of town, take Country Club Road west to Sixteenth Street and turn south. The ranch is about a mile down the road. Call (405) 222–4910 for information or visit www.musclecarranch.com.

TOP EVENTS IN CROSS TIMBERS

**Festival of the Arts, Myriad
Botanical Gardens,**
Oklahoma City, mid-April;
(405) 270–4848
www.artscouncilokc.com

**Chuckwagon Festival, National
Cowboy and Western Heritage
Museum;**
Oklahoma City, May;
(405) 478–2250
www.nationalcowboymuseum.org

**Oklahoma Cattleman's Association
Range Round-Up,**
Guthrie, May;
(405) 282–7433
www.lazye.com/arena

**Red Earth Native American
Cultural Festival,**
Oklahoma City, June;
(405) 527–5228
www.redearth.org

**Aerospace America
International Airshow,**
Oklahoma City, June;
(405) 685–9546
www.aerospaceokc.com

Jazz in June,
Norman;
(405) 325–3388;
www.jazzinjune.org

International Bluegrass Festival,
Guthrie, October;
(405) 282–4446
www.oibf.com

peppered with comments such as "Best since El Paso!" There is no menu, just sirloin steaks, ribs, chicken, and brisket smoked over mesquite wood. Owner Ken Morrison and his wife, Ola, also serve fried okra, pinto beans, and salad. Diners can purchase T-shirts with caricatures of Ken and the legend "We Eat Barbecue Buck Nekkid"—a reference to the fact that Ken doesn't use any sauce in the preparation. Ken's is 3 blocks east of the intersection of Highway 92 and Amber's Main Street. Call (405) 222–0786 for information.

Highway 9

Highway 9 angles northeast across more ranch country and then crosses I–35, just south of **Norman,** www.visitnorman.com. From the looks of its picture-book downtown, the news that Norman is Oklahoma's third-largest city is a bit of a surprise. Most of the population lives away from downtown, to the south and west, leaving the business district in a pleasant time warp. Case in point: **The Diner,** at 213 East Main, has been operating as an eating establishment in the same narrow spot for a hundred years. There are a dozen stools in front of the cook and grill, a dozen gold-tufted vinyl booths with pink Formica tables, black-and-white tile on the floor, and four kinds of hot sauce on every table. Tamales and chicken-fried steak are served with eggs for breakfast, along with more traditional omelets, blueberry pancakes, and biscuits. Lunch, which, like breakfast, is served all day, is a short list of burgers, sandwiches, burritos, Frito pies, and cornbread. The restaurant is open daily from 6:30 A.M. to 2:00 P.M. Call (405) 329–6642 for information.

Tin ceilings and a rustic wooden floor make a good backdrop for the Native American art displayed at *Tribe's Gallery,* at 307 East Main. The gallery sells paintings (originals and prints), photography, pottery, and sculpture by Oklahoma artists, along with jewelry, kachinas, and fetishes from New Mexico. The gallery also sells books, Native American drumming and flute tapes, and CDs. Gallery shows are held during Oklahoma City's Red Earth Festival in June and in December. A table by the door is stacked high with notices and fliers about Native American events and powwows, along with information about other Norman events. Call (405) 329–4442.

A few blocks north of Main Street is the ***Montford Inn Bed and Breakfast,*** www.montfordinn.com, a buttery-yellow 4,000-square-foot inn designed and built to have the feel of an old house. It comes pretty close to the mark. The inn is owned by bed-and-breakfast pros Phyllis and Ron Murray and their son William Murray; Ron and Phyllis travel the country giving seminars on hospitality. The creature comforts of the rooms are unsurpassed in Oklahoma: Each of the ten antiques-filled rooms in the main house has a private bath; most have gas fireplaces, and all are stocked with coffeepots and gourmet coffee, candles, scented soaps, magazines, and piles of pillows. Three 1,000-square-foot cottages across the street are as charming and comfortable as the inn, with bonuses: whirlpool baths and tiny kitchens. Hidden Hollow is a whole house unto itself— the restored bungalow has a full kitchen and a yard and is perfect for families.

The inn is named for one of Phyllis Murray's ancestors, a Chickasaw cattle rancher named Montford Johnson. Johnson's license to operate in Indian Territory is framed and hanging on the wall; a kachina doll collection and University of Oklahoma football memorabilia fill other rooms. (Helen Hunt stayed in the hunting-and-fishing-themed Trophy Room while she was in Oklahoma filming the movie *Twister.*) The Murrays cater to business as well as leisure travelers and provide guests with a photocopying machine, fax, modem hookups, and workouts at a nearby gym. The inn is at 322 West Tonhawa; (405) 321–2200.

The ***Cutting Garden Bed and Breakfast,*** www.cuttinggardenbandb.com, at 927 West Boyd, (405) 329– 4522, is more impressive inside than it appears from the street. What makes it special are the backyard gardens and innkeeper

Connie Byrum's intense interest in green, growing things. Fresh flowers are in every room, bouquets of fragrant herbs are tucked in out-of-the-way spots, and figs wait to be plucked from a tree by the front door.

Just a few blocks east, on the corner of Boyd and Chautauqua and on the western edge of the University of Oklahoma campus, is *The Jacobson House,* www.jacobsonhouse.com, a 1918 house that once belonged to OU art professor and painter Oscar Jacobson and is now a contemporary Native American arts center. When a social worker named Susan Peters noted the exceptional talent of a group of Kiowa students in Anadarko in the 1920s, she arranged for them to move to Norman to study art with Jacobson. The professor took the students under his wing and arranged for their work to be shown and published in, among other places, Prague and Paris. The artists, known as the Kiowa Five, are generally credited as the first modern Native American painters. The Jacobson House carries on the tradition of nurturing Native American artists and hosts exhibits that showcase emerging Native American artists and art forms, including sculpture, photography, and film. An Indian art market is held in October. The house, at 609 Chautauqua, is open Tuesday through Friday from 10:00 A.M. to 6:00 P.M. and on weekends from 1:00 to 5:00 P.M.; (405) 366–1667.

Visitors will not want to miss another attraction along the west side, the *Sam Noble Oklahoma Museum of Natural History,* located at 2401 Chautauqua Avenue. This museum holds fascinating natural and cultural wonders for young and old. There are four permanent galleries: the Siegfried Family Hall of Ancient Life, which showcases the Age of Dinosaurs; the Noble Drilling Corporation Hall of Natural Wonders, which lets visitors experience Oklahoma's natural land-scapes; the Merkel Family Foundation Gallery of World Cultures, which includes a variety of antiquities from Greece, Rome, Egypt, Tibet, Africa, and other coun-

Oklahoma Gold Rush

The Chickasaw Legislature, now in session at Tishomingo, Indian Territory, has placed a royalty on all gold that is hereafter mined in the Chickasaw Nation. This act was brought about by Indian citizens who live near Purcell, in the Chickasaw Nation taking out samples of ore. Some of the Chickasaws, who have investigated the matter, are under the belief that the "Klondike is a small and insignificant goldfield compared with the one discovered near Purcell." The secret of the location of the gold is locked in the bosoms of the discoverers and a few prominent men of the nation, who are guarding it sacredly.

—reported in the *Oklahoma State Sentinel,* Thursday, September 30, 1897

tries; and the McCasland Family Hall of the People of Oklahoma, which presents the more than 15,000 years of Native American history in Oklahoma. This gallery also displays the oldest painted art in North America, on a bison skull dating 10,000 years old. The museum is open Tuesday through Saturday from 10:00 A.M. to 5:00 P.M. and Sunday 1:00 to 5:00 P.M. Admission is $5.00 for adults, $4.00 for seniors (age sixty-five and older), and $3.00 for children (ages six to seventeen). Children ages five and under are free. For more information call (405) 325–4712 or visit www.snomnh.ou.edu.

Oscar Jacobson also founded the ***Fred Jones Jr. Art Museum,*** www.ou.edu/fjma, a few blocks east of the Sam Noble Oklahoma Museum of Natural History, on the University of Oklahoma campus. It was a fine little museum until 1996—then it became a great little museum by acquiring the Fleischaker collection, 400 major pieces of art assembled by an Oklahoma family. Among its highlights are works by Thomas Hart Benton, Mark Cagoule, Henry Madest, Joan Miró, and Pablo Picasso. Its Native American collections include work by potter Maria Martinez and Oklahoma-born sculptor Allan Houser. The museum is open Tuesday through Saturday from 10:00 A.M. to 5:00 P.M. and on Sunday from 1:00 to 5:00 P.M. When the OU football team plays home games, the museum closes at kickoff time. The museum is at 410 West Boyd Street; (405) 325–3272.

The campus holds another Jacobson namesake—Jacobson Hall, now home to the ***University of Oklahoma Visitors Center.*** The center is on Parrington Oval, which intersects with Boyd Street. In addition to information about campus attractions, such as the Western History Collection, a trove of historic Native American and Western photographs and manuscripts, visitors will find the center stocked with brochures and other information about state and local attractions. Another nod to Jacobson's passion for Native American art and culture is a 31-foot mural, *The Grand Entry,* which shows Native American dancers in full regalia. The center, at 550 Parrington Oval, is open weekdays from 8:00 A.M. to 5:00 P.M. and on Saturday from 9:00 A.M. to noon.

Travelers can stay near campus at the ***Holmberg House,*** a 1914 two-story Craftsman bungalow, which was built as the home of Fredrik Holmberg, the first dean of the university's fine-arts department. Still artful, it's now owned by two OU professors, who have furnished the house with period wallpaper and arts and crafts–style furniture. Rates for the three guest rooms, each with a private bath, range from $65 to $85. The house is at 766 DeBarr; (405) 321–6221.

Misal's Bistro of India specializes in tandoori cooking, accomplished with an imported clay oven. Diners sit under a brightly colored *shamiana,* a tentlike awning used for special events in India, and watch chefs at work in the glass-enclosed kitchen, preparing such specialties as tomato-cardamom soup; *saag*, a classic Indian dish of chopped spinach sautéed with tomatoes and cumin; or lamb marinated in spices and yogurt. For dessert, try *kheer*, an Indian rice dessert; or a mango shake. Misal's of India is at 580 Ed Noble Parkway, Norman, and is open for lunch Monday through Friday from 11:00 A.M. to 3:00 P.M., Sunday to Thursday evenings from 5:00 to 10:00 P.M., and Saturday from 5:00 to 11:00 P.M. Call (405) 579–5600.

When the weather is fine, drummers assemble at Reaves Park, one block north of the Lloyd Noble Center, home of the Oklahoma Sooner basketball team. Each April, an estimated 300,000 visitors attend the Medieval Fair in Norman, for music, crafts, food, and entertainment, including a Royal Court, a human chess game, jesters, and more. For information about the festival, call (405) 366–8095 or (800) 767–7260. You may also want to visit their Web site at www.medievalfair.org.

Just north of downtown Norman sits **The Crucible Foundry,** 110 East Tonhawa. Artists here use a mixture of art and science to create beautiful bronze sculptures. Visitors can walk through the 1,400-square-foot indoor gallery and see sculptures, paintings, and other exhibits free of charge. Sculptures include Pat Kennedy's "Clydesdales," Scott Adams' "Before the Rut," and David Phelps' "Hornytoad." Stepping into the outdoor gallery, guests are treated to more sculptures and a bronze fountain. Gallery hours are Monday through Saturday 10:00 A.M. to 5:00 P.M. Call (405) 579–2700 or visit www.thecruciblellc.com for more information.

Travel farther south, all the way through Noble, for a look at some of Nature's handiwork at the **Timberlake Rose Rock Museum,** www.roserockmuseum.com. Rose rocks are the official Oklahoma State Rock, but, actually, they aren't rocks at all; they are crystals that formed from barium sulfate and

For the Love of Chocolate

Visitors come from miles around to sample some of the finest chocolate products at the Annual Chocolate Festival held in Norman every February. This festival was voted number 5 of the Top 10 Food Festivals in America by the Food Network. Besides trying chocolate samples, visitors can enjoy the many chocolate competitions including the Adult and Kids Chocolate Sculpture Contest, Most Delicious Dessert, Brownie Bake-Off, and the People's Choice. For more information call (405) 329–4523 or visit www.normanfirehouse.com.

sand as a prehistoric sea evaporated at the end of the Permian age. Iron oxide in the sand gives the round crystals a rosy cast, further enhancing their resemblance to roses. The rocks are found throughout central Oklahoma but are concentrated most heavily east of Noble. The museum is filled with some of the most unusual crystals that have been unearthed, including ones that resemble, among other things, butterflies and a miniature poodle. The museum is in a white house with blue shutters, at 419 South Highway 77, Noble, and is open Tuesday through Saturday from 10:00 A.M. to 6:00 P.M. Admission is free. Call (405) 872–9838.

Highway 9 takes travelers to *Shawnee,* www.visitshawnee.com, east of Norman and north of Tecumseh. Shawnee was first known as Shawnee Town and was originally a trading post for the Indians living on the Shawnee reservation. Non-Indian settlement began in 1892 with the opening of Shawnee and Potawatomi lands.

A mall built north of town near I–40 a few years ago has drained vitality from Shawnee's downtown. To see how the city once bustled, head to the *Santa Fe Depot Museum,* www.santafedepotmuseum.org, at 614 East Main. The betowered 1903 depot was built of Bedford limestone with cantilevered ceilings and reportedly was designed by a homesick Scottish architect. Along with railroad memorabilia, the museum holds vintage photographs, a life-size model of a horse that stood in the window of a Main Street western-wear store, a Native American doeskin wedding dress, and a Model T. The museum is open Tuesday through Friday from 10:00 A.M. to 4:00 P.M. and on weekends from 2:00 to 4:00 P.M. For information call (405) 275–8412.

The railroad is responsible for the presence of St. Gregory's College, which moved to Shawnee in 1913 when the railroad bypassed its original location farther south. St. Gregory's grew out of the Sacred Heart mission, which was established by Benedictine monks in Indian Territory in 1876 among members of the Potawatomi Tribe. The art collection of one early twentieth-century priest, Father Gerrer, forms the nucleus of the *Mabee-Gerrer Museum of Art,* www.mgmoa.org, on the campus grounds. Before joining the order, Gerrer played the clarinet on horseback in a circus. As a monk, Gerrer showed the same flair for the unexpected; he studied painting in Europe and put together an eclectic collection of art on the prairie. Today, the museum collection includes works by American painters, as well as by Raphael, Whistler, and Rembrandt, and such artifacts as medieval armor and two Egyptian mummies. The museum, at 1900 West McArthur Drive, Shawnee, is open Tuesday through Saturday from 10:00 A.M. to 5:00 P.M. and on Sunday from 1:00 to 4:00 P.M. Admission is $5.00 for adults, $4.00 for senior citizens, and $3.00 for children. For information call (405) 878–5300.

What's still standing of Sacred Heart Mission is a half hour away. Travelers, however, should stop along the way at the **Potawatomi Heritage Center,** at 1901 South Gordon Cooper Drive. The Potawatomi Tribe is closely related to the Chippewa and Ottawa Tribes, who first lived on the upper shores of Lake Huron and migrated west under pressure by white settlement. The Potawatomi came to Indian Territory in the 1870s. Along with the shells, baskets, and beadwork on display at the tribal headquarters

Santa Fe Depot Museum, Shawnee

are dioramas and vintage photographs of the mission school. The annual Potawatomi Homecoming and Powwow is held at the tribal headquarters at the end of June. Call (405) 275–3121 to learn more.

Even though **Seminole** is a small town struggling to survive in a post–oil-boom economy, resident Jasmine Moran saw no reason why Seminole's children shouldn't have a hands-on, educational museum as well-equipped and spacious as any in the country. Four years after planning began, the **Jasmine Moran Children's Museum** opened, and at 20,000 square feet, it is indeed one of the largest children's museums in the country. Inside, children enact real-life occupations ranging from television anchor to supermarket checker. The museum, at 1714 Highway 9, is open Tuesday through Saturday from 10:00 A.M. to 5:00 P.M. and on Sunday from 1:00 to 5:00 P.M. Admission is $7.00 per person; admission for children younger than three is free and persons age sixty or older pay $6.00. Call (405) 382–0950 or visit www.jasminemoran.com for information.

The **Bus Station Cafe,** at 411 East Broadway, has been open since 1929, and owners saw no reason to close down—or to change the name—just because bus service to Seminole ceased. The nostalgic little cafe serves country breakfasts with biscuits, hamburgers, and chicken-fried steak Monday through Saturday from 6:00 A.M. to 2:00 P.M. Call (405) 382–3353.

Route 66 Revisited

If you drive due north on Highway 99, you'll intersect with Route 66. The historic road is particularly easy to follow between Tulsa and Oklahoma City and is filled with quirky surprises.

A Monk's View

The Citizen Band Potawatomi Tribe sold its allotments in Kansas and bought a reservation in Indian Territory. In 1876 Sacred Heart Mission was established on a square mile of land given to the monks of the Order of St. Benedict, who built a church, an abbey, convents, schools, and a farm. Father Thomas Bergh, a monk who traveled to Indian Territory from Ramsgate Abbey in England, was at the mission from August 1885 to February 1886. His observations are preserved in the archives of St. Gregory's College. About the land, he wrote, "The prairies are broken up by thickets and glades for all the world as if the landscape was studied and artificial. I was continually thinking of a huge but ill-kept English park . . . . It is good land, undulating and well watered and where cultivated, grows the usual European crops . . . . There can be no doubt that the U.S. Government will not be able much longer to restrain the covetousness of the Whites who hover all around the Territory and only wait the chance to rush in."

One such offering is in Stroud: *The Rock Cafe,* a two-story filling station and cafe, was built out of the stones unearthed when Route 66 was built in the late 1920s. Owner Christian Herr, a native of Switzerland, serves a diverse menu that stars buffalo burgers, schnitzel, sauerbraten, spaetzle, pork ribs, and brisket and keeps a cozy fire going when it's cold outside. Route 66 is a particularly beloved destination for German and other international travelers, as a peek inside Herr's guest book shows. The Rock Cafe is at 114 West Main. Call (918) 968–3990 for information.

The revival of interest in Route 66 has spawned a number of antiques shops and specialty stores in Stroud, www.stroudok.com, that make window-shopping a treat. Southwest of Stroud, in Davenport, barbecue enthusiasts will want to stop at *Dan's Bar-B-Que,* (918) 377–2288. Owners Alice and John Vandever smoke pork and beef and mix up mountains of old-fashioned side dishes such as brown beans and potato salad.

Seven more miles to the west is *Chandler,* www.chandlerok.com, which has become something of a meeting place for Route 66 enthusiasts. Everyone from bicyclists tracing the route to Europeans traveling in rented convertibles turns up at the *Lincoln Motel,* a fixture on the road since 1939. The rooms are clean but spartan, each detached and equipped with old-fashioned metal lawn chairs out front for watching the world roll by. The motel is at 740 East First Street. Call (405) 258–0200 for reservations.

In downtown Chandler, the *Museum of Pioneer History* has an outstanding assortment of artifacts and photographs dating back to the town's founding in 1891. The museum also has what amounts to a collection of town home movies; a newsreel photographer for Pathé News was based in Chandler. Films of town parades, Fourth of July celebrations, and other events are in the museum's archives. The museum, at 717 Mantel Street, Chandler, is open Tuesday through Friday from 10:00 A.M. to 4:00 P.M.; (405) 258–2425.

Westfall's Gas Station on Eighth Street was a popular stop for travelers on Route 66. The 1927 redbrick station looks more like a cottage than a Phillips 66.

The pride of the little town of **Arcadia,** www.townofarcadia.com, 26 miles to the west, is its red **Round Barn.** In the days when Route 66 was the way west, the red round barn was a landmark for travelers, marking the shift from the hilly eastern portion of the road to the trek through the plains. The four-story-high barn was designed and built in 1898 by a German farmer, who thought the circular structure would withstand tornadoes. (It never got hit.) The barn was a popular spot for barn dances well into the twentieth century; two Oklahoma governors played the fiddle upstairs. The barn was saved from ruin by an army of volunteers who were given a National Preservation Award for their efforts, and the barn celebrated its centennial in grand style in 1998.

The barn is now something of a cottage industry. There is a gift shop selling Route 66 souvenirs downstairs, and the barn is open for tours Tuesday through Sunday from 10:00 A.M. to 5:00 P.M. Be sure to climb upstairs and look at the roof bracing, which resembles the inside of a basket. There's also a board posting photographs and information about round barns around the United States. Arcadia's round barn is distinguished by the fact that it is the only one in the world with a freestanding second floor and a hemispherical roof. Call (405) 396–2761 for information.

rainingbricks androllingpins

Ever since Stroud, Oklahoma, and Stroud, Gloucester, England, discovered that both towns have brick-making plants, the two towns have challenged each other to participate in an annual brick-throwing contest; results are compared over the telephone. Now Stroud, Australia, has gotten into the act. The Australians manufacture rolling pins, so Stroud (Oklahoma) now has expanded the contest to the "International Brick and Rolling Pin Competition," held every July.

Right across the street is **Hillbillee's Cafe,** (405) 396–9600, 206 East Highway 66. The old Western-style rock building was once a gas station but now serves fried chicken, chicken-fried steak, and barbecue, with cobbler for dessert. Hillbillee's is open every day except Sunday from 11:00 A.M. to 3:00 P.M. Local country-and-western bands play Wednesday through Saturday nights from late spring until Labor Day, and Friday and Saturday nights year-round. **Hillbillee's Bed and Breakfast,** outfitted with Western-style furnishings, sits

Arcadian Inn Famous Maple Walnut Cookies

Want to bring a little of the Arcadian Inn to your home? Bake up a batch of the inn's signature cookies and keep them in your cookie jar. Martha Hall keeps them in hers.

1 cup butter-flavored Crisco

1 cup sugar

½ cup brown sugar

2 eggs

1 tsp. vanilla

1 Tbsp. maple flavoring

4 Tbsp. flour

1 tsp. salt

1 tsp. baking soda

2 cups flour

1½ cups chopped English walnuts

Cream together Crisco, sugars, eggs, vanilla, and maple flavoring. Add 4 Tbsp. flour, salt, and soda. Fold in 2 cups flour and walnuts. Drop by teaspoons onto an ungreased baking sheet. Bake at 350 degrees for ten minutes.

behind the restaurant. Rates are $45 to $55 and include breakfast. Call (405) 396–2982 or visit www.hillbillees.com for information.

Less than a mile from where Route 66 intersects with I–35 in Edmond is **Arcadia Lake,** a municipal impoundment notable in landlocked Oklahoma for the 500 tons of imported river sand spread on three swim beaches every year just before Memorial Day. There are changing rooms and lakeside rinse showers, as well as volleyball nets and a playground. There is also a series of mountain-biking trails blazed around the lake, ranging from easy rides cut with switchbacks to more rigorous routes. Admission to the lake is $6.00 per day per car. Call (405) 216–7470 for information.

A few more miles west, and a half mile north on Air Depot Road, you will find the **Mountain View Weavery,** 5621 East Mountain View Road. Wanda Nobbe, owner and textile artist, welcomes visitors who are interested in learning about the art of weaving and spinning. In her studio, guests will marvel at the completed projects, while the Weavery itself offers opportunities for the beginner and advanced to buy materials—fiber, spinning wheels, floor looms—for projects of their own. For information about private classes, commission work, or just to learn about the latest fiber festivals and where to discover wool and alpaca in Oklahoma, contact Wanda at (405) 341–4998.

One-half block from Route 66 is the ***Arcadian Inn Bed and Breakfast,*** (405) 348–6347 or www.arcadian inn.com. Owner Martha Hall had a friend paint a celestial scene on the dining-room ceiling; under it she serves guests heavenly breakfasts such as pumpkin pancakes and apples swimming in cinnamon-hazelnut cream. The house is filled with Victorian antiques, lace, and Martha's collections of angels and glass sheep. All eight guest rooms have Jacuzzis and private baths, but the Crown Jewel Villa is particularly luxurious. The private cottage has a king-size canopy bed, a fireplace, and a European shower for two. Most rooms come with a private candlelight breakfast. The Crown Jewel Villa rents for $229 on weekends and $209 on weekdays. Room rates range from $119 to $229. The Arcadian Inn is at 328 East First Street.

grape expectations

For their first Cinco de Mayo festival at the ***Tres Sueños Vineyard*** near Edmond, owners Richard Kennedy and Gene Clifton expected only 1,000 guests. Four thousand people showed up. The Three Dreams (its English-language name) began when Richard made his first bottle of wine from Concord grapes in 1993, and the winery officially opened in May 1999. The vineyard now has 2,500 vines producing four tons of grapes annually. The Mexican fiesta now includes tours, live music, food, and wine tasting. From Edmond take Route 66 east to Luther Road; call (405) 277–7089 or visit www.tressuenos.com.

Cimarron Valley

History buffs will want to continue north on I–35 to ***Guthrie,*** www.guthrieok.com, the territorial capital of Oklahoma. Guthrie never did recover from the loss of its state capital status in 1910, which turned out to be a fine thing, since the town can now boast the largest urban district (400 blocks) listed on the National Register of Historic Places. The town's 1,300 pre-1910 Victorian cottages and 22-block commercial district are remarkably intact, with hundreds of stained-glass windows, working transoms, and original light fixtures. In Guthrie even the gazebo in the park is an antique; the white wooden bandstand in Mineral Wells Park was built before 1900, and there are remnants of an old-fashioned English garden planted by club ladies soon after the turn of the twentieth century. The park is 3 blocks south of the intersection of Harrison Avenue and Second Street.

The commercial district is built almost entirely of redbrick on redbrick streets in a style that locals call "Prairie Gingerbread." The abundance of cupolas, round windows, and ornate detailing was due largely to the influence of Belgian-born architect Joseph Pierre Foucart, who came to Guthrie on the day of the 1889 Land Run. Foucart designed several downtown buildings and residences, including the Victor Building at Second Street and Harrison Avenue, before moving on.

Foucart designed both residential and commercial buildings, including the **State Capital Publishing Museum,** at 301 West Harrison. The museum holds both early newspaper and town history; the presses that printed Guthrie's first paper are still in the basement. The museum is open Thursday through Saturday from 9:00 A.M. to 5:00 P.M. Admission is free. Call (405) 282–4123 for information.

Across the street from the museum is the **Blue Belle Saloon,** where movie cowboy Tom Mix worked as a bartender before going to Hollywood. The original tile floor and oak bar are in place where visitors can still belly up and have a cold one. The Blue Belle is at 224 West Harrison, (405) 282–8111.

Behind the Saloon and upstairs, travelers will want to visit **Miss Lizzie's Bordello.** This restored Victorian bordello has a large parlor surrounded by 16 rooms of various shapes and sizes. In its heyday, the bordello boasted "purty girls and they was clean." The madam here was well respected and took an active role in church and civic affairs around town. Miss Lizzie's was connected to the Elks Club Hotel across the alley by a cast-iron sky-walk at second-floor level. This discreet entrance was used by early politicians, businessmen, and prominent Guthrie gentlemen.

Today, there is no need to be discreet; visitors can walk right in the front door to find seventeen shops housing souvenirs and collectibles. Each of the sixteen rooms is different and items range from dolls and stuffed animals to a Christmas shop and a bath shop.

The Bordello is open Monday through Saturday from 10:00 A.M. to 5:00 P.M. and Sunday from 1:00 to 5:00 P.M. The owners invite you to come on up and see why "all of our customers leave satisfied." Call (405) 282–6477 for more information.

The **Oklahoma Frontier Pharmacy Museum,** 214 West Oklahoma, Guthrie, is operated by a state pharmacists' association, whose members donated the apothecary bottles, old advertising cards, and intriguing logs that record the dispensation of arsenic and cocaine. The Apothecary Garden next door contains native plants used for medicinal purposes. A soda fountain up front is mostly for show, although visitors can buy bottles of cream soda and

Victor Building, Guthrie

sarsaparilla. The museum is open Tuesday through Saturday from 10:00 A.M. to 5:00 P.M. and on Sunday 1:00 to 4:00 P.M.; closed Monday. Call (405) 282–1895.

First-time visitors to **_Byron Berline's Double Stop Music Hall,_** at 121 East Oklahoma, might take the linoleum floors and folding chairs as an indication of a lack of polish—but it takes just a few moments of playing for the Byron Berline Band to shatter that misperception. Berline is a Grammy-nominated three-time national fiddle champ who has played with musicians including Elton John, Bob Dylan, and the Rolling Stones. The fiddle player grew up on a farm in north central Oklahoma and worked for three decades in Los Angeles before moving back to Oklahoma (to his wife Bette's hometown) to open just such a place as the music hall. Music shows at the Music Hall are scheduled erratically, as are the Sunday afternoon jam sessions. (At the latter, you never know which of Berline's old musical pals will show up. One Sunday, it was Vince Gill.) Berline is the organizer of the International Bluegrass Festival, held each October in downtown Guthrie, which features top-flight American bluegrass bands and bluegrass bands from Europe and even Asia. A fiddle shop where Berline sells and swaps fiddles and mandolins is downstairs. For information call (405) 282–6646 or check out Berline's Web site at www.doublestop.com.

Up the hill from the music hall, atop a hill, sits the world's largest **_Scottish Rite Temple,_** a 252,000-square-foot architectural tour de force. The major rooms of the marble-and-stone building were designed to reflect great periods in human history, including Imperial Rome, ancient Egypt, Renaissance Italy, Georgian England, and Gothic France. The structure was built in the 1920s, on a site originally intended to hold a state capitol building, and is lavishly

The Travels of Elmer McCurdy

A story that seems too odd to be true appears on the wall of the Oklahoma Territorial Museum, in a section devoted to outlaws and marshals. The story unfolded, weirdly enough, from the set of a 1970s episode of *The Six Million Dollar Man*, set in a Los Angeles fun park. When a member of the crew knocked the arm from what he thought was a dummy, he tried to repair it with electrical tape and discovered a human bone. The "dummy," it turns out, was the long-lost corpse of Oklahoma outlaw Elmer McCurdy. When McCurdy was shot in 1911 in Osage County, his body was taken to a funeral parlor in Pawhuska, where it was embalmed with arsenic. No one claimed the body, and the funeral store owner propped the (very well-preserved) corpse in the corner. Men claiming to be McCurdy's relatives took the corpse from Pawhuska in 1911, and rumors filtered back that the pair was traveling with the body as a sideshow attraction they called "The Hundred-Year-Old Man." The corpse traveled in sideshows for decades, coming finally to rest as "The Dope Fiend" at a California fun house—the same fun house where the television show was being filmed. After the corpse's discovery, the county coroner and police traced the body back to Oklahoma. Elmer McCurdy was given a proper burial on April 23, 1977, in the Summit View Cemetery in Guthrie.

appointed with such materials as stone taken from the same quarry as King Solomon's Temple and a Czechoslovakian crystal chandelier. Exhibits that explain Masonic organizations are in the basement, next to a billiards hall decorated in a Native American theme, complete with tepee light fixtures. Guided tours are given on weekdays at 10:00 A.M. and 2:00 P.M. and on Saturdays at 10:00 A.M. There is a $5.00 charge for adults; children and Masons are admitted free. The temple is at 900 East Oklahoma. Call (405) 282–1281 for information.

The **Beacon Drive-In** in Guthrie is one of ten remaining in Oklahoma, but it was among the first in the country to give members of a burgeoning car culture a place to sit, look, eat, and be entertained. The souvenir program at its grand opening in 1950 read "The guy who designed the [drive-in] theatre had the lazy man at heart." The theater is located at 2404 South Division, Guthrie. Shows start at dusk and run nightly during the summer. Adults pay $4.00 and admission is free for children eleven and under. Steamed hot dogs cost $1.25.

Travelers who like the charm of a bed and breakfast will not be disappointed with Guthrie. With its numerous Victorian houses it is the Bed and Breakfast Capital of Oklahoma, www.guthriebb.com. Choosing from the thirteen located here will not be easy. If you like a little mystery though, the **Stone Lion Inn**, www.stonelioninn.com, may be your cup of tea. This 1907 Victorian mansion offers not only six rooms, but Murder Mystery Weekends. Call innkeeper Becky Luker at (405) 282–0012 to make your reservations. Visitors who want to explore downtown Guthrie will enjoy a stay at the **Pollard Inn,** www.thepollardinn.com. Located on the corner of Harrison and First, the inn is within easy walking distance of the **Guthrie Historic District.** The Pollard Theatre is next door, as well as several eateries. Call (800) 375–1000 to book one of their twenty available rooms.

Among Guthrie's many antiques stores and collectible shops is one particularly apt for the region. **Vic's Place,** at 124 North Second Street, is a former gas station filled with memorabilia from the oil and gas industry. Among its wares are oil cans, gasoline pumps, service station signs, and oil company promotional items, both vintage and reproduction. Vic's is open Monday through Friday from 8:00 A.M. to 5:30 P.M. and on Saturday 9:00 A.M. to noon. Call (405) 282–5586.

Granny Had One, at 113 West Harrison, started out as an antiques store, with a tearoom as a sideline, but the food was such a big hit, it took over the business. The restaurant got its name from patrons who eyed the antiques and said "granny had one of those." Originally in a narrow storefront, it took over a neighboring building and today has expanded upstairs, where on weekends you'll find live entertainment in the dinner theater. Large hand-painted murals of early Guthrie life, featuring present-day townspeople, cover the east and west walls. Wooden floors and pressed-tin ceilings give the eatery a feeling of days gone by. Whether you eat the blue plate special or order items from the menu, everyone will find something to enjoy. Menu items, named after the owner's family members, include Aunt Texie's Tuna Salad Sandwich, Grandpa's Old-Fashioned Burger, and Papa Don's Chicken-Fried Steak Dinner. Bumbleberry Pie, made with blackberries, raspberries, and apples, and homemade ice cream are just a few of the desserts to try. Another favorite, Dill Bread, can be eaten with the meal or ordered to go. Hours are Monday through Wednesday 11:00 A.M. to 2:00 P.M. and Thursday through Saturday 11:00 A.M. to 9:00 P.M. Call (405) 282–4482 or visit Granny's Web site at www.grannyhadone.biz to sign up for their newsletter.

The **Oklahoma Territorial Museum and Carnegie Library,** located at 406 East Oklahoma, should be on every visitor's schedule. This museum tells the story of the pioneers and the determined individuals who fought for Oklahoma's future. When Oklahoma became a state in 1907, the first governor was sworn in at the Carnegie Library. Besides artifacts, photographs, and paintings, the museum offers educational programs as well. The museum is open Tuesday through Saturday from 9:00 A.M. to 5:00 P.M. A $2.00 donation is requested. A guided tour by one of the museum's staff takes about an hour. Call (405) 282–1889 for more information.

Just west of the police station, you'll find **The Sweet Pea,** 312 West Oklahoma. This restaurant offers the warmth of Victorian days gone by with its rich dark wood and thick drapes hanging from the ceiling. Serving breakfast, lunch, and dinner, the restaurant's specialties include crepes, hand-cut prime rib sandwiches, and homemade tamales. The Sweet Pea is open Tuesday through Saturday 10:30 A.M. to 2:30 P.M. and Friday and Saturday from 5:30 to 9:00 P.M. Call (405) 282–1114.

On the south side of the street is the **Oklahoma Sports Museum,** www.oklahomasportsmuseum.com. This museum recognizes professional and Olympic athletes as well as coaches and teams with Oklahoma ties. Exhibits include thousands of items from hundreds of athletes like Jim Thorpe, Troy Aikman, Mickey Mantle, and Shannon Miller. Home to the Oklahoma High School Baseball Coaches Hall of Fame, this museum is proud to promote all aspects of Oklahoma's athletic heritage. Hours are Monday through Thursday 1:00 to 5:00 P.M. and Friday and Saturday 10:00 A.M. to 5:00 P.M. Appointments for extended hours can be arranged by calling (405) 282–1342. Admission is free.

If art is your cup of adrenaline, don't miss the **Double Starr Studio and Gallery,** 322 West Oklahoma Avenue; (405) 282–4050. Three blocks west of Division on Oklahoma, across from the Santa Fe Depot, the open gallery and working studio's wooden sign hangs proudly outside the front door. The owners, Sheldon and Nancy Russell, purchased and remodeled the building in 1996. Built in 1890, it was a wholesale produce store for the Tannery District of Guthrie in its early days. Today, Sheldon, an author of historic frontier and suspense novels, and Nancy, a clay, bronze, wood, and alabaster sculptor, can be found working in the studio producing more award-winning art. The Russells periodically hold open houses, inviting other artists in the area to display and sell their pieces. On any given day, in the gallery, you may find works not only by Nancy, but by Bert Seabourn, Cherokee pen-and-ink artist and teacher; Cletus Smith, watercolors; Elizabeth Kramer, oils; and Buck Dollarhide, pottery. While there, be sure to check out the bristlecone pine impressionistic *Crucifix* sculpture. The wood used to make this piece is rare, and the Russells have to be licensed to use it. The artists welcome visitors to their studio Tuesday through Saturday from 10:00 A.M. to 4:00 P.M.

After your fill of art, pop across the street to **Artie's Bakery**. It's located on the north side of the restored Santa Fe Depot, where hungry travelers can enjoy the bakery's signature pizzas and sandwiches, or the European-style pastry items that Artie, an American Culinary Federation–certified pastry chef, has put together. Call (405) 282–1700. Next door, you'll want to visit the Santa Fe

Depot, www.theoldsantafedepotofguthrie.com, restored to its 1903 splendor, and view the model train exhibit. Six model train displays race around tracks showing visitors not only how people traveled to and from early Guthrie but other areas as well. The depot is open Saturday from noon to 6:00 P.M. Call (405) 260–0707.

Capital Region

Oklahoma's capital city likes to say it was "born grown," claiming 10,000 residents on April 22, the day of the 1889 Land Run. It has stayed haphazard and sprawling, so spread out that it is difficult to find its center (especially because an underground concourse downtown siphons most of the pedestrians from the sidewalks). Finding its essence, however, is easier. Oil money built many of the downtown skyscrapers and old mansions to the north, but **Oklahoma City** had an even earthier, earlier incarnation. You can find old Oklahoma City at **Stockyards City,** www.stockyardscity.org, centered around Agnew and Exchange Boulevard, 1 mile west of downtown. Railroads and the meatpacking industry were Oklahoma City's first economic underpinnings, and the brick stockyards were built for the cattle and hogs brought by rail to the slaughterhouses. Today, cattle are trucked in, but cowboys still pen and sort stock on horseback, shouting, "In!" (keep the cow in that pen) or "By!" (cull it). A metal catwalk takes visitors over the cattle pens, where in the spring the stock comes in smelling of green wheat, to a huge brick barn where the National Stock Yards Company holds one of the world's largest weekly cattle auctions. The auction itself is a blend of decades-old hand signals and computers, bawling calves, and stoic buyers, who keep in touch with their markets with dingy telephones bolted on the backs of chairs. Over all the action hangs a cloud of cigarette smoke and, as the old joke goes, the smell of money. The two auctioneers, decked out in starched white shirts and big hats, are among the best in the business; their chant is practically an art form. (Auctioneer Ralph Wade has been named world champion.) Monday is the biggest auction day—things get underway at 8:00 A.M. and last until 8:00 or 9:00 P.M. The auction winds up earlier on Tuesday. The stockyards' administrative offices are at 2501 Exchange Boulevard, Oklahoma City (you'll walk or drive under a gate with a large steer head). The auction barn is just west of the offices. For information, call Stockyards City Main Street at (405) 235–7267.

A good next stop is **Cattlemen's Steakhouse,** www.cattlemensrestaurant .com, at 1309 South Agnew Avenue; (405) 236–0416. The restaurant was established in 1910 as Cattleman's Cafe, a little coffee shop where current cattle prices were posted on a blackboard over the counter so ranchers and farmers who stopped in didn't miss anything. In 1945 a man named Gene Wade won the cafe in a game of craps by rolling a hard six. Wade kept the original counter, added a dining room, and got serious about the steaks: Cattlemen's ages its own beef and hand-cuts it in its butcher shop. The restaurant is filled with old photos that show the area in its heyday; sketches of such locally revered figures as John Wayne and Hopalong Cassidy; and a 20-foot photographic mural of Wade and his father, Percy, on horseback in a sea of Herefords. Wade sold the restaurant, but his rocking chair is still in the old north cafe section, inviting patrons to feel at home. Cattlemen's opens at 6:00 A.M. for a breakfast of grits, steak, and biscuits, and stays open until 10:00 P.M., Sunday to Thursday, and until midnight on Friday and Saturday.

Some of the most sought-after saddles in the country come out of the unassuming-looking storefront next door to the restaurant. The building that houses the **National Saddlery,** at 1307 South Agnew, Oklahoma City, has been a saddle shop since 1926. (Before that it was a grocery that sold coffins, lanterns, and windmills, along with more conventional supplies.) The original brass ceiling tiles are still in place, but if you look up, you'll see what looks like a cowboy stuck in the ceiling.

When replacement tiles couldn't be found to fix a hole in the ceiling, owners John David and Dona Kay Rule filled the spot with a pair of stuffed jeans attached to cowboy boots. Rule makes custom saddles and belts for the likes of Garth Brooks. Prices start at $1,400, but some of his best work takes more than money to own: Rule makes all the trophy saddles for the Professional Rodeo Cowboy Association's National Finals Rodeo. The saddle shop is open Monday through Friday from 9:00 A.M. to 5:30 P.M. and Saturday from 9:00 A.M. to 3:00 P.M. Rule's workshop is in the back; visitors are welcome to come back and watch him work. Call (405) 239–2104 or visit www.nationalsaddlery.com for information.

The namesake at **Shorty's Caboy Hattery,** www.shortyshattery.com, on the next block at 1206 South Agnew Avenue, is Lavonna Koger, who bills her shop as the only female-owned hattery in North America. Koger makes hats from 100 percent beaver "blanks" she imports from France, shaping them with her collection of vintage wooden hat blocks and machinery. Koger, who's called on by Hollywood from time to time, specializes in jobs requiring vanishing expertise, like putting a tight "pencil curl" around the brims of hats. Koger also is happy to have visitors watch her work, and she also likes to show off her equipment, most of which is nearly impossible to come by anymore. Prices for Koger's hats range from about $300 to $450. The hattery is open Monday through Friday from 8:30 A.M. to 6:00 P.M. and Saturday from 8:30 A.M. to 5:00 P.M.; (405) 232–4287.

There are numerous boot shops and saddle makers in the area, and then there is *Langston's,* at 2224 Exchange Avenue, which covers a whole city block and sells boots and Western clothing from infant sizes on up. The store's facades were recently stripped of 1950s aluminum siding, so it now looks much as it did in the 1930s and 1940s. Call (405) 235–9536 or go to www.langstons.com for information.

You can continue to explore old Oklahoma City by driving east on Exchange Avenue to the *Public Market Antiques* and the *Farmer's Market,* www.okcfarmersmarket.com, which sit at an angle to Exchange at 311 South Klein. The three-story Spanish Mission–style Public Market was considered a showplace when it was built in 1928 as a community center and a place where farmers could sell produce.

The decaying main building is now an antiques mall, with about two dozen cluttered shops selling everything from old bicycles to crystal stemware. Bob's Sporting Collectibles on the top floor has a great assortment of wooden lures, rods and reels, baseball cards, and old hunting and fishing magazines. The antiques stalls continue into a building next door. For information about the antiques stores, call (405) 239–2273. The area immediately west is the real draw: a farmers' market, where dozens of vendors sell produce in season and a few stay open year-round. Produce stands sell everything from garden-grown tomatoes and herbs to French bread and roasted peanuts. Regional specialties are for sale here, too: pecans, muscadine preserves, gooseberry jam, apple cider, sorghum, honey, corn, green-tomato relish, and bread-and-butter pickles. The market is open seven days a week.

The Grandison at Maney Park, a bed-and-breakfast established in a beautiful 1904 three-story Victorian house, is a good base for exploring downtown Oklahoma City. The Grandison has nine bedrooms, each with a private bath, with decor ranging from the Treehouse Room, a third-floor fantasy with painted blue skies, tree branches, and glow-in-the-dark stars and furnished with rubber duckies to play with in the Jacuzzi, to elegant suites with tapestry canopies overhanging carved beds. The salmon-pink house is trimmed in teal, with rockers and settees on the porch and polished maple floors throughout. A full breakfast is served on the weekends; a continental breakfast is available on other days. Room rates range from $75 to $145. The Grandison at Maney Park is at 1200 North Shartel. Call (405) 232–8778 or go to www.grandison inn.com to make reservations.

The bed-and-breakfast is adjacent to Heritage Hills, a historic neighborhood where many of the city's founding families first settled. *The Overholser Mansion,* a 1904 three-story French château–style house, was built by Henry Overholser, who came to Oklahoma Territory in the 1889 Land Run. Some of the walls of the fifteen-room house are hung with hand-painted canvas, and the rooms are filled with heavy mahogany, oak, and teak furniture, brocade-covered sofas, and French stained-glass windows. The house, at 405 Northwest Fifteenth Street, is now owned by the Oklahoma Historical Society. Tours are conducted every day except Monday. For information call (405) 528–8485.

A visit to Oklahoma City isn't complete without stopping at **Bricktown,** www.bricktownokc.com. In the early 1980s, Oklahoma City began renovating its warehouse district. Today, it is the "happening" place to be. Visitors can attend concerts at the Ford Center, catch baseball games at the Bricktown Ball-park, or watch movies at the Harkins Theatres. Other attractions include the Bass Pro Shop, Oklahoma City Museum of Art, Oklahoma City Bombing Memorial, and the Bricktown Canal where guests can take a ride on a water taxi. Over forty restaurants and nightclubs are located here including Toby Keith's I Love This Bar & Grill, Rio del Fuego, and Earl's Rib Palace. No matter what the palette craves, food is just a street away. Besides museums, shopping, and sports, special events are also on the ticket. Brewer Entertainment, www.brewer entertainment.com, arranges many of the festivals and happenings for Brick-town throughout the year. Events range from the St. Patrick's Day Celebration to the Reggae Festival and the Fourth of July event to the Haunted Warehouse in October. Whatever interests visitors may have, they'll find it at Bricktown.

Tucked away in a neighborhood that's a patchwork of well-kept homes and urban blight is a surprising 2-block-long arts district known as **The Paseo Arts District,** www.thepaseo.com. The Paseo, which curves south of North-west Thirtieth Street, near Dewey Avenue, was built in 1929 and intended as a miniature version of the Country Club Plaza in Kansas City. The district's dress shops, laundries, and other businesses were built in the Spanish Mission style, finished with glazed ceramic-tile entries, red tile roofs, and wrought iron. As the neighborhood around the shopping center shifted, so did the building's tenants, and by the 1960s, artists had staked out the territory for their own. Always interesting, the street has lately attracted established artists, and the area is flourishing. A pottery studio, a handful of artists' cooperatives, and gift shops are sprinkled in among individual artists' studios. In the summer, a farm-ers' market sells fresh produce every Saturday from 9:00 A.M. to 4:00 P.M. The Paseo Arts Festival, held each Memorial Day, features one hundred or so artists and three days of local music. Call (405) 525–2688.

Oklahoma's territorial period, from 1889 until statehood in 1907, is the focus of the **Harn Homestead Museum,** at 313 Northeast Sixteenth Street, Oklahoma City. The museum is a collection of houses, barns, a school, and outbuildings sitting on what was originally the homestead of William Fremont Harn, a lawyer who came to the Territory in 1891 to sort out the hundreds of land disputes that clogged the territorial courts after the run. When his job was abolished two years later, Harn stayed and set up a private practice. He settled on a 160-acre homestead in 1896 and built the Queen Anne–style farmhouse that's now the centerpiece of the museum. The stone-and-wood exhibit barn, enclosing part of a windmill, was based on the original Harn barn. In addition to a carriage and farm equipment, the barn holds historical photos from pre-statehood days. Two more farmhouses and another barn, along with vegetable and herb gardens, are intended to illustrate the daily life of pioneer families. The museum does a good job, hanging laundry out on a clothesline and positioning washtubs and lye soap nearby. Hourly tours of the house are conducted Monday through Friday from 2:00 to 4:00 P.M., and a self-guided tour of the grounds is available. Admission is $5.00. Children three and under are free. For information call (405) 235–4058.

From the museum grounds it's possible to spot Oklahoma's **State Capitol** 5 blocks north, significant in this setting because Harn donated forty acres to Oklahoma City in 1910 as a site for a capitol. The capital was moved (read: wrenched away) from Guthrie, 30 miles to the north, to Oklahoma City, following a spirited campaign and referendum that Guthrie appealed all the way to the U.S. Supreme Court.

One of the more long-lived debates about the state capitol concerned what wasn't there: a dome. The capitol was built between 1914 and 1917 in what was once Harn's pasture; a set of plans for a dome was drawn up, but the legislature didn't appropriate money to build it. The steel shortage created by World War I put off any discussion of topping off the capitol until the 1920s, and by then, a politician risked seeming fiscally irresponsible in supporting the addition of what would essentially be a frill. By the mid-1920s, ideas for functional additions to the top of the capitol were floating around; the state board of affairs proposed that a seven-story office tower be added. In the 1960s a state senator even proposed that a revolving restaurant be built on top. Now after nine decades, the domeless capitol has a dome and a 22-foot bronze statue of an Indian called *The Guardian*.

everyday inventors

Ardmore grocer Sylvan N. Goldman, noticing that his customers bought only as many groceries as they could carry, introduced the world's first grocery-shopping cart. A bronze sculpture of Goldman and his invention is on display at the **Kirkpatrick Center** in Oklahoma City, 2100 Northeast Fifty-second Street. (Goldman personally selected the contents of the sculpted grocery cart, which holds a loaf of bread, a carton of eggs, a carton of milk, a box of cereal, and a bunch of celery.) Another inventive first: An Oklahoma City man built the world's first parking meter.

Wild Mary

The wildest runaway oil well in history was the No. 1 Mary Sudik, a well drilled in south Oklahoma City on land leased from dairy farmer Vincent Sudik and his wife, Mary. On March 26, 1930, the No. 1 Mary Sudik blew out its four tons of drilling pipe, sending a gusher of gas and sand, and then crude oil 175 feet into the air. Two hundred men at a time worked feverishly to cap the well as Wild Mary continued to blow 20,000 barrels of oil into the sky a day, blackening farms and houses in the immediate area and spattering clotheslines as far away as Norman, 12 miles to the south. The gusher was capped four days later, but within a few hours, she blew again. By the time a crew reined her in for good on April 6, Wild Mary had raged for 11½ days, raining 227,000 barrels of oil down on Oklahoma City. One of the blow-out valves from Wild Mary is on display at the Oklahoma State Museum of History, just across the street from the state capitol.

The inside ceiling has been painted with a series of murals that romantically depict Oklahoma's history, from Coronado's visit to the area in 1541, to the forced march of southeastern tribes to Indian Territory in the 1830s, to the 1889 Land Run. Artist Charles Banks Wilson also painted full-length portraits of state heroes, including Sequoyah and Will Rogers.

Oklahoma's state capitol is the only one in the nation with oil wells dotting the lawn: Petunia No. 1, just outside the north door, was named for the flower bed in which it was drilled. East of the drilling rig (nonoperational now) is a plaza where the flags of all thirty-seven of the federally recognized tribes headquartered in Oklahoma are flown. The state capitol is at Twenty-third Street and North Lincoln Boulevard. Tours of the capitol are conducted hourly Monday through Friday from 9:00 A.M. to 3:00 P.M. Closed for lunch. A self-guided-tour brochure is available for weekends. The capitol is open every day except Thanksgiving and Christmas. Use west entrance lower level. For tour information call (405) 521–3356.

Directly across the street, on the northeast side of Lincoln and Twenty-third, is the ***Oklahoma History Center,*** www.okhistorycenter.org. This 18-acre, three-story, 215,000 square-foot center houses five state-of-the-art galleries, a huge library, and archives. Visitors will learn not only about the Native American culture of Oklahoma, but its sports heroes, arts and crafts, and dust bowl days. The Center also exhibits some Oklahoma landmark inventions like the shopping cart, parking meter, and trencher. The Gemini 6 space capsule, a Civil War cannon, and a Land Run wagon also have homes here. After visitors absorb Oklahoma history through the exhibits, they might want to check out their ancestry. The center's library and archives is a must for genealogists and those looking to see if they might be on the Indian Rolls. While exploring this complex, visitors may find they are hungry. By taking the stairs or elevator upstairs to the Winnie Mae Café located on the third floor, they'll discover drinks and sandwiches. The Oklahoma History Center is open Monday through

Oklahoma History Center

Saturday 9:00 A.M. to 5:00 P.M. and Sunday from 12:00 to 5:00 P.M. Admission is $5.00 for adults, $4.00 seniors (sixty-two and older), $3.00 students, and five and under are free. Call (405) 522–5248 for more information.

Oklahoma's Dutch Colonial *Governor's Mansion,* once leaky and dowdy, recently received a $1 million facelift—and coverage in *Architectural Digest.* Highlights of the renovations to the 1928 mansion, made through a collaboration of seven interior designers, are rugs woven with the names of Oklahoma's governors and replicating the state seal, a Montgolfier chandelier, and art on loan from Oklahoma museums. Tours are conducted on Wednesday from 1:00 to 3:00 P.M., except in December and January. The mansion is at 820 Northeast Twenty-third, Oklahoma City; (405) 557–0198.

Military history buffs will want to stop at the *45th Infantry Museum,* named after the division that General George Patton called "one of the best, if not the best, divisions in the history of American armies." The museum covers the history of Oklahoma soldiers from 1841 to the present, but some of the most popular exhibits are connected with the 45th. Division member and cartoonist Bill Mauldin first drew "Willie & Joe" for the 45th Infantry newsletter, and a collection of his drawings is on display. The 45th was the first division to reach Munich and to enter Adolf Hitler's apartment there; consequently, the museum displays the world's largest collection of items that were once Hitler's private property. Outside, military vehicles, weapons, and aircraft are on display. The museum is at 2145 Northeast Thirty-sixth Street, and is open Tuesday through Friday from 9:00 A.M. to 4:15 P.M., Saturday from 10:00 A.M. to 4:15 P.M., and Sunday from 1:00 to 4:15 P.M. Admission is free. Call (405) 424–5313 or visit www.45thdivisionmuseum.com.

Since 1967, *Eddy's Steakhouse,* 4227 North Meridian, is the place to visit for great food. The Elias family serves some of the finest lobster, steak, quail, and lamb chops in Oklahoma City. Before the entree arrives, visitors are served appetizers like tabouli, hummus with carrots, celery, and baby corn, and cabbage rolls, all made from family recipes. The restaurant is open Tuesday through Saturday from 4:15 to 9:30 P.M. and on Easter, Mother's, and Father's Day. Chris and Patricia Elias, the owners, recommend reservations, as they fill up fast. Call (405) 787–2944.

A quarter mile north is the **Rose Garden Tea Room,** 4413 North Meridian. Sitting next door to an antiques store, this Victorian-style cottage brings a charm all its own as one steps through the door. Here visitors are served by the "Jolly Women of the Tea Room." House specialties are chicken salad, broccoli salad, and, some say, the "best quiche in the state." After your main course, don't leave without trying dessert—baked fudge, buttermilk pie, or bread pudding with rum sauce. Open Tuesday through Saturday 11:00 A.M. to 2:00 P.M., the Tea Room fills up fast, so call (405) 495–2252 for reservations.

About 15 miles due east is the little town of **Choctaw,** www.choctaw city.org, population 7,500, which started out as a trading post in 1890 and is now the unlikely home to **The Old Germany Restaurant.** The restaurant opened in 1976 and from 1986 to 2003 (when the awarding organization began charging restaurants to be on the list) received the Wine Spectator Award of Excellence, thanks to its assortment of fine German estate wines. The wine cellar, with stone walls, linen napkins, and candlelight, is the best place to sample authentic German cuisine, including everything from Wiener schnitzel, red cabbage, potato dumplings, and extraordinary rye bread to assorted domestic and imported beers. The restaurant is open Tuesday through Saturday for lunch (11:00 A.M. to 2:00 P.M.) and dinner (5:00 to 9:00 P.M.). On Friday and Saturday nights, a strolling accordionist in lederhosen plays German folk songs and obliges diners who request it by playing a Western swing tune. The restaurant is at 15920 Southeast Twenty-ninth; (405) 390–8647.

Route 66 West

Yukon, due west of Oklahoma City, is a farming-turned-bedroom community. You can reach it easily on I–40 or along Route 66. The name of Yukon's most recent claim to fame is painted in proud letters on the city's water tower: HOME OF GARTH BROOKS. Pre-Garth, the town was best known as an enclave of Czech families who established wheat farms on their claims following the 1889 run. The grain elevators are still there, and the citizenry recently relit the electric lights that advertised YUKON'S BEST FLOUR. Along with the flour company, the Czech bakeries and delicatessens have vanished, but a polka band still plays every Saturday night at the **Czech Hall,** www.czechhall.com, a 1925 wooden-floored ballroom where entire families come to polka, dance the schottische, and, with a nod to Brooks and local country band the Boot-Scooters, dance the

Cotton-Eyed Joe. (But no rock 'n' roll.) The dances are sponsored by a local lodge, which sells Polish sausages, hot dogs, popcorn, and beer. Admission varies between $3.00 and $6.00, depending on the band, and the dancing may continue until midnight, especially if the band is from, say, Nebraska. Czech Hall is at 205 Czech Hall Road, and is reached by driving south on Cornwall Boulevard on the east end of town. (That road's name changes to Czech Hall Road.) Call (405) 324–8073 for information.

On the first Saturday in October, the town holds its annual Czech Festival with a parade, Czechoslovakian music and dancing, and mountains of kolaches, fruit- or cheese-filled pastries. For information about the festival, visit www.yukoncc.com or call (405) 354–3567.

A few more miles down Route 66 is **El Reno,** www.elreno.org, first established as Reno City. The town is near **Fort Reno** and the Darlington Agency;

kolachefestival

Every May, the small town of Prague, www.pragueok.org, celebrates its Czech heritage and culture with the annual **Kolache Festival**. A parade, carnival, arts-and-crafts show including Czech gift items, polka street dancing, and a contest for homemade kolaches (fruit- or cheese-filled patries), bread and wine are only a few of the events visitors will enjoy. For more information call (405) 567–4866.

both were built in the 1870s after the Battle of Little Big Horn and the removal of the Southern Cheyenne and Arapaho from the northwest United States to Indian Territory. Fort Reno was a cavalry outpost when it was built in 1874, and the army used it through World War II, when Italian and German prisoners of war were held there. It was also used to keep supply horses for cavalry troops through World War I. Decades of horse droppings helped prepare the soil for its current use, as the Grazing Lands Agricultural Research Station for Oklahoma State University. The hundred-year-old brick commissary building is now used for storage, but most of the original buildings have crumbled or have been removed. The most potent reminder of the fort's history is its cemetery, which holds headstones ranging from Indian scout Ben Clark to markers for prisoners of war. At one time, the fort had polo fields and a racetrack; one prisoner painted a mural of an officer playing polo, which now looks over a research lab. Fort Reno is 5 miles west of El Reno on old Route 66 and is open Monday through Friday 10:00 A.M. to 5:00 P.M. Call (405) 262–3987 for information.

El Reno grew up around the Rock Island Railroad, which went through in 1890. The old passenger depot now is headquarters for the **Canadian County Historical Museum,** which holds artifacts pertaining to many different elements of local history: the land runs, Fort Reno, the Cheyenne-Arapaho agen-

OTHER ATTRACTIONS IN CROSS TIMBERS

National Cowboy and Western Heritage Museum,
Oklahoma City
www.nationalcowboymuseum.org

Frontier City Amusement Park,
Oklahoma City
www.sixflags.com/parks/frontiercity

Myriad Botanical Gardens,
Oklahoma City
www.myriadgardens.com

Omniplex Science Museum,
Oklahoma City
www.omniplex.org

Seminole Nation Museum,
Wewoka
www.wewoka.com/museum.htm

cies, even Route 66, which turns north on its course through town a few blocks from the museum. The western starting line for Oklahoma's first land run in 1889 was right out front. (Soldiers from Fort Reno held order and shot the cannons that started the run.)

Three years later, the line was the eastern boundary for the 1892 run, which opened western lands that had belonged to the Cheyenne-Arapaho Tribes. El Reno was also one of the registration stations in 1901, when federal officials opted for a lottery rather than a run to divide up Kiowa and Comanche land in the southwest. (The runs, it was decided, were too messy.) General Phil Sheridan's log cabin has been moved from Fort Reno and now holds an exhibit dedicated to African-American soldiers, called "buffalo soldiers" by the Native Americans because of their thick hair. A jail cell moved from the Darlington Indian Agency is on the grounds, along with a one-room school, a caboose, a passenger car, and an old two-story hotel. The depot, where valleys on the wooden floors made by lines of waiting passengers remain and where the ticket office is still cluttered with schedules, exhibits Cheyenne-Arapaho paintings, quill and beadwork, antique toys, and other household items. The museum, at 300 South Grand, El Reno, is open Wednesday through Saturday from 10:00 A.M. to 5:00 P.M. and Sunday from 1:00 to 5:00 P.M. Admission is free; (405) 262–5121.

For a more pungent taste of history, stroll from the museum over to **Robert's Grill,** at 300 South Bickford, (405) 262–1262, for an onion-fried burger. There's a faction in town that believes El Reno cooks actually invented the onion-fried burger; others are just happy they caught on so well and for so long. Robert's, low-slung and built of ancient white cement, has room for fewer than a dozen stools and usually only one conversation. Only hamburgers, French fries, and the El Reno version of the coney are found on the menu.

(The coney is topped with the requisite chili, plus a tangy cabbage slaw.) On the first Saturday in May, the town celebrates Onion-Fried Burger Day by cooking the world's largest onion-fried burger; it weighs in at 150 pounds and sits in a 110-pound bun. Musical entertainment and a classic car show accompany the burger celebration. For information about the festival, call the El Reno Main Street office at (405) 262–8888.

Underneath the opera house's tin ceilings and old ceiling fans at the **Old Opera House Antiques Mall** are dozens of consignment booths holding a little bit of furniture and lots of collectibles: salt and pepper shakers, 1950s fruit- and flower-printed tablecloths and embroidered pillow slips, china, Fiestaware, baskets, crocks, even old saddles. The antiques mall and a craft mall beside it cover most of the east side of the 200 block of South Bickford. The mall is open Monday through Saturday 10:00 A.M. to 4:00 P.M. (405) 422–3232.

More nostalgia is waiting at **Denny's Restaurant** on I–40. The restaurant was first established on Route 66 in 1939 and moved to the interstate in the 1960s. The building may be modern, but the menu is old-fashioned, with daily specials, steak, baked ham, and roast beef dinners and a pie list as long as your arm. (The specialty is Peanut Butter Pie.) Rolls are baked fresh for every shift. The restaurant caters to truckers and solo diners: In one dining room, there are three television sets, with their remotes in easy reach. Denny's is south of exit 123; there's a windmill in back and an oil derrick out front. Call (405) 262–3535 for information.

The only reason to drive the dozen miles along Highway 81 from El Reno to Okarche is a good enough one: **Eischen's Bar.** The bar, the oldest in Oklahoma, is more tavern than honky-tonk, and on Saturday nights whole families come in to play pool and eat the famed fried chicken. The owners still throw down handfuls of chalky floor sweep, a tradition left over from the days when the patrons were apt to spit on the floor. Open Monday through Saturday 10:00 A.M. to midnight. Eischen's is off Main in Okarche, at 101 Second Street; (405) 263–9939.

Places to Stay in Cross Timbers

CHANDLER

Lincoln Motel
740 East First Street
(405) 258–0200

Lost Creek B&B
Highway 18 North
(405) 258–0166

CHICKASHA

Holiday Inn Express
2610 South Fourth Street
(405) 224–8883

EL RENO

Best Western
Country Club Road and I–40
(405) 262–3630

Goff House Inn
506 South Evans
(405) 262–1980

GUTHRIE

**Best Western
Territorial Inn**
223 Territorial Trail
(405) 282–8831

The Magnolia
222 South First Street
(405) 623–7194

Pollard Inn
124 West Harrison Avenue
(405) 282–1000 or (800)
275–1001

**The Railroad House Bed
and Breakfast Inn**
316 West Vilas
(405) 282–1827

Victorian Garden Inn
324 South Broad
(888) 792–1092
or (405) 282–8211

White Peacock
616 East Warner
(405) 282–0012

NORMAN

**The Cutting Garden Bed
and Breakfast**
927 Boyd Street
(405) 329–4522

**Holmberg House Bed
and Breakfast**
766 DeBarr
(405) 321–6221

**The Montford Inn Bed
and Breakfast**
322 West Tonhawa
(405) 321–2200

Thunderbird Lodge
1430 Twenty-fourth Avenue
Southwest
(405) 329–6990

OKLAHOMA CITY

Carlyle Motel
3600 Northwest
Thirty-ninth Street
(405) 946–3355

**Grandison Inn
at Maney Park**
1200 North Shartel Avenue
(405) 232–8778

SHAWNEE

Hampton Inn
4851 North Kickapoo
(405) 275–1540

STILLWATER

The Atherton
Student Union Building
Washington Street
(405) 744–6835

Places to Eat in
Cross Timbers

CHANDLER

Pete's Diner
912 Manvel
(405) 258–0202

**Steer Inn Family
Restaurant**
102 North Oak
(405) 258–3155

CHICKASHA

**Eduardo's Mexican
Restaurant**
3127 South Fourth Street
(405) 222–5566

J&W Grill
501 West Choctaw
(405) 224–9912

Jake's Rib
100 Ponderosa
(405) 222–2825

EDMOND

Cafe 501
501 South Boulevard
(405) 359–1501

Dot Wo's
64 Southeast Thirty-third
(405) 341–2878

Jason's Deli
78 Southeast
Thirty-third Street
(405) 330–1663

Twelve Oaks Restaurant
6100 Midwest Boulevard
(405) 340–1002

EL RENO

Denny's Restaurant
I–40 West
(405) 262–3535

Opera House Cafe
106 South Bickford
(405) 262–3663

Robert's Grill
300 South Bickford
(405) 262–1262

GUTHRIE

Blue Belle Saloon
224 West Harrison
(405) 282–8111

Granny Had One
113 West Harrison
(405) 282–4482

The Stables Cafe
223 North Division
(405) 282–0893

Woody's
3001 West Minister
(405) 282–2658

NORMAN

Al Eschbach's Hall of Fame Bar & Grill
769 Asp Avenue
(405) 364–2352

Cafe Plaid
333 West Boyd
(405) 360–2233

Coach's
102 West Main
(405) 360–5726

Deighan's Indian Hills Restaurant and Club
6221 North Interstate Drive
(405) 364–7577

The Diner
213 East Main
(405) 329–6642

La Baguette
924 West Main
(405) 329–5822

Legend's
1313 West Lindsey
(405) 329–8888

Misal's Bistro of India
580 Ed Nobb Parkway
(405) 579–5600

The Mont
1300 Classen
(405) 329–3330

Van's Pig Stand
320 North Porter
(405) 364–0600

OKLAHOMA CITY

Many restaurants are found along "Restaurant Row," a 3-mile stretch of Western Avenue between North Thirty-sixth Street and Wilshire Boulevard. Fast-food and chain restaurants are found along Memorial Road in north Oklahoma City and along Meridian near the airport.

Ann's Chicken Fry
4106 Northwest Thirty-ninth Street
(405) 943–8915

Charcoal Oven
5911 Northwest Expressway
(405) 722–7588

FOR MORE INFORMATION

Chandler Chamber of Commerce
824 Manvel Avenue
Chandler 74834
(405) 258–0673
www.chandlerok.com

Chickasha Chamber of Commerce
P.O. Box 1717
Chickasha 73023
(405) 224–0787
fax (405) 222–3730
www.chickashachamber.com

Edmond Convention and Visitors Bureau
2000 Southeast Fifteenth Street, Building 300
Edmond 73013
(405) 341–2808
fax (405) 340–5512
www.visitedmondok.com

El Reno Chamber of Commerce
206 North Bickford
El Reno 73036
(405) 262–1188
www.elrenochamber.com

Guthrie Convention and Visitors Bureau
212 West Oklahoma Avenue
Guthrie 73044
(405) 282–1948, (800) 299–1889
www.guthrieok.com

Norman Convention and Visitors Bureau
224 West Gray
Norman 73069
(405) 366–8095, (800) 767–7260

Oklahoma City Convention and Visitors Bureau
189 West Sheridan
Oklahoma City 73102
(405) 297–8912, (800) 225–5652
www.okccvb.org/

**Chelinos Mexican
Restaurant**
15 East California
(405) 235–3533

Coach House
6437 Avondale
(405) 842–1000

County Line Restaurant
1226 Northeast
Sixty-third Street
(405) 478–4955

Eddy's Steakhouse
4031 North Meridian
(405) 787–2944

Gopuram Taste of India
4559 Northwest
Twenty-third Street
(405) 948–7373

Ingrid's Kitchen
3701 North Youngs Road
(405) 946–8444

**La Baguette
Bistro & Bakery**
7408 North May
(405) 840–3047

Rose Garden Tea Room
4413 North Meridian
(405) 495–2252

Ted's Cafe Escondido
2836 Northwest
Sixty-eighth Street
(405) 848–8337

SHAWNEE

Jay's Classic Steak House
US 270 and Coker Road
(405) 275–6867

Van's Charcoal Room
717 East Highland
(405) 273–8704

Van's Pig Stand
717 East Highland (upstairs)
(405) 273–8704

Southwest Passage: Southwestern Oklahoma

Travelers driving west along Route 66 soon find themselves in a world made almost entirely of grass and sky, a landscape the Kiowa writer N. Scott Momaday called "the middle and immeasurable meadow of North America." "Nowhere on earth," Momaday wrote, "was there a more perfect equation of freedom and space."

The immensity of the plains can exhilarate or overwhelm travelers, depending on their tastes, but the reward for driving the region's two-lane roads is found in some of the most striking scenery in the state. The ancient Wichita Mountains, a 60-mile-long chain of pastel-hued granite mountains, cross the region in the south, and to the north, the plains are marked with red mesas and wooded canyons.

Interstates 44 and 40 outline the region, while state highways, many of them ruler-straight, link towns in a symmetrical grid. Travelers along scenic Highway 49 may spot bison as they pass through the Wichita Mountains Wildlife Refuge.

Southern Plains

A prime example of the surprises the southwestern plains hold is found a few miles south of I–40 along U.S. Highway 281.

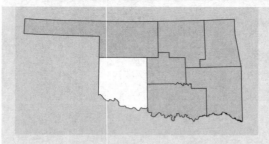

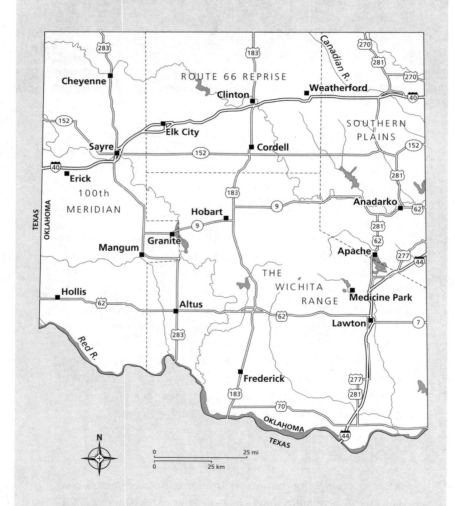

Cheyenne

283

ROUTE 66 REPRISE

183

Canadian R.

270

281

270

Clinton

Weatherford

40

152

Elk City

SOUTHERN
PLAINS

Sayre

152

Cordell

152

40

Erick

281

100th
MERIDIAN

183

TEXAS
OKLAHOMA

Hobart

9

Anadarko

62

281

Mangum

Granite

9

62

Apache

277

44

Hollis

THE
WICHITA
RANGE

62

Medicine Park

Altus

62

Lawton

7

Red R.

283

Frederick

277

281

183

70

OKLAHOMA

TEXAS

44

N

0   25 mi

0   25 km

Two hundred million years ago, the banks of a prehistoric sea began to stir, and the shifting land cut canyons 100 to 200 feet deep and a few miles long into the sandstone of the Permian Red Beds. The red-walled canyons of what is now **Red Rock Canyon State Park,** ½ mile south of Hinton on US 281, were once a well-protected winter camp for the Cheyenne, Comanche, and Kickapoo. According to local legend, the area was also used as a hiding place for horse thieves during the nineteenth and early twentieth centuries. A local civic group sandblasted a winding road down into the canyon in the 1930s and built a park, which was deeded to the state in 1954. Today, there are RV and tent campsites on the canyon floor, picnic areas, a swimming pool, hiking trails along the canyon's rim, and a small lake. Rappelling is allowed at several points along the 90-foot-tall rock wall.

More than thirty species of trees have been identified in the park, including brilliant sugar maples that look as if they are on loan from New England. The canyon is the only place in the area where native sugar maples have survived; it's thought that the maples survived in the canyons because they were shielded from the wind that forced maples off the plains thousands of years ago. There are two places in the park where ruts made by wagons traveling to California during the gold rush are still visible. Call (405) 542–6344 for information.

Rock Mary, an impressive 60-foot-tall red sandstone monument west of Hinton, was a landmark for nineteenth-century travelers. The stone appears in travelers' journals beginning in 1849, when a lieutenant traveling with Captain Randolph Marcy noted the formation and named it after an Arkansas traveler named Mary Conway. To see the formation drive 1½ miles east on Highway 37, then 1 mile north, another 1½ miles west, and then south for approximately 1½ miles.

Anadarko, south along Highway 8, bills itself as "The Indian Capital of the Nation." The modern town was built just south of the old Anadarko Agency that

AUTHOR'S FAVORITES IN THE SOUTHWEST PASSAGE

Altus-Lugert Wildlife Management Preserve	Old Greer County Museum and Hall of Fame
Fort Sill Military Reservation	Quartz Mountain State Park
Kiowa Tribal Museum	Red Rock Canyon State Park
Mohawk Trading Post	Route 66 Museum
Museum of the Great Plains	Wichita Mountains Wildlife Refuge

was established after the 1867 Treaty of Medicine Lodge relegated the Kiowa, Comanche, and the Kiowa-Apache to a reservation between the Washita River and the North Fork of the Red River. Seven tribes were served by the agency: the Kiowa, Comanche, Apache, Western Delaware, Fort Sill Apache, Caddo, and Wichita. The Bureau of Indian Affairs is still on the grounds, on the west side of US 281 just north of Anadarko's city limits. The grounds are also home to the **Riverside Indian School,** established in 1871 by a Quaker agent who taught eight students. Call (405) 247–6673 for information.

A restored early twentieth-century farmhouse, perched on a hill, holds **Nicoli's Italian Restaurant,** where Nicolas Scaffetta serves diners steaks and rustic Italian dishes he makes using his grandfather's recipes. The restaurant is open Thursday, Friday, and Saturday nights from 5:00 to 9:00 P.M.; (405) 247–6340.

The one-room **Western Delaware Tribal Museum** holds traditional clothing, drums, bowls, beadwork, jewelry, moccasins, and other artifacts of tribal history. The Delaware Nation are the descendents of the Lenape, a group prehistorically and historically located on the Northeast coast. Through forced migration the Lenape left their aboriginal home. In their journey westward four groups formed. One went into Canada, and another into Wisconsin. The third, the Absentee Delaware (Delaware Nation), traveled through Missouri to Arkansas and finally to Texas. The fourth, the Delaware Tribe, traveled through Missouri to Kansas and settled with the Cherokee in Eastern Oklahoma. The Absentee Delaware (Delaware Nation) were later forcibly moved from the Brazos Indian Reserve in Texas to Caddo County, Oklahoma. The ninety survivors settled near present-day Anadarko. Today the Delaware Nation is flourishing with over 1,600 members. Tribal members take an active role in the preservation of their culture and history by holding periodic activities and language classes. The museum is 2 miles north of Anadarko. Open Monday through Friday 9:00 A.M. to 5:00 P.M. Call (405) 247–2448.

thechampion boxelder

The third-largest box elder in the United States grows in Red Rock Canyon State Park. The trunk measures 11½ feet around, the tree is 64 feet tall, and its branches spread 70 feet across. Part of the reason for the tree's growth is the fact that the canyon protects it from the wind.

During the summer, travelers may spot the Native American version of the summer house, the brush arbor, built with hardwood tree trunks and lashed with green willow branches, along the highways west and south of Anadarko. Downtown Anadarko, however, looks much like any other slowpoke Western town, save for the stylized sidewalks on Main and Broadway, built with colored stones that resemble beadwork.

A good first stop is the ***Anadarko Visitor Center,*** www.anadarko.org, housed at the ***National Hall of Fame for Famous American Indians,*** (405) 247–6651, at the intersection of U.S. Highway 62 and Highway 8. The center is staffed by volunteers who are knowledgeable about area attractions as well as Native American history. The museum is open Monday through Friday 9:00 A.M. to 5:00 P.M. and Saturday 1:00 to 5:00 P.M. Outside, along a rectangular walkway, are more than three dozen bronze busts of Native American notables, including Kiowa chiefs Stumblingbear, Satanta, and Kicking Bird and such figures as Geronimo, Sequoyah, Jim Thorpe, and Hiawatha. A ten-page publication carries profiles of each of the Native Americans inducted into the National Hall of Fame, along with brief tribal histories. In summer, the ½-mile-long walk is most enjoyable in the morning—Oklahoma can be very hot in August.

Immediately west of the outdoor sculpture garden is the ***Southern Plains Indian Museum and Crafts Center,*** at 725 East Central, Anadarko, (405) 247–6221. An Indian-owned-and-operated crafts cooperative, it started in 1955 and is nationally known for the quality of craftsmanship found there. Beadwork, fans, nickel-silver jewelry (known as German silver), dance regalia, moccasins, musical instruments, and dolls are all sold. The gift shop also sells cassette tapes of Native American drumming and singing. A permanent museum exhibit displays mannequins dressed in traditional dress and regalia of the Kiowa, Comanche, Kiowa-Apache, Southern Cheyenne, Southern Arapaho,

TOP EVENTS IN THE SOUTHWEST PASSAGE

Apache Rattlesnake Festival,
Apache, April;
(580) 588–2880

Black Leggins Ceremonial,
Anadarko, May;
(405) 247–6651

Route 66 Car Events,
Clinton, held throughout the year;
(580) 323–7866;
www.route66.org

American Indian Exposition,
Anadarko, August;
(405) 247–6651

International Festival,
Lawton, September;
(580) 581–3470

Cheyenne-Arapaho Labor Day Powwow Celebration,
Colony, September;
(580) 323–0340

Wichita, Caddo, Western Delaware, and Ft. Sill Apache Tribes. The brilliant beaded buckskin clothing and moccasins are shown against dioramas painted by Chiracahua-Apache painter and sculptor Allan Houser, who grew up near Anadarko. Twice during the summer, Native American tepees dot the museum lawn. Two are put up for the town's Fourth of July celebrations, and eight tepees, put up by eight different families, all members of Southern Plains tribes, are displayed during the American Indian Exposition held each August.

The museum is open Tuesday through Saturday from 9:00 A.M. to 5:00 P.M. Closed Sunday and Monday; (405) 247–6221.

Melton's Drug and Soda Fountain Eatery, at 108 West Broadway, serves sandwiches, sodas, and limeades (made from real limes) from a fountain counter. There's a grill, but owners Phillip and Phyllis Melton use it to toast bread for their pimento cheese and chicken-salad sandwiches. (The chicken salad is the top seller.) There's a daily special, soup in the winter, and salads in the summer, and Phyllis makes a special dessert every day, from chocolate cake to a concoction she calls Pig-Out Cake. Ice-cream sundaes are also available. The fountain is open Tuesday through Friday 11:00 A.M. to 2:00 P.M. (405) 247–3800.

Three members of the Kiowa Five, Stephen Mopope, James Auchiah, and Spencer Asah, were commissioned during the 1930s by the federal government to paint murals on the walls of the ***Anadarko Post Office Building,*** at the corner of First and Oklahoma Streets downtown. Open Monday through Friday 8:30 A.M. to 5:00 P.M., (405) 247–6461. Mopope, the lead artist, painted sixteen panels illustrating life on the plains before the arrival of European settlers, including scenes of hunting buffalo and moving camp, along with twentieth-century Native American singers, drummers, and dancers.

More art by Mopope and a case holding some of Susan Peters's belongings (see box "The Kiowa Five") are among the items found at the ***Philomathic Museum,*** housed at 311 East Main, Anadarko, (405) 247–3240, in the old Rock Island Depot. The museum was founded in 1935 by a women's study circle called the Philomathic Club—*Philomathic* means "love of learning." The seven rooms in the museum hold pioneer items, railroad memorabilia, and Native American items such as cradleboards, beaded dresses and vests, and art. Peters's riding skirt is displayed along with the buckskin dress she wore after she was adopted by the Kiowa tribe.

For a Native American festival that more Indians than tourists mark on their calendars, visit the ***American Indian Exposition,*** held the third week in August at the Caddo County Fairgrounds (follow Main Street east of town). The exposition began in 1931 as an Indian version of the county fair, with ribbons for corn, wheat, and ponies. Over the years it has evolved into today's event: a festival filled with Native American dancing and foods, an all-Indian rodeo, Indian arts and crafts, and a historical pageant. (The pageant has been described by one non-Indian visitor as "a cross between opera and a church service.") Brush arbors sprout up on the county fairgrounds, where participants camp out as their grandparents did before them. Non-Indian visitors should abandon their expectations that events should adhere to the printed schedule—along with their watches. Starting "on time" has nothing to do with clocks in traditional Native American culture. Noncompetitive powwows begin with families honoring their members or others and the exchange of gifts, a tradition that is not hurried. For information about the exposition, call (405) 247–6651.

Take Anadarko's pulse by ordering a burger at the little cafe at the ***Indian City Lanes*** bowling alley at 131 East Broadway, a popular local hangout. Or try the smoked kidneys at ***K.I.G. Que*** at 115 East Market Street. The owner smokes the customary beef and pork but added the kidneys for his Native American clientele. Call (405) 247–2454.

From Anadarko follow US 62 west out of town and south to US 281 to ***Apache,*** a little cowboy town of 1,200 with a largely Native American population. The few downtown storefronts are filled with colorful tenants, including the headquarters for the Apache Rattlesnake Hunt and a retail store called ***"Mo" Betta.*** Maury Tate is an Apache resident and rodeo cowboy who tired of seeing five other competitors wearing the same shirt he was and thought he could make one that was "more better." Tate bought some hot-pink fabric and black piping and had a local seamstress whip up a shirt to his specifications. The

The Kiowa Five

A young field matron named Susan Peters, who worked at the Anadarko Indian Agency beginning at the end of World War I, spotted what she thought was exceptional artistic ability in a group of young Kiowa students. Their sketches and paintings incorporated elements of Native American traditions that Peters's supervisors were actively working to stamp out; nonetheless, Peters rounded up art supplies and brought in an art instructor for the young artists. The students, who came to be known as the Kiowa Five, came to the attention of University of Oklahoma professor Oscar Jacobson, who, in turn, brought their work to the attention of the art world at large. Those early paintings of regalia, battles, and scenes from everyday life done in a detailed, flat style are generally regarded as the genesis of modern Native American painting.

shirt caught the attention of other rodeo cowboys, who started buying the shirts off Tate's back, and Tate assembled more seamstresses to put together the shirts. The shirts were eventually brought to the attention of Garth Brooks, who began to wear them almost exclusively during his stage act and started a stampede on Tate's inventory. Today, the "Mo" Betta Store, at 104 East Evans, looks like the inside of a kaleidoscope, with racks of brilliantly colored shirts and deerskin, canvas, and denim jackets for sale. Also sold are rope cans, hand-painted carriers for carrying your ropes from rodeo to rodeo and that also work as makeup bags. The "Mo" Betta Store is open Monday through Friday 9:00 A.M. to 5:00 P.M. and Saturday from 10:00 A.M. to 4:00 P.M. They will give group tours, but not individual ones. Call (580) 588–9222 or (800) 259–9222.

Just down the street, at the corner of Coblake and Evans, is the ***Apache Historical Museum,*** a 1902 sandstone building that was formerly a bank. The sandstone was quarried southwest of town and carried to the site in wagons. The original bank ledgers are still stacked on shelves, and the original teller cages are in place. The bank is filled with period furniture and tools and holds art exhibits from time to time. There is a little unsigned mural painted on the bank wall; it is said to have been made by one of the Kiowa Five, who was commissioned by a bank executive. The museum is open Monday through Friday 9:00 A.M. to 5:00 P.M. in June and July and Monday to Saturday from 1:00 to 5:00 P.M. from August through May; (580) 588–3392.

Carnegie, population 1,500, is small enough that almost all directions begin at the same starting point: the junction of Highways 58 and 9, the town's only four-way stop. From the junction drive north for 8 miles and turn back east for 1¼ miles to tour the ***Horn Canna Farm,*** www.cannas.net, the largest producer of canna bulbs in the nation. The farm grows nineteen kinds of cannas—reds, yellows, pinks, salmons, and so on—on 150 acres and sells bulbs at the

The End of the Buffalo Road: A Kiowa Legend

Straight to Mount Scott the leader of the herd walked. Behind him came the cows and their calves and the few young males who had survived. As the woman watched, the face of the mountain opened. Inside Mount Scott the world was green and fresh, as it had been when she was a small girl. The rivers ran clear, not red. The wild plums were in blossom, chasing the red buds up the inside slopes. Into this world of beauty, the buffalo walked, never to be seen again.

—Kiowa legend

farm. Cannas have been grown on the farm since the 1920s and have been a large-scale commercial operation since 1946. Carnegie hosts a Canna Festival the last Saturday in September, during which special events are held at the farm and visitors are invited to cut and carry all the cannas they want. (You can fill your whole car if you like.) Harvest begins the day after the festival, which means all of the blooms will be cut down. Cannas bloom from late June until the first frost. Call (580) 637–2327 for information.

Continue west from the four-way stop on Highway 9 to the **Kiowa Tribal Museum,** housed in the Kiowa Tribal Complex. The one-room museum holds ten richly colored 16-feet-by-8-feet murals, which were painted by three preeminent young Kiowa artists in consultation with tribal elders. The Kiowa had no written language but preserved their heritage with stories. The murals depict creation stories, the tribe's emigration from Yellowstone to southwestern Oklahoma in about 1750, and the importance of the horse to the tribe. Each of the artists painted three murals, and the artists collaborated on the last, which shows a warrior dance society over the modern Kiowa landscape. The painting shows trophies that are still used in the ceremonials today, including a cavalry bugle. Historic photographs and beadwork and models of powwow grounds and tepees round out the collection. The museum is open Monday through Friday from 8:00 A.M. to 4:30 P.M.; (580) 654–2300.

The Wichita Range

As Highway 58 drops south into Comanche County, the blue line of the Wichita Mountains appears on the horizon. Pick up Highway 19 and travel east to Highway 115, which takes visitors to the north entrance to the **Wichita Mountains Wildlife Refuge,** (580) 429–3222, www.wichitamountains.fws.gov/. The mountain range, which extends for about 60 miles and is 30 miles across at its widest point, is 650 million years old, making it one of the oldest mountain ranges in the United States. It is also one of the oldest looking; the boulder-strewn granite and quartz peaks are colored blue, pink, and gold and are barren save for scrubby post oak trees. The mountains were named for the Wichita Indians, farmers who lived in circular grass houses and believed the boulders held the spirits of their ancestors.

The heart of the mountain range is contained in the 60,000 acres of the refuge land set aside by the federal government when the Kiowa-Comanche reservation was opened to settlement in 1901. In 1905 the refuge was designated as a game preserve by President Theodore Roosevelt. (Roosevelt had close acquaintance with the environs; he traveled to the territory that same year to take part in a wolf hunt.)

Less than a century before, Edwin James, a member of the Long Expedition, which traveled across the plains in 1819, had written: "The bison paths in this country are as frequent and almost as conspicuous as the roads in the most populous parts of the United States." By 1905, however, bison had vanished from the Oklahoma prairies, and there were fewer than 1,000 of the animals left in North America. The bison herd at the Wichita Mountains was started with fifteen bison, shipped by rail from a zoo in New York and escorted into the refuge in 1907 by cheering cowboys, soldiers from Fort Sill, and Native Americans in full regalia. The herd is now maintained at just over 500 bison.

Pure longhorn cattle once faced extinction as well. In the summer of 1927, refuge officials found a pureblood herd of longhorn cattle in the Gulf Coast region of Texas and imported twenty cows, three bulls, three steers, and four calves to the refuge. Today, the herd is maintained at around 280 cattle. Along with buffalo and longhorns, visitors also spot Rocky Mountain elk, white-tailed deer, prairie dogs, and hefty raccoons (some refuge raccoons weigh in at twenty-five pounds).

A visitors' center at the intersection of Highways 49 and 115 is a worthwhile stop. The center's multimedia exhibits are designed to appeal to a wide range of interests and attention spans; visitors can simply admire a stuffed wooly bison or study panels that explain the interwoven life systems on the plains. Recordings of animal sounds likely to be heard on the refuge are a big hit with children.

Visitors will find maps to refuge hiking trails at the visitors' center. The most heavily used are the trails in the Dog Run Hollow Trail System, which offers hikers 1-, 2-, or 6-mile-long loops. The trails lead to such picturesque points as Twin Falls and Lost Lake. The Elk Mountain trail hikes are on a higher elevation and are a little more challenging.

On the west side of the refuge is the *Charon's Garden Wilderness Area,* a 5,000-acre area that offers hiking through canyons and past waterfalls. The Sunset picnic area is just off the road, and a trail leads along the west edge of The Valley of the Boulders, a valley strewn with boulders of all shapes and sizes. Backcountry camping is allowed in the area by permit, which can be reserved by writing to the Department of the Interior, U.S. Fish and Wildlife Service, R.R. No. 1, Box 448, Indiahoma 73552; (580) 429–3222. Only ten overnight permits are issued to campers each day; reservations are taken one month in advance. Campsites at Doris Campground, which offer showers, RV hookups, and a sanitary dump station, are available on a first-come basis. Fees are $6.00 for campsites without electricity, $10.00 for campsites with electricity.

At present the preserve is also the only federal refuge to allow technical rock climbing and rappelling. Refuge officials fear the effects climbers will have on the residents of rock crevices—canyon wrens, golden eagles, and great horned owls—but so far haven't been successful at banning climbing. Mountain bikers can also use a trail built for that purpose. Bikers have to write for a permit (fifteen are issued each day). The trails traverse terrain with loose rock, steep hills, and sudden drop-offs.

The **Holy City of the Wichitas,** (580) 429–3361, a collection of about twenty picturesque rock buildings surrounding a stone amphitheater, was constructed in the 1930s within the refuge by members of the Works Progress Administration. Workers quarried the rocks from the mountain, and the buildings, which were meant to resemble the city of Jerusalem, were constructed to accommodate an annual passion play started by a local priest in the 1920s—"The Longest Running Outdoor Passion Play in America." By 1939 the crowd had grown to about 200,000, but attendance at the performance, held the evening before Easter Sunday, is now only a few hundred. The Holy City Chapel, painted with angels and saints and holding wooden benches, is open all year.

It's nearly obligatory for visitors to spiral up the 3½-mile road that leads to the top of Mount Scott, which, at 2,364 feet, is the second-highest elevation in the refuge.

Highway 115 takes travelers to Meers, on the northern edge of the refuge, or, more accurately, to **Meers Store,** (580) 429–8051. Formerly a general store and now a restaurant, the wooden building is all that's left of a little flurry of a gold rush that brought prospectors to the mountains in 1903. The population of Meers once hovered around 500; it's now down to 4. Meers Store, formerly a post office and currently a federal seismographic station, is still a gathering point for information, by way of hundreds of business cards tacked on the wall. The specialty of the house is a Meersburger, a 7-inch-diameter longhorn beef patty, served with mustard, pickle, onion, lettuce, tomato, and a fork. The

Meers Store

french fries come on a tray of their own. Meers Store is a good place to pick up local tales of buried treasure and to get directions to a nearby *arrasta*, an ore grinder that is believed to have been used by Spanish miners.

Tales of lost gold and other legends are also found in **Medicine Park,** www.medicinepark.com, east on Highway 49. Medicine Park was incorporated as Medicine Park Summer Resort and Health Spa and opened on the banks of Medicine Creek on the Fourth of July, 1908. Today, on the eastern edge of the Wichita Mountain Wildlife Refuge, guests can experience the same relaxing atmosphere at the **Star Dust Inn.** The inn is secluded and is as close to the wildlife refuge as one can stay. Thousands of Native Americans used to camp at the creek, which runs along the property, and white-tailed deer, painted buntings, and raccoons are only a few of the animals spotted by guests. A white deer, reported to bring good luck, is seen by one out of every forty guests. The inn has four rooms, all with outside entries, private bathrooms, and cable television, that range in price from $115 to $135. An eighty-year-old cabin in Medicine Park is also available for rent. Peggy Brown, the owner and innkeeper, uses art from local artists to decorate her bed-and-breakfast. She says the area, besides having a spiritual feel, is magical. Call (580) 529–3270 or visit www.star dustinn.com to learn more.

The little community of Medicine Park fell onto hard times in the 1930s. Since then, the town has waxed and (mostly) waned. Today, however, visitors find the early stages of a revival, evidenced in such places as the **Riverside Cafe,** (580) 529–2626. A wooden deck behind the cafe overlooks Medicine Creek and is arguably the best place in the entire region to linger over dinner. The versatile menu offers catfish and grilled salmon, grilled chicken, chicken-fried steak, shrimp and pasta, steamed veggies served with honey-wheat bread, cappuccino, and beer. The interior is done in soothing neutrals, with a Maxfield Parrish–style mural painted by the owner.

Next door is the friendly **Park Tavern,** www.medicineparktavern.com, operated by Bill and Jeannette Patty. The Pattys renovated a narrow cobblestone cottage that they used as a weekend retreat before they moved to Medicine Park permanently and bought a bigger house. The Treehouse, their carriage-house apartment, has a queen-size bed, sitting area, kitchen, deck with a view, grill, and books, including a three-volume set of the writings of Freud. None of the secondary streets in Medicine Park have names, so homes do, Jeanette Patty explained. The apartment can be rented for $100 a night; call (580) 529–2945.

The **Fort Sill Military Reservation** abuts the wildlife refuge; to reach historic Fort Sill, take I–44 south to the Key Gate entrance. (The polo fields, a bit farther south, are on the spot where scouts found an abandoned Wichita village in 1849.) Fort Sill has a romantic, tragic history: Wild Bill Hickok and Buffalo Bill Cody served as scouts and Indian fighters with the Seventh and Tenth Cavalries stationed there; soldiers were on hand for the destruction of the buffalo; and Bat Masterson and Wyatt Earp both hunted buffalo on the plains. They also saw the anger and frustration of the leaders of the Plains tribes, who saw their way of life disappear in a matter of decades. To learn about Fort Sill's history as a western outpost, take the first right to Randolph Road and follow it around to the visitors' center, housed in an 1875 stone building erected as a warehouse and later used as infantry barracks. The center's exhibits cover all aspects of the fort's history and changing function, both during its early years as a base of operations for the Indian Wars and as an artillery training grounds beginning in World War I. It also was the base for the nation's first aero squadron; don't miss photographs of soldiers wing-walking on biplanes. The visitors' center children's area, Cricket's Corner, is furnished with a brush arbor, a life-size model of a saddle horse, and lots of old-timey equipment just asking to be tried out: a washboard, a pump, a butter churn, old slates, and a school bell. The building immediately to the west is the Old Post Headquarters, which was built in 1870, a year after the post was established. The building is now the museum office and also holds archival materials that are available to the public on weekdays. The center is open Monday through Saturday from 8:30 A.M. to 4:30 P.M. and on Sunday from 12:30 to 4:30 P.M. Call (580) 442–5123.

One of the most visited structures at the fort is the *Guardhouse,* which was built in 1873 and held hostile Indian leaders, civilian outlaws, and soldiers. Its most famous resident was Geronimo, one of the leaders of a Chiricahua-Apache band who were arrested after leaving their Arizona reservation. The band was first moved to a prison in Florida, where a quarter of them died in the swampy heat. In 1894 the band was moved to Fort Sill, where they were given allotments and raised pumpkins and corn. In the guardhouse an entire exhibit is devoted to debunking the myths that have grown up around the name *Geronimo.* These include the misconception that he was so fierce and untamed a warrior, he was imprisoned in chains for years. The truth is that Geronimo spent only a night or two in the guardhouse when he had too much to drink. Geronimo left the fort frequently to travel with Pawnee Bill's Wild West Circus.

Just north of the guardhouse is *Cannon Walk,* a display of artillery from 1600 to the present. Also built around the old parade grounds are the Old Post Chapel, built in 1875, and a stone stockade built in 1870 after the cavalry's horses were raided by the Kiowa. Just southwest of the chapel is the *Prairie Crafters Gift Shop,* which sells craft items made by Fort Sill soldiers and their families. The cheery shop, in vintage noncommissioned officer housing, fills several rooms with folk art, baskets, toys, country and Victorian crafts, candles, and other items. The shop, in Building 372, is open Monday through Saturday from 10:00 A.M. to 5:00 P.M.; (580) 353–7055.

In the nineteenth century Fort Sill was regarded as one of the most beautiful posts in the West. To see part of the reason for that reputation, take Randolph Road to Fort Sill Boulevard, then turn north and follow that road to King Road. Travel west to the end of the road and turn north across a bridge. The first left turn will take you to *Medicine Bluff,* where Medicine Creek flows through two rocky outcroppings, a spot sacred to Indian tribes. Each Memorial Day, during the Fort Sill Heritage Fair, descendants of the Apache prisoners come to the fort from New Mexico and dance the sacred Fire Dance. Tribal members gather sage and wildflowers from the base of Medicine Bluff and take it home for use in ceremonies. The Heritage Fair and dance are open to the public. There are picnic tables and a fishing dock near the creek. To the north is a small animal park, featuring species native to western Oklahoma, such as coyotes and white-tailed deer.

On Fort Sill Boulevard, signs direct visitors to *Chief's Knoll,* sometimes called the "Indian Arlington" for the number of Native American leaders buried there. A monument and marker for Geronimo are at the cemetery.

Lawton, www.cityoflawton.ok.us, is Oklahoma's fourth-largest city and was settled by a lottery of the Kiowa, Comanche, Wichita, Caddo, and Apache land that was left after allotments were made to tribal members. The earlier land runs were unfair, Congress decided, and dangerous to boot. In 1901 more than 165,000 people registered at Fort Sill and El Reno for 15,000 claims. The first name drawn was that of J. F. Woods, who took his 160-acre claim in one long choice strip adjoining the Lawton town site—which was bounded on the other three sides by federal and school land—and earned himself the nickname "Hog" Woods.

Ten Bears

In 1867 the U.S. government persuaded the chiefs of the Kiowa, Comanche, Cheyenne, and Arapaho Tribes to sign the Treaty of Medicine Lodge, which provided for tribes to settle on reservations in Indian Territory. The treaty was opposed by Ten Bears, chief of the Comanche, who made a stirring speech: "The Comanches are not weak and blind . . . they are strong and far-sighted, like grown horses. . . . I was born upon the prairie where the wind blew free and there was nothing to break the light of the sun. I want no blood upon my land to stain the grass. I want it clear and pure and I wish it so that all who go through among my people may have peace when they come in and leave it when they go out."

Hackberry Flat

At the turn of the twentieth century, settlers drained a large, shallow lake with mules and a steam shovel and converted the marshy land to wheat and cotton production. In 1995 the Oklahoma Wildlife Department began to re-create the wetland habitat into a 7,000-acre refuge for migrating waterfowl and shorebirds. Restoration of the habitat is basically completed, and visitors spot sandhill cranes, avocets and stilts, ducks, geese, and a variety of songbirds, including meadowlarks, painted buntings, Savannah sparrows, red-winged blackbirds, and scissor-tailed flycatchers. Roads in the wildlife management area are mostly gravel; many of the planned boardwalks have been built. To get to the **Hackberry Flat Wildlife Restoration Project,** travel 1 mile southeast of Frederick along Highway 183, then travel east on Airport Road for 3 miles. A sign marks a paved road, which takes travelers to Hackberry Flat, 4 miles to the south. A birding checklist is available by calling (580) 335–5262.

The second name drawn was attached to a much more lovable figure. Twenty-two-year-old Mattie Beal, a telephone operator from Wichita, Kansas, entered the lottery hoping to gain a farm for herself and her widowed mother. Miss Beal also chose land near the town site, valued at $20,000 to $40,000 at the time, and received 500 marriage proposals in the mail. She married a local man who owned a lumberyard, and together they built a neoclassical Greek Revival mansion, now open as the **Mattie Beal House.** The house, which has stained-glass windows depicting the nearby Wichita Mountains, is open for tours the second Sunday afternoon of each month or by appointment; 1006 Southwest Fifth Street; (580) 678–3156. Admission is $3.00.

Also in Lawton is the newly expanded **Museum of the Great Plains,** dedicated to the cultural and natural history of the plains, from prehistoric to contemporary times. A mammoth skull unearthed in Kiowa County is on display, along with information and artifacts from the nearby Domebo site, a canyon where a group of prehistoric hunters, the Clovis people, killed an imperial mammoth circa 9000 B.C. Among the museum's more contemporary artifacts are the contents of an Indian store in Anadarko, established in 1910 to sell beadwork and clothing made by Kiowa and Cheyenne tribal members, and a collection of Indian peace medals, engraved coins given to Indian chiefs and prominent tribal members by the federal government to commemorate treaties and other occasions. The museum does a good job of recalling just how remote the area was 160 years ago when U.S. soldiers held their first meetings with the "Camanchees" and "Kioways" (as old documents put it) in the Wichita Mountains. Until 100 years ago, what's now called the North Fork of the Red River

Miles of Prairie Dogs

In 1852 there were an estimated twenty to twenty-five million prairie dogs scattered over a 400,000-acre area in what's now southwestern Oklahoma—one 22-mile-long prairie-dog town stretched from El Reno to Okarche. No friend to ranchers, the black-tailed prairie dog (actually a member of the squirrel family) has declined considerably in numbers since then. There are plenty of places left to observe the sociable little animals in southwestern Oklahoma, including at the Wichita Mountains Wildlife Refuge and the Museum of the Great Plains. A prairie-dog town is flourishing, too, at a state-operated traveler's information center on the H. E. Bailey Turnpike (I-44) about 20 miles south of Lawton. Visitors should keep in mind that feeding prairie dogs salty snacks and other human treats can make them very sick—prairie dogs are adapted to living in dry climates and get water from their food, including grass.

was considered the main branch, and the land south was Spanish territory, then Mexican, and then belonged to the Republic of Texas. A reproduction of a Red River trading post, with stockade walls, cabins, blockhouses, and a trade house, has been erected on the museum grounds and is the setting for living-history events held the first weekends in May and November. The museum also has a prairie-dog town on the grounds. The museum, at 601 Ferris Avenue, Lawton, is open Monday through Saturday from 10:00 A.M. to 5:00 P.M. and Sunday 1:00 to 5:00 P.M.; the museum stays open an hour later during the summer. Call (580) 581–3460 or visit www.museumgreatplains.org, for information.

Next door is the ***Percussive Arts Society Museum,*** with an amazing assortment of marimbas, xylophones, vibraphones, chimes, and, of course, drums collected from around the world. Best of all there's a hands-on section where visitors can bang on a variety of percussive instruments for themselves. The museum is at 701 Northwest Ferris Avenue, Lawton, and is open Monday through Friday from 8:00 A.M. to 5:00 P.M. and on weekends and holidays from 1:00 until 4:00 P.M. For information, call (580) 353–1455 or visit www.pas.org.

Travelers leaving Lawton on US 62 will pass through Cache, www.cacheok coc.org, where Quanah Parker built his twelve-room ***Star House,*** now the centerpiece of Eagle Park Ghost Town. This stop is poignant because the buildings in the ghost town and a nearby fly-specked trading post have seen better days. Parker's house is open only by appointment; someone at the trading post has to go and open the gate. Call (580) 429–3238. The trading post is on the southwest corner of US 62 and Highway 115.

Due west of Lawton on US 62 is ***Altus,*** home to Altus Air Force Base. For those landlocked seafood lovers, a stop at ***Fred's Famous Fish and Steak-house*** may be just the fix. Located downtown at 2011 North Main, (580)

480–0555, its blue ocean waves and neon lights beckon all who pass to a hearty meal. Seafood, fresh-cut steaks, chicken-fried steak, and barbecue are just a few of the items on the menu. It's open seven days a week from 11:00 A.M. to 10:00 P.M. A steak and seafood buffet is served from a boat on Friday and Saturday nights. Sunday-morning brunch is served from 11:00 A.M. to 2:00 P.M. If guests are still hungry, they can order cheesecake, bourbon pecan pie, or the Magnificent 7—a seven-layer all-chocolate decadent dessert. Just down the street you'll find the *Main Street Grill,* (580) 482–1440. The 6,000-square-foot restaurant offers dining and a sports bar. For those who like to keep up on the scores, don't worry; there are plenty of televisions for viewing. Serving American cuisine in a sports-bar atmosphere is what this eatery is all about. Open Monday through Saturday for lunch from 11:00 A.M. to 2:00 P.M. and for dinner from 4:00 to 10:00 P.M.; closed on Sundays.

Straight north up U.S. Highway 283 is *Quartz Mountain State Park,* where the Wichita Mountains crop up again, creating more striking landscapes and good hiking terrain. The park's namesake mountain rises 1,800 feet above the flat plain, its pink-and-orange granite boulders contrasting against the blue of Lake Altus. The New Horizon Trail treats hikers to spectacular views.

Overlooking Lake Altus is the new *Quartz Mountain Resort.* Built from native Oklahoma stone and timber, its simple architecture only adds to the landscape. Eight murals depicting life in southwestern Oklahoma decorate the lobby, and the huge stone fireplace is the centerpiece. Students of the Oklahoma Arts Institute spend summers there and add to the lodge's art collection—their work hangs in hallways and rooms throughout the building. Visitors can take walks along Sunrise Trail, eat in the Sundance Cafe, or watch local

Quanah Parker

Quanah Parker was born in 1845, the son of a leader of the Quahadi band of the Comanche and Cynthia Ann Parker, a white woman who as a child had been taken captive in Texas. Quanah became the last Comanche leader to surrender during the Indian wars that were waged on the western plains of Indian Territory. Parker turned himself in after the Battle of Adobe Walls in 1875, and, after his surrender, he was recognized as chief of all the Comanche. Parker served as a judge in an Indian court, and, after a reunion with his white relatives in Texas, negotiated a deal with Texas ranchers to lease Comanche grassland to Texas ranchers. Parker built a big house near Cache where he lived with his several wives. The house became known as the Star House for the fourteen stars Parker painted on the roof after a visit from a multistarred army officer.

jazz musicians play in the Performing Arts Hall. Room rates are flexible according to season. Call (580) 563–2424 or visit www.quartzmountainresort.com.

Several other peaks ring the reservoir; locals dammed the North Fork of the Red River in the 1930s for irrigation. The landscape has always drawn artists and photographers, and today it's home to the Quartz Mountain Arts Institute. For active outdoor recreation, visitors can choose swimming, boating, go-carts, fishing, paddleboats, and technical rock climbing. Rio Grande turkeys and mourning doves are abundant in the spring and fall in the ***Altus-Lugert Wildlife Management Preserve*** adjacent to the park, where hunting is allowed; (580) 683–4249. The North Shore Beach, a naturally sandy fringe with a view of purple mountains, fluctuates with the lake level, ranging from almost a half mile wide to nearly nothing.

The park is prime wildflower country. There are so many species that the park hosts an annual Wildflower Weekend in April with park naturalist–led identification walks and workshops. Eagle spotting replaces wildflower watching in winter: Quartz Mountain Park is one of the best spots in the state to see them, fishing under the dam off Highway 44. There's an eighteen-hole golf course, too, shaded by native trees transplanted from elsewhere in the park and rimmed with wildflower plots.

100th Meridian

A large chunk of southwestern Oklahoma used to be included in what was called Old Greer County, encompassing all the land south of the North Fork of the Red River. The designation as "fork" didn't come until 1896, when the U.S. Supreme Court ruled that the branch of the river that flowed farther south was the main track and, therefore, the border between Texas and Oklahoma Territory. In other words, part of Oklahoma used to be Texas.

Texans, notoriously proud of their heritage, do things on a grand scale, and those tendencies may have stuck around in far southwestern Oklahoma. ***Granite,*** on Highway 9, is the site of a huge granite quarry; there's so much of the rose-colored rock that the town's curbs are made of it. Bill Willis, the quarry's owner, was carving portraits of three of Oklahoma's heroes—Will Rogers, Jim Thorpe, and Sequoyah—on an eleven-story mountain until he retired. Today visitors can drive by and admire the completed Will Rogers bust and dream of what might have been.

Willis's granite was also used in ***Mangum,*** at the ***Old Greer County Museum and Hall of Fame,*** 222 West Jefferson. The museum, four stories high, holds photographs and artifacts relating to the settlement of the area. It has been praised as "a workingman's museum," with far greater emphasis on everyday implements than on parlor pianos and Sunday china. Out front, more than 200 granite monuments have been erected, each one engraved with the portrait and biography of a person born or living in the county before 1896. The museum is open Tuesday through Friday from 9:00 A.M. to 4:00 P.M. and Saturday from 3:00 to 6:00 P.M.; (580) 782–2851.

The ranch country around Mangum has few state roads. Highway 9 heads straight west and intersects with Highway 30. The drive north toward Erick takes travelers into the ***Sandy Sanders Wildlife Management Area,*** a 19,000-acre preserve that area residents refer to as "The Breaks." Here, pastures give way to small red mesas and gullies, covered with scrubby pinchot juniper trees. The area is remote and mostly undeveloped; there are picnic tables, rest rooms, campsites, fishing ponds, and 45 miles of unpaved roads for hiking and mountain biking. Call (580) 683–4249 for information.

Uniquely Oklahoma

Oklahomans are proud of their food products. My mother, who now lives in Kansas, and my brother in Utah, buy cases of Griffin's Syrup when they are in town to take home because "it's the best on the planet." Bar S meat products, Shawnee Best, and Field's Pies have a similar reputation. When my brother-in-law goes on vacation, his first stop when returning to Oklahoma is Braum's, where he buys one of their famous banana splits. Visitors can find other Oklahoma products by visiting www.madeinoklahoma.net, www.oklahomafood.coop, or www.miocoalition.com.

Famous around these parts are Indian Tacos. Below is the recipe.

Oklahoma Indian Tacos

Fry Bread

2 cups flour

3 tsp. baking powder

1 tsp. salt

1 cup milk (you can also use dry milk and water to make 1 cup liquid)

Mix dry ingredients. Pour in milk slowly to make dough. After dough is kneaded, pinch off medium sized balls and flatten. Deep fry in fat for approximately five minutes or until golden brown.

Meat Sauce

1 pound ground meat (beef, pork, lamb, venison, turkey)

1 8-ounce can tomato sauce

1 tsp. chili powder

½ tsp. oregano

½ tsp. basil

1 16-ounce can chili beans

1 4-ounce can chopped green chilies (optional)

Brown meat and add seasonings. Stir in chili beans and green chilies. Spoon on top of flat bread.

Toppings

Top meat mixture with shredded lettuce, diced tomato, diced onions, grated cheddar cheese, sour cream, and sliced black olives.

In *Erick,* travelers meet up again with Route 66. The path the historic highway makes through western Oklahoma has a distinctly different feel than it does in the eastern part of the state, because out west, the modern interstate and the old road are intertwined for long stretches. Even as travelers barrel along the interstate, Route 66 keeps I–40 company, appearing as a narrow access road (distinguishable by its creamy Portland cement) and disappearing, in some places, for a tree-lined detour. Staying precisely on the old road requires doubling back and measuring mileage down to ⅒ mile. Another option for driving Route 66 is to take the easy-to-find old alignments, such as the 23-mile-long stretch from Texola to Sayre, and hop on the interstate to take you to Route 66 towns such as Elk City and Clinton, where you'll find plenty of old landmarks.

Just west of Erick is a genuine roadside attraction, the *Erick Honey Farm.* The farm is down a few hives from its heyday, but there are enough to fill a little gift shop with beeswax candles and jars of honey. There is a cross-section of a hive under glass, and tours of the facility where the honey is taken from the combs are conducted. The farm and shop are open Monday through Saturday from 9:00 A.M. to 5:00 P.M. from March through September. A restaurant serves hamburgers Monday through Friday from 10:00 A.M. to 2:00 P.M. For information call (580) 526–3759.

The address of the *100th Meridian Museum* in downtown Erick is proof that the town is proud of its own: The little museum sits at the intersection of Roger Miller Boulevard and Sheb Wooley Avenue. Miller wrote "King of the Road"; Wooley penned "Purple People Eater." The museum is named in honor of the nearby one hundredth meridian, a state line that museum curators brag is "the most perfect exact line in the United States." (The jog in the line across the state, along the Arkansas-Oklahoma border, was due to a surveying error.) The museum is housed in what was once a bank building and has eclectic holdings, including a marble collection and a mammoth's tooth. It is open regularly only on Friday and Saturday mornings during July and August, and Friday and Saturday afternoons the rest of the year; (580) 526–3221. Ask for J.W. Docents' names and phone numbers are posted on the door, along with the assurance that they can be at the museum in a flash if someone wants in.

Route 66 from Erick takes travelers east to *Sayre,* www.sayreok.net. The *Beckham County Courthouse,* at the east end of Main Street, is of interest to Route 66 buffs, because it appeared in the movie *The Grapes of Wrath*, which "starred" Route 66 as the highway that took Dust Bowl refugees to California.

Attractions include the *RS&K Railroad Museum,* at 411 North Sixth Street, 2 blocks west of Route 66. The little museum holds railroad memora-

Battle at Washita

In a blizzard, General George Custer, led by Osage scouts, moved south from Fort Supply toward the Antelope Hills in search of a raiding party returning from Kansas. Instead, he found the village of a peaceful chief who had worked for years to prevent war between the southern Cheyenne and the white settlers. At dawn on November 27, 1868, the regimental band played "Gary Owen," an Irish drinking song Custer liked, signaling the attack. Black Kettle and his wife tried to escape but were shot off their horse and died in the Washita River. Custer's Seventh Cavalry killed an estimated forty Cheyenne, including women and children. He also destroyed the pony herd (about 800 horses), camp equipment, and winter food stores. Today, guided tours of the *Washita Battlefield National Historic Site* are available through the National Park Service. For information call (580) 497–2742.

bilia, including 250 trains. Eleven different track layouts are on display, too. Owner Ray Killian, who didn't play with model trains until he retired from the postal service, likes to run trains on all tracks at once. The museum is open daily from 9:00 A.M. to 9:00 P.M.; (580) 928–3525.

Built in 1932, the Rock Island train depot has been restored and re-opened as the *Shortgrass Country Museum.* The depot displays rotating exhibits on various aspects of early-day life on the western plains. The museum is at 106 East Poplar; (580) 928–5757. It's open Tuesday through Friday from 2:00 to 4:00 P.M. Route 66 continues north of Sayre and intersects with I–40.

This is a good place to detour north to *Cheyenne,* (580) 497–3318 or www.cheyenneokchamber.com, a little town adjacent to the 31,000-acre *Black Kettle National Grasslands.* The grasslands were named in honor of Cheyenne Chief Black Kettle, who was massacred by Colonel George Custer and members of the Seventh Cavalry in November 1868. (The battle site itself is west of Cheyenne along Highway 47 and north on Highway 47A.) Here, the grasslands are broken by hardwoods along the bottomlands and populated by prairie chickens, Canada geese, and nesting Mississippi kites. The grasslands have some of the best wild-turkey hunting in the country.

Military maps, Cheyenne beadwork, cavalry artifacts, and a historical perspective are on hand at the *Black Kettle Museum* in Cheyenne. A new children's area has several hands-on exhibits, including a large dinosaur puzzle and animal pelts. The museum, on Highway 47, is open Monday through Friday 10:00 to 11:45 A.M. and 1:00 to 4:00 P.M. and Saturday and Sunday from 9:00 A.M. to 5:00 P.M.; (580) 497–3929.

Also on Highway 47 in Cheyenne is a tearoom, antiques store, and art gallery named after a white woman captured by the Cheyenne Tribe. Efforts were being made for her release when she was killed in the Washita massacre. *Clara's Cottage* is part of a colony of art galleries and studios that carry Native American items made by local artists.

A good base camp is *Coyote Hills Guest Ranch,* www.coyotehillsguest ranch.com, situated in red, rugged rolling hills. Lodging is in a rustic bunkhouse where each of the twenty rooms has a private bath; a hot tub overlooks the mesas. Meals are taken in the cavernous Social Barn, where you can drink a glass of wine in the afternoon, dip into the library, and then dance to a cowboy band at night. The best part of Coyote Hills, however, is the horseback riding. The owners have a string of about twenty-eight steeds, lovingly cared for and suited to every level of riding expertise. Owners Devey Napier and Kass Nickels can come up with just about any Western entertainment you might want, ranging from cowboy poets, to a tepee overnighter, to chuck-wagon cookouts, to cattle drives. In November the ranch opens to members of the Cheyenne Tribe, who hold a memorial service for tribal members killed in the 1868 massacre. To reach the ranch from Cheyenne, travel 4 miles west on Highway 47 and then 2 miles north and 2 miles west to the ranch. For reservations call (580) 497–3931.

Tepee at Coyote Hills Guest Ranch

Route 66 Reprise

In *Elk City,* www.elkcitychamber.com, 15 miles east, the most recent path of Route 66 is marked "Business 40" and runs north of town on Third Street.

One block south, shady, brick-lined Broadway Street was an earlier alignment of Route 66. Broadway intersects with Pioneer Road; take it to the *Old Town Museum,* (580) 225–2207. The museum, housed in a gingerbread-covered Victorian-style building, holds collections of early-day tools, furnishings, memorabilia, and a "Rodeo Hall of Fame," a tribute to the Beutler Brothers Ranch. The Hall of Famers in this case are bulls and broncos; the Beutler Brothers Ranch, west of Elk City, has provided stock to regional and national rodeos for decades. The museum is adjacent to Ackley Park, which holds historic buildings, including a livery stable, schoolhouse, and a working gristmill. All were moved from nearby Elk Creek, the town's namesake. (Elk City was first named Busch, in a failed effort to lure the Anheuser Busch Company to town.) The newest addition to the museum complex is the *National Route 66 Museum,* displaying memorabilia related to the highway.

Five blocks east is the seventeen-story Parker Drilling Rig No. 114; at 179 feet high, it's billed as the tallest nonoperating drilling rig in the world. It was the world's tallest rig when it was built in the 1960s to drill shafts for underground nuclear testing. It was brought to Oklahoma in the 1980s when Elk City was the epicenter of drilling in the Anadarko Basin, an enormous oil reserve that runs underground from Denver to southern Oklahoma. The rig sits outside the *Anadarko Basin Museum of Natural History,* housed in what was once a landmark Route 66 stopping place, the Casa Grande Hotel. The museum displays Oklahoma fossils, petrified wood, and oil- and gas-related exhibits. The museum is at 105 East Third Street. Call (580) 243–0437 to arrange special tours.

boosting66

"When we came here we lived on the prairies, no road, we made our trails. White man came, he made big trails and now we have the long wide trail and I am backing 66 to the limit."— Unidentified Cheyenne-Arapaho man, addressing an Elk City gathering of the Highway 66 Association in May 1931.

Next up, 28 miles east, is *Clinton,* www.clintonokla.org, home to the state-operated *Route 66 Museum,* www.route66.org. Take the Business 40 exit from I-40, then travel north on Randolph Gary Boulevard to 2229 Gary Boulevard. The museum is on the west side of the road—not that you're likely to miss it. The museum building, which opened in 1995, sports glass bricks, tail fins, and lots of pink neon. Beginning in the front room, where a vintage

Corvette is parked, exhibits illustrate the development of the historic highway decade by decade, from the 1920s, when the highway was constructed with mule-drawn graders, to the 1970s, when the interstate system finally superseded the road. Along the way, homage is paid to family station wagons, Volkswagen-driving hippies, Dust Bowl refugees, the trucking industry, World War II, and 1950s-era diners. Touch-screen computers, video, and push-button audio add other dimensions such as vacation home movies, old black-and-white films of military caravans pulling onto the highway during World War II, and Elvis singing "Heartbreak Hotel."

With the profusion of curio-shop treasures, Technicolor-tinted postcards, matchbooks, and motor-court ashtrays, you can almost smell the hot asphalt and hear the whir of old window air-conditioning units. The museum is open Monday through Saturday from 9:00 A.M. to 7:00 P.M. and Sunday from 1:00 to 6:00 P.M.; it is run by the Oklahoma Historical Society. Call (580) 323–7866 for information. Admission is $3.00.

As it happens, a living example of the archetypal 1960s motel is found just across the street at **Doc Mason's Best Western Tradewinds Motel,** 2128 Gary Boulevard; (580) 323–2610. The motel's most famous guest was probably Elvis, who stayed at the hotel during road trips to Las Vegas. (The King didn't like to fly, according to the motel owner.) Ask for rooms 215 or 238; both are "Elvis Rooms."

Built in 1963, the motel has been updated over the years but still manages to exude nostalgia, from the cactus out front to the clattering coffee shop. The front desk will deliver a card table to your room, and you can order steak, pork chops, and chicken-fried steak from room service.

The sandstone arch and entrance to **McLain Rogers Park,** (580) 323–4572, at Tenth Street and Opal, was built in 1936 by the Works Progress Administration, as was its sandstone amphitheater. The amphitheater hosts live, free entertainment—everything from gospel to country cloggers to bluegrass—every Saturday night from Memorial Day weekend straight through to Labor Day. The park has playgrounds, sand volleyball courts, and a big pool where visitors can take a swim.

Just across the Washita River and on the south side of the road, a canvas tepee serves as a marker for the **Mohawk Trading Post,** situated where Business 40 begins to curve south to rejoin the interstate. The trading post is deceptively nondescript from the highway; the tepee on the front lawn is the only thing that distinguishes the redbrick building. The trading post, the oldest Indian-goods store in Oklahoma, was first established in 1892 in Colony, a Cheyenne-Arapaho community southeast of Clinton. The operation was moved to Clinton in 1942 to take advantage of the Route 66 traffic. Cheyenne and Arapaho women kept the shop supplied with beadwork, and over the years, the trading post's two owners kept examples of some of the most exquisite artistry for themselves, displaying it in the shop with early twentieth-century studio portraits of Cheyenne chiefs and photographs of tribal gatherings. Today, the collection is breathtaking; the rows of beaded pouches and buckskin dresses glow with the patina of age and from the quality of the pre–World War II Czechoslovakian cut-glass beads (still the choice of Native American artists). Some of the old Indian beadwork is for sale, and visitors can also buy pottery, hides, appliquéd dance shawls and moccasins made by hand by Cheyenne seamstresses, beading supplies, Pendleton blankets, and other items. Outside, near the tepee, the wooden Seger House has been moved to Clinton from Colony; inside its walls, generations of Cheyenne-Arapaho women have gathered to make moccasins and dresses. The Mohawk Trading Post is open Monday through Saturday from 9:00 A.M. to 5:00 P.M.; (580) 323–2360.

The **Cheyenne Cultural Center,** (580) 323–6224, is just east of the trading post on I–40. Echinacea, yarrow, aloe, and other plants with medicinal and ceremonial value to Plains tribes grow along the walk to the front door. Under a pavilion, artists sculpt, paint, and string beads while visitors watch. Peace Chief Lawrence Hart built the center to keep the Cheyenne heritage alive; he didn't want Cheyenne traditions, especially the language, to die with the tribe's elders. The center houses an art gallery, gift shop, and a learning center with computers that teach the Cheyenne language.

South of Clinton, on Highway 183, you will find **Cordell.** The town may be small, but its people are big in heritage and heart. The first and only city in Oklahoma to receive the "Great American Main Street Award" from the National Trust for Historic Preservation in 1999 for its historic and community development, the town has continued its restoration efforts despite the many setbacks Oklahoma weather has dealt them. Cordell is centered around a town square where the Washita County Courthouse is located. Several buildings are listed on the National Register, one of them being the Carnegie Library Building, now home to the Washita County Historical Society. One of the oldest buildings in town was built in 1903. The City National Bank of New Cordell was one of the first brick buildings built in the National Register District. Fifth-generation proprietors Phil and Milli Kliewer have renewed the building and turned the upstairs into studio apartments called **The Bank Lofts,** www.thebanklofts.com. Museums, galleries, antiques shops, restaurants, bed-and-breakfasts, Oklahoma history and its spirit await visitors when they visit Cordell. For a walking-tour map of Cordell or for more information, call (405) 832–5888 or go to www.cordellmainstreet.org.

Places to Stay in the Southwest Passage

ALTUS
Best Western
2804 North Main Street
(580) 482–9300

ANADARKO
Payless Inn
1602 East Central
(405) 247–2538

CHEYENNE
Ivy Rose Cottage
210 South Cearlock
(580) 497–3505
www.ivyrose.net

CLINTON
Best Western Tradewinds
2128 Gary Boulevard
(580) 323–2610

Travelodge
2247 West Gary Boulevard
(580) 323–6840

ELK CITY
Holiday Inn
I–40 and Highway 6
(580) 225–6637

Motel 6
2604 East Highway 66
(580) 225–2241

Ramada Inn,
I–40 and Highway 6
(580) 225–8140

LAWTON
Best Western Lawton Hotel
and Convention Center
1125 East Gore Street
(580) 353–0200

Red Lion Hotel
3134 Cache Road
(580) 353–1682

Places to Eat in the Southwest Passage

ALTUS
Main Street Grill
1220 North Main Street
(580) 482–1440

Val's It's About Time
800 North Main Street
(580) 482–4580

ANADARKO
Indian City Lanes Cafe
131 East Broadway
(405) 247–3060

K.I.G. Que (barbecue)
115 East Market
(405) 247–2454

Nicoli's Italian Restaurant
north of town on
Highway 8
(405) 247–6340

FOR MORE INFORMATION

Anadarko Chamber of Commerce
Kentucky and Mission Streets
Box 366
Anadarko 73005
(405) 247–6651
www.anadarko.org

Clinton Chamber of Commerce
400 Gary Boulevard
Clinton 73601
(580) 323–2222
www.clintonok.org

Elk City Chamber
1016 Airport Industrial Road
(580) 225–0207
www.elkcitychamber.com

Lawton Chamber of Commerce
607 East Avenue
Lawton 73502
(580) 355–3541
www.lawtonfortsillchamber.com

APACHE

Farmer's Roost Cafe
(family style)
109 Evans Street
(580) 588–2899

CHEYENNE

B & H Restaurant
102½ North Cearlock Road
(580) 497–2339

Las Casuelas
209 Li Males
(580) 497–3433

CLINTON

Cafe Downtown Clinton
502 Frisco
(580) 323–2289

Jigg's Smokehouse
west of town on I–40
(580) 323–5641

Oakwood Steakhouse
1200 South Tenth
(580) 323–5550

Pedro's Mexican Food
1223 Avant
(580) 323–2944

**Wong's Chinese
Restaurant**
712 Opal
(580) 323–4588

ELK CITY

**Country Dove Gifts & Tea
Room**
610 West Third
(580) 225–7028

**Lupe's Mexican
Restaurant**
905 North Main
(580) 225–7109

LAWTON

Empress of China
2910 Northwest
Cache Road
(580) 357–8411

Martin's (fine dining)
2107 Cache Road
(580) 353–5286

Sophie's Gyros
312 Southwest Sheridan
Road
(580) 355–0656

MEDICINE PARK

Mercantile Hall
Creekside
(580) 529–2525

Riverside Café
Eastlake Drive
(580) 529–2626

High Plains:
Northwestern Oklahoma

Coronado, who crossed through the Panhandle in 1541, was one of the first travelers to record remarks on the flatness of the land in northwestern Oklahoma. "One can see the sky between the legs of the buffalo," he marveled, "and if a man lay down on his back, he lost sight of the ground." Today, roads here are so straight, there's even a truck stop named "The Curve," in reference to a rare bend in the highway. But for all its flatness, northwestern Oklahoma holds some of the most unusual geology in the state: Salt plains, sand dunes, red buttes, wooded canyons, and vast underground caverns wait for travelers who venture off the main roads.

Highway 3 bisects the region, connecting to nearly every major thoroughfare in the state. The most scenic stretch of road, Highway 325 from Boise City to Kenton, wasn't paved until after World War II.

Canyon Country

Just north of where U.S. Highway 281 crosses the Canadian River is **Watonga,** population 3,500, named for the Arapaho chief Watonga, whose name means "black coyote." The town

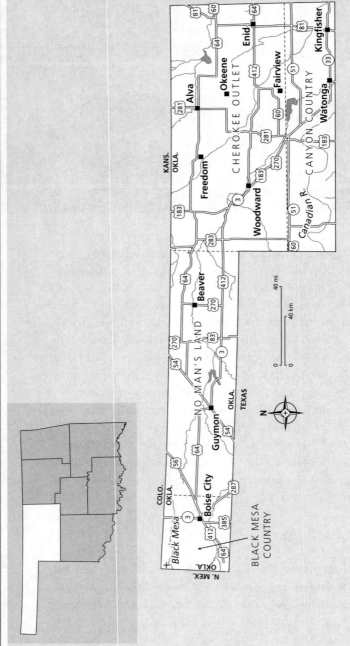

was settled after the 1892 opening of the Cheyenne and Arapaho reservation and was home to one of the most listened-to people of all time: Clarence Nash, the voice of Donald Duck.

Watonga's small downtown retains a historic quality, thanks to renovations like the *Noble House Restaurant.* Located in a 1912 two-story building that was once a rooming house and has been recently restored, the place looks as good as—maybe better than—the day it opened. Outside, the redbrick building's wood trim and second-story porch are painted a soft green and cream. Inside, the three dining rooms, with polished pine floors, dark green walls, and lace curtains, are usually packed for lunch. The regular menu offers a long list of hearty sandwiches, soups, and salads, augmented with a couple of daily specials, such as chicken-fried steak or lasagna. Noble House rolls and bread pudding are always available, along with an assortment of pies, cakes, and other desserts. A specialty is Watonga Cheese Soup, made with cheddar cheese from a local cheese factory. The restaurant is open Monday through Saturday from 7:00 A.M. to 8:00 P.M. and on Sunday from 11:00 A.M. to 2:00 P.M. The restaurant is at 112 North Noble; (580) 623–2559.

Next door, *The Place To Be* offers weary travelers hour-long massages, reflexology, European hot-towel facials, and foot baths. To make an appointment call (580) 623–2451.

History buffs and fans of the novelist Edna Ferber should head straight to the *T. B. Ferguson Home,* the former residence of newspaper publisher and territorial governor Thomas Benton Ferguson and his wife, Elva. Ferguson was thirty years old when he staked a claim near Oklahoma City during the 1889 Land Run; he sold the claim and moved to Kansas, where he became a newspaper editor. He returned to Oklahoma after the 1892 opening of Cheyenne and Arapaho lands, hauling printing equipment in a covered wagon. He started the Watonga *Republican* and became an outspoken proponent of statehood.

AUTHOR'S FAVORITES IN THE HIGH PLAINS

Alabaster Caverns State Park	Plains Indians and Pioneer Museum
Black Mesa State Park	Roman Nose State Park
Little Sahara State Park	Salt Plains National Wildlife Refuge
Museum of the Cherokee Strip	Selman Bat Cave
No Man's Land Historical Museum	Sod House Museum

TOP EVENTS IN THE HIGH PLAINS

Bitter Creek Frontier Daze,
Roman Nose State Park, mid-February;
(580) 623–7281

Cimarron Territory Celebration,
Beaver, mid-April;
(580) 625–4726

Kenton Easter Pageant,
Easter Sunday;
(580) 261–7424

Tri-State Festival,
Enid, last weekend in April;
(580) 237–4964

Pioneer Days Rodeo and Celebration,
Guymon, first weekend in May;
(580) 338–3376

Santa Fe Trail Daze,
Boise City and Kenton, early June;
(580) 544–3344

National John Deere 2-Cylinder Tractor Show,
Fairview, mid-July;
(580) 227–2527

Selman Bat Watch,
Woodward, July;
(405) 424–0099

Freedom Rodeo,
Freedom, mid-August;
(580) 621–3276
www.freedomokla.com

Earthbike Fellowship Mountain Bike Ride,
Roman Nose State Park,
third week in September;
(580) 623–4215

Watonga Cheese Festival,
Watonga, mid-October;
(580) 623–5452

Appointed governor of Oklahoma Territory in 1901, Ferguson served until 1906. He built the two-story white house in 1907, the same year Oklahoma became a state. After Ferguson's death in 1921, Elva continued to publish the paper until her retirement in 1930. Edit the story and rearrange the details and you have the plot of *Cimarron*, Edna Ferber's novel about the settlement of Oklahoma and a fiery young newspaper man, which was made into a movie of the same name. Ferber stayed at the house in 1927, gathering material. The house is filled with period furnishings and memorabilia, including a first edition of *Cimarron*. The back porch holds records and historical photographs of the family and early twentieth-century Watonga. An 1870 U.S. Cavalry log remount station and the old Watonga city jail have been moved to the backyard. The house is at 519 North Weigel, Watonga, a block west of Noble, and is open for tours Thursday through Saturday from 10:00 A.M. to 4:00 P.M.; (580) 623–5069.

As you drive south on North Weigel, look out for a little white clapboard church with a bell tower on the corner of Second Street and Weigel. The Presbyterian church was built in 1903 and has recently been restored. No longer used for services, it's open only by appointment; call (580) 623–7397.

Another Watonga institution is the **Watonga Cheese Factory,** (888) 270–5915 or www.watongacheese.com, built in 1940 as a cooperative by local dairy farmers looking for a market for the surplus milk they produced. The invention of refrigerated trucks eliminated the need for such local factories, and now the Watonga Cheese Factory is the only one left in the state. Today workers in a low, one-story, white building make between 2,000 and 8,000 pounds of cheddar cheese daily. A retail store operates in the front of the building, where a window has been installed so visitors can look in on the manufacturing process. Along with Oklahoma-shaped bricks of cheddar, the store sells an array of specialty cheeses and made-in-Oklahoma sausages, jellies, salsas, and mixes. The cheese factory is at 314 East Second Street. In mid-October, Watonga hosts a Cheese Festival downtown, featuring foods made in Oklahoma, a parade, and crafts shows.

From Watonga, head north on Highway 8 for 3 miles and then west on Highway 8A to **Roman Nose State Park,** built around a cedar-filled canyon tucked into the red prairie. After miles of prairie landscape, the small red mesas that dot the park are a visual treat. There's more to come: A subterranean river pumps a million gallons of water a day into the Springs of Everlasting Water. The cold spring water fills a lake and a rock-lined swimming pool and waters the park's many hardwood trees. The canyon is sheltered from the cold winds that blow during the winter, and the springs attract wild game, making an ideal winter camp for the Cheyenne who hunted buffalo on the plains. The park is named for Cheyenne Chief Henry Caruthers Roman Nose, who came to the Cheyenne-Arapaho reservation with his family after they were removed from North Dakota in 1868. Roman Nose was among a group of twenty-eight Cheyenne arrested for raiding white settlements in 1875 and imprisoned in St. Augustine, Florida. Roman Nose became chief in 1889. In 1891, before the opening of the reservation lands, he chose his old campgrounds as his allotment. Roman Nose died in 1917, and the canyons became a city park, later deeded to the state. Civilian Conservation Corps crews built the rock-lined swimming pool and the paths that lead down to the springs. In addition to a forty-seven-room lodge, there are cabins, tent campsites, electricity and water for RVs, and a circle of canvas tepees pitched on a concrete pad with electrical outlets on the center pole. It's rugged country, good for moun-

topride

Outside magazine included the 10-mile Roman Nose Trail in Roman Nose State Park in its rankings of the top fifty mountain biking rides in the United States. The magazine praised the scenic 200-mile views but warned riders of "wild dips and swoops over 'roots' that can turn out to be rattlers."

tain biking: A loop takes bikers through the gypsum hills, with plenty of cactus and boulders to make things interesting along the way. The terrain makes for rugged horse trails as well.

Wranglers dress in authentic nineteenth-century cowboy gear for interpretive Roman Nose Trail Rides through the backside of the canyon, telling stories collected from local Arapaho and pioneer families along the way. The Roman Nose Stables has a collection of nineteenth-century cowboy saddles and cavalry saddles for guests to use, and even the horses are in historical context. Many of them are wild mustangs, broken to the saddle by inmates in an innovative program at a state prison. Rides—the most challenging that travelers will find short of the Rockies—are one or two hours long, or guests can sign up for a campfire cookout with steaks, corn on the cob, and brown beans cooked over an open fire. The campfire ride requires reservations and a minimum of four people. Trail riders have to be at least eight years old. Open-range riding is available. Call (580) 623–4121 for more information.

Cowboys, cavalry, U.S. dragoons, marshals, outlaws, and cattle drovers are among the characters who are brought to life during **Bitter Creek Frontier Daze,** held in February. In this event, subtitled "A Walk Through Oklahoma History Featuring the Period 1830–1890," reenactors station themselves along a path cleared into the woods so that visitors walk through Indian and buffalo hunters' camps, drop in on an outlaw gang, or visit a moonshiner's still. Western heritage arts and crafts are for sale in an enclosed building. Even golf gets a little wild and woolly at Roman Nose: One golf pro sighted a mother bobcat and her cubs sunning themselves on the number-seven green. As lush as irrigation and modern science can make the western prairie, the nine-hole course is also rife with canyon hazards and round bits of gypsum masquerading as golf balls. Duffers are advised not to try to retrieve balls that go down in the canyons; golfers may encounter rattlesnakes. For information about the park or for lodge or cabin reservations, call (580) 623–7281.

themarryingtree

Along U.S. Highway 81 north of Hennessey stands a lightning-damaged, disease-ravaged old cottonwood tree. The only tree around, it at one time provided more than shade for the settlers. It was a sacred place of matrimony for several couples, who, at the last minute, realized they had to get married in the same county where they had obtained their marriage license. Several couples got licenses in Enid, in Garfield County, and had their weddings in Hennessey, which is in Kingfisher County. Often, not realizing the error until the ceremony, the minister would move the wedding party 3½ miles north, to the county line. A legal wedding would take place under the branches of the old cottonwood tree.

Okeene's Rattlesnake Hunt

In western Oklahoma, killing rattlesnakes in spring used to be considered the neighborly thing to do, practically a civic duty. The contemporary hunt, held the first weekend of each May, was started by the Jaycees in 1939. The sixty-year-old tradition makes for some mind-bending contrasts: the juxtaposition of a pancake breakfast with "The Den of Death" display of live rattlers, for example. Visitors can rent "snake-catchers"—long sticks with hooks on the end—and snake bags from the Jaycee Headquarters. They are also soberly instructed to head straight for the Okeene Municipal Hospital in the event of a snakebite (and then contact a member of the Jaycees).

According to the Okeene Chamber of Commerce, no one has ever died from a rattlesnake bite sustained during the hunt. Those who are bitten get a consolation prize—a plaque and membership in the White Fang Club. Information about the hunt is linked to the Web page at www.okeene.com or you can call (580) 822–3101.

Next to rattlesnakes, *Okeene* is best known for wildflowers. Freddie Lorenz, second-generation owner of *Lorenz's Seeds,* (580) 822–3655, harvests and packages wildflower seeds from local pastures. He sells dozens of varieties, including Indian blanket, Indian grass, and Indian paintbrush. The seed of the latter is so fine, it must be handpicked; one worker can harvest about half a pound on a good day. Okeene has only one stoplight; Lorenz's is next to the light.

Cherokee Outlet

Highway 51 crosses the Cimarron River east of Okeene and intersects with Highway 81, which picks up the course of the Chisholm Trail to *Enid,* (580) 233–5914, www.enidchamber.com. If you look on a highway map, you'll see a little jog just north of the Garfield County line. When the highway was widened a few decades ago, it deviated from its straight path to detour around an old historic tree that marked the boundary for the 1889 Land Run and the opening of the Cherokee Outlet in 1893. The tree is gone now, done in by old age and lightning strikes, but there's a marker commemorating the 1889 Land Run where the tree once stood.

The 1893 run into the Cherokee Strip wasn't the first of the five land runs in Oklahoma, but it was by far the biggest; the country was in an economic slump and 100,000 settlers turned out to race for 50,000 claims.

The Cherokee Outlet

The Treaty of New Echota of 1835 gave the Cherokee Tribe ownership of land in northwestern Oklahoma; it was called the Cherokee "Outlet" because it guaranteed the Cherokee a right-of-way to western hunting grounds. After the Civil War, the federal government took the position that the Cherokee had broken their treaties, since some tribal members fought for the Confederacy. Beginning in 1866, the Cherokee ceded land to other Indian tribes, including the Tonkawa, Ponca, Pawnee, Cheyenne, and Arapaho, who were forced to the territory by the settlement of other states. After the Civil War, cattle trails, including the Chisholm, crossed over the grasslands, and cattle ranchers began to lease the remaining Cherokee lands from the tribe. After the 1889 opening of Old Oklahoma Territory in the central part of the state, the populace began to clamor for the federal government to make the Cherokee Outlet available to homesteaders. In 1890 President Benjamin Harrison negotiated to purchase absolute title to the land from the Cherokee, ordered all the ranchers out, and prepared to open the lands for settlement.

The whole story of the run is unfurled in Enid at the *Museum of the Cherokee Strip,* which underwent extensive renovations and additions when the one-hundredth anniversary of the run of 1893 was celebrated. Most significant is the *Humphrey Heritage Village,* a collection of vintage buildings so immaculately restored they look like they could be on Disneyland's Main Street. There's a turreted two-story frame house that belonged to a homesteader-turned-banker, a church, a 1902 schoolhouse, and a real prize: the only known U.S. land office still in existence. The land office had been used in the interim as a house, but, beneath lathe and plaster, restorers found relics of the land-run days: old railroad advertisements, a spot where the original registrar signed his name, and the admonition, DON'T SPIT ON THE FLOOR.

The museum is next to the lush, expansive *Government Springs Park,* established around springs that watered cattle and horses along the Chisholm Trail. The museum and the park are at the corner of Fourth Street and Owen Garriott Boulevard, also the path of U.S. Highway 412 through town. The museum, which is operated by the Oklahoma Historical Society, is open Tuesday through Saturday from 9:00 A.M. to 5:00 P.M.; closed Sunday and Monday. Call (580) 237–1907 for information.

The *Railroad Museum of Oklahoma,* north on Grand then 3 blocks west on Chestnut Street to 702 North Washington Street, features rolling stock including cabooses, a baggage car, and motor cars. It also has an exhaustive collection of model railroads, signs, dining-car china, and railroad esoterica, such as examples of the paper currency used by railroads between 1834 and

1878 collected from 108 different lines. Housed in a restored Santa Fe Freight Depot, the museum displays 6,000 postcards of railroad depots. The museum is operated by a nonprofit organization and staffed by enthusiastic volunteers. Museum hours are Tuesday through Friday 1:00 to 4:00 P.M., Saturday from 10:00 A.M. to 1:00 P.M., and Sunday from 2:00 to 5:00 P.M., or by appointment; call (580) 233–3051.

Rockhounds will love the quirky **Midgley Museum**, (580) 234–7265, the former home of Dan and Libbie Midgley, who not only filled their house with their collections of fossils, rocks, crystals, and petrified wood but also covered the facade with a mosaic of stones, Texas horn crystal, and geological oddities. Among the museum's treasures are a 7,000-pound petrified redwood stump and a bone from a woolly mammoth. The museum is open Wednesday through Friday from 10:00 A.M. to 5:00 P.M. and on Saturday from 2:00 to 5:00 P.M. The museum is at 1001 Sequoyah Drive, 1 block south of the intersection of US 412 and US 81. (The Enid Convention and Visitors Bureau operates a visitors' center at the southwest corner of the intersection.)

Astronaut and Enid native Owen K. Garriott provided seed money for the foundation that created **Leonardo's Discovery Warehouse**, a hands-on arts-and-sciences museum housed in two stories of what was once a wholesale grocery warehouse. (That's *Leonardo* as in *da Vinci*.) Science exhibits change weekly, and there is a sandy area in which to dig for fossils, as well as a 750-gallon fish tank, computer and music labs, a carpentry shop, and a Castle Courtyard stocked with royal garb and equipped with thrones, scepters, and a maze. Adventure Quest across the street is the most spectacular playground in the state and features a three-story slide and a host of other kid-pleasing features. (Builders made sure kids would like it by including Enid children on the design committee.) Admission to Leonardo's is $6.00 per person; admission for children under two is free. The museum is open Tuesday through Saturday from 10:00 A.M. to 5:00 P.M. and on Sunday from 2:00 to 5:00 P.M. The street address is 200 East Maple. Call (580) 233–2787 for information.

Enid's historical downtown is anchored by a courthouse square surrounded by antiques malls and stores. To experience true Oklahoma hospitality, you might want to stay at **Maple Place Bed and Breakfast**, www.mapleplace.com, located in the heart of Enid and built in 1902. The owners, Brent and Jennifer Kisling, welcome guests with a cheese and fruit basket when they check in. Four rooms are now available—the State Room, decorated in blue and white, showing off the elegance of Oklahoma; the Redbud Room, named for the state tree, done in burgundy and red with a king-size bed and Jacuzzi; the Amber Waves Room, where guests will enjoy the hardwood floors, farming antiques, red-white-and-blue decor, and glassed-in shower; and the Scissortail Cottage, named for Oklahoma's state bird. The cottage offers visitors all the comforts of home and includes a king-size bed, big-screen television, and two-person Jacuzzi with rainfall shower. Prices start at $40 a night for extended stay in the rooms, to $115 a night in the cottage. Call (580) 234–5858.

Many descendants of the 1893 homesteaders still make their living on their great-grandparents' claims—some in ways their ancestors could never have imagined. A case in point is found at the **Robert Bartunek Winery** in south Enid, where a fledgling vineyard has been planted on a claim staked by Robert Bartunek's wife, Jean's, great-grandfather. The tree where he tied his horse to actually claim the property is still standing just north of the parking lot. Robert Bartunek has planted a few acres of *vinifera* grapes—Chardonnay, Cabernet Sauvignon, and Muscat Blanc—and makes wine from those and other Oklahoma-grown grapes. Bartunek is convinced that Enid's climate and soil, which make it a prime wheat-growing area, are also ideal for growing grapes. (Judge for yourself with a tasting.) The winery, housed in an addition to the Bartuneks' home, is open for tours on Friday and Saturday from 1:00 to 5:00 P.M. The Bartuneks are available to give tours at other times, too; make an appointment by calling (580) 233–6337, or, if you drive by, look for the yellow flag with a red lion that signifies that the winery is open. In addition to wine, a little shop sells Oklahoma-made mustards, jellies, jams, and sauces as well as grapevine-cutting gift baskets and T-shirts and sweatshirts with the winery's logo. The winery is south from US 412 on Cleveland Street, west of the intersection of US 412 and 81, then about ½ block west on Rupe Street.

US 412 west of Enid intersects with a farm-to-market road leading south toward Ames and **Island Guest Ranch.** *Island* refers to the location—straddling the sandy Cimarron River—but the 4,800-acre ranch can also be considered a refuge from ringing telephones and gridlock.

Accessible along a farm-to-market road, the cattle ranch has been in the White family for more than a century; in the 1980s ranchers Carl and Mary White built some Southwest-style cabins, had a pool put in, and opened for business as a guest ranch as a hedge against unpredictable cattle markets. Fishing in two lakes and horseback riding entertain guests in the daytime. (Depending on their level of skill, guests can ride out with Carl to check the cattle.) If there isn't a local rodeo or powwow within easy driving distance (the Whites provide transportation), wranglers demonstrate and teach the fine points of team penning. Meals are served in a lodge built with cedar, cottonwood, yellow pine, and catalpa logs. The average rate is $120 a day for adults, all meals and activities included. Open April through September. For reservations and directions call (580) 753–4574 or (800) 928–4574.

From Enid, take US 81 north to where it ends at its intersection with U.S. Highway 64; then take US 64 west to Jet. Drive north from Jet along Highway 38 to the entrance to **Salt Plains National Wildlife Refuge,** where the wheat fields of alfalfa country have given way to a landscape that looks like the surface of a pale moon. The crumbly salt on a 7-mile-long, 3-mile-wide swath was deposited underground more than 200 million years ago. An inland sea once covered northwest Oklahoma, and as it receded and dried, it left tons of sea salt behind. In the salt plains, groundwater brings the salt steadily upward; some flows into the Salt Fork of the Arkansas River, and some is left behind on the ground. The Osage, who hunted buffalo in the area, knew the area as "Big Salt" and used the area's salt to preserve buffalo meat. Animals came to the plains for salt, which also attracted a human population. The area was so important to Native American hunters for both salt and game that when the government negotiated with the Cherokee Tribe in the 1830s for their Cherokee Strip, the salt plains were excluded so that other tribes could continue to hunt and gather salt there.

An estimated 250 species of birds have been spotted at **Great Salt Plains State Park,** www.greatsaltplains.com, on the east side of the reservoir and also off Highway 38. The park has cabins, ninety campsites, picnic areas, a nature trail, and showers.

Keep the showers in mind, because from May to October an area in the southwest portion of the refuge is opened so visitors can dig for tea-colored

A Sea of Salt

Daniel Boone's son Nathan, a captain in the army, traveled to survey the salt plains with a company of soldiers in 1843 and noted in his journal: "Such was the effect of Mirage on the plain that we could not see across it. . . . The buffalo bones whitening in the sun looked like large white animals in the distance. Buffalo appeared to be standing in water, and, in fact, the whole plain appeared as if surrounded by water."

Today the salt plains are still owned by the government. The federal wildlife refuge was formed in 1930, and the Arkansas River was dammed to create the Great Salt Plains Reservoir in 1939.

Together, the more than 32,000 acres of shoreline, marshes, and salt plains are a powerful draw for wildlife, particularly migratory birds. Every winter, the refuge is host to golden and bald eagles, snowy plovers, pelicans, sandhill cranes, and even a family of whooping cranes. Interior least terns nest on the refuge in elevated platforms. A 2½-mile-long road takes visitors past land flooded to create habitat for waterfowl, and a hiking trail has an observation tower that looks out over the plains.

selenite, and it's very dirty work. Selenite is a crystallized form of gypsum, a mineral that is abundant just below the surface of the plains. When saline water passes through the gypsum, crystals are formed. The crystals are formed in wet sand, so bits of clay and soil often form a distinct hourglass shape within the crystal. Oklahoma's Great Salt Plains are the only place in the world where the hourglass crystals are found. Both single crystals and starlike clusters are found in the sand; some individual crystals measure up to 7 inches long, and one thirty-eight-pound cluster was unearthed. The area open for public digging is rotated every year to allow crystals to form and to protect the area, which is a refuge for endangered least terns. Wildlife officials once worried that allowing the public to dig for crystals might have a negative effect on the birds, but they learned that the terns nest in the holes left behind by crystal diggers and are hidden from predators.

To reach the digging area, travel 6 miles west of Jet on US 64, then north on a dirt road for 3 miles. A paved road takes travelers 1 mile east to the crystal-digging area. There are no nearby facilities, save for rest rooms.

About 20 miles south on Highway 8, south of the little town of Aline, is the ***Sod House Museum,*** (580) 463–2441, which shelters the last sod house still standing on the Oklahoma prairies. The earthen houses once dotted the area, because the Homestead Act required all settlers to improve their claims with a dwelling within a year. On those claims that lacked timber or even hills where dugouts could be constructed, settlers cut blocks of sod from the prairie and used them as if they were bricks. The structures remained plenty earthy; sheets were generally draped overhead to catch the snakes that dropped into the houses. The sod house at Aline was built in 1894 by Marshall McCully, a homesteader who made the walls a foot thick and plastered the insides with alkali mud dug from a riverbed. Part of the reason McCully's soddy was so

Shorebird Sanctuary

The Salt Plains National Wildlife Refuge is one of fewer than three dozen sites in the Western Hemisphere named to the Western Hemisphere Shorebird Reserve Network, a list of sites recognized as critical to the survival of shorebirds. The refuge is along the Central Flyway and is a stopover for birds making migrations from Canada to South America. Thirty-six species of shorebirds have been spotted at the refuge, including American avocets, sandpipers, piping plovers, long-billed curlews, and Hudsonian godwits. The Sandpiper Trail, with a wooden observation deck and high-powered scope, is just off Highway 11, northeast of Cherokee.

May and June are the best times to spot the shorebirds.

Digging for Selenite Crystals

Selenite crystals are fragile, particularly when wet, so local rock hounds advise this method of uncovering the crystals: Dig a hole about 2 feet wide and 2 feet deep and wait for it to fill with water. (The water table is very high and it won't take long.) With your hand or with a cup, gently pour water down the sides of the hole. Sand will wash away, revealing the selenite crystals below. Continue to wash the sand gently away with water—tugging on the crystals may break them. Once they are excavated, the sun and wind will dry them out, and they will become much sturdier. Experienced diggers bring an old towel or plastic sheeting for kneeling on in the muddy, salty sand, plenty of water to drink, and empty egg cartons to carry home treasure. They also avoid the midday sun and slather on the sunscreen. Hands-on instruction is available the first weekend in late April or early May, when the town of Cherokee hosts a Crystal Digging Festival and experienced selenite "miners" are on hand to teach novices how to uncover the best specimens. In town, the Cherokee Volunteer Fire Department and the Cherokee Police Department sponsor a carnival and "Crystal Bingo."

sturdy, a story goes, is that he dug packed, compacted sod from a buffalo wallow. (Even though buffalo vanished from the prairies more than a century ago, buffalo wallows remain and become apparent after heavy rains.) The McCully family lived in the house until 1909, when they moved into a frame house built right next to the soddy. The soddy was well maintained over the years— because the family continued to use it as a pantry—and even outlasted the farmhouse, which burned a few decades ago. Today, a frame building has been constructed around the soddy to preserve it, and the artifacts on display—tools, saddles, dishes—are intended to interpret early farm life on the prairies. For a Pioneer Christmas, held during December, the museum staff decorates for the holidays using the same materials settlers of that region would have: a stack of tumbleweeds trimmed with crocheted doilies, wheat weavings, and "icicles" made of twisted strips of tin cans. On Pioneer Craft Day, held the Saturday of Labor Day weekend, artisans demonstrate early-day household skills, such as weaving, spinning, and rug making. The museum is open Tuesday through Friday from 9:00 A.M. to 5:00 P.M. and Saturday and Sunday from 2:00 to 5:00 P.M.

Not far from the sod house is another distinctive, even odd, structure, the **_Heritage Manor Bed and Breakfast,_** www.1aj.org, a rambling twenty-room Victorian-style dwelling created from a 1903 house and a 1906 house pieced together, with the stairways, moldings, light fixtures, stained-glass windows, and other architectural elements taken from dozens more houses. The result is highly individual (and a bit chaotic): There are eight staircases, a suspension bridge, three decks, four verandas, and a rooftop spa. The house sits in splendid isolation on twenty acres of dirt roads and wildflower meadows, looking a little like the mansion in *Giant*. Longhorn cattle wander the property, but the ostriches are penned up. There are four guest rooms, a dining room where breakfast, lunch, and dinner are available (innkeepers Carolyn and A. J. Rexroat used to run a restaurant), and a 5,000-volume library. For reservations call (580) 463–2563.

havecarwill travel

Ready to check out some of Oklahoma's wildlife? Look no farther than the western part of the state. The Oklahoma Wildlife and Prairie Heritage Alliance, www.owpha.org, with its partners and volunteers has unveiled the *Great Plains Trails of Oklahoma.* These trails consist of thirteen loops that cover 1,777 miles and include 33 counties. Travelers will be able to view some of Oklahoma's unique and diverse wildlife species including prairie chickens, "horny" toads, scissor-tail flycatchers, and elk plus experience some of the state's small-town hospitality. Visit www .wildlifedepartment.com/wildlifetrails .htm or call (800) 652–6552 for a Great Plains Trails of Oklahoma map.

U.S. Highway 60 and US 412 intersect just south of Orienta. South of the intersection is *Fairview,* an agricultural community where a large population of Mennonites have made their homes. The founding families of Fairview's Mennonite Brethren Church emigrated from Russia, bringing with them red winter wheat, which flourished on the prairies.

One family bequeathed a quarter-section farm to the local historical society, which built the *Major County Historical Museum.* The museum has a nice collection of artifacts, but the real excitement occurs behind the museum, where pastures are slowly filling up with historical buildings donated and restored by local residents. The section is also plowed and planted with wheat each year, to feed the "thrashers" at the Major County Threshing Bee, when vintage steam-powered threshing machines are demonstrated. Local cooks also demonstrate the proper way to feed a threshing crew, with pots of *bierocks* (meat-and-cabbage-stuffed biscuits), German cherry soup, and cheese dumplings.

In July the grounds are a sea of yellow and green: The National John Deere 2-Cylinder Tractor Show brings old tractor lovers to Fairview from as far away as Canada.

The cooks come out in force, too, for the Mennonite Relief Sale, held annually on the weekend after Thanksgiving at the Major County Fairgrounds. A grilled chicken dinner is served on Friday night, there's a pancake breakfast on

Saturday morning, and Saturday lunch features *veranki* (filled dumplings with onion gravy), sauerkraut, and cherry soup. If you're still hungry, you can sate your appetite at food booths selling German sausage, sugar-coated raisin cookies, apple butter, pastries, and homemade bread. Saturday's highlight is the quilt auction, where upward of one hundred quilts made by community members are sold. All proceeds go the Mennonite Central Committee for hunger relief. The museum is 1½ miles east of Fairview on Highway 58. Call (580) 227–2265 or visit www.mchsok.com for information.

No restaurants in Fairview regularly sell *veranki* or *bierocks,* but the blue-plate special at **Frank's Country Kitchen,** (580) 227–2242, at 508 South Main, includes homemade bread and dishes such as skillet-fried chicken, meat loaf, roast beef, turkey and dressing, and barbecued ribs and briskets, followed by blackberry pie, chocolate cake, or cherry crisp. The noon buffet, which offers two meats, a vegetable, salad bar, dessert, and iced tea or coffee, is a little over $5.00.

The drive west on US 412 takes travelers through Oklahoma's painted desert, the **Glass Mountains,** a series of red buttes striped with gypsum and sparkling with millions of selenite crystals. Some older maps list the buttes as the Gloss Mountains; according to an old story, the words *glass* and *gloss* became confused after a surveyor with a thick English accent came through. The buttes rise along both sides of US 412; a county road 10 miles west of the highway junction offers the chance to slow down and get a closer look. (If you get out of your car in warm months, watch for snakes.)

Ancient deposits of quartz and volcanic rock have eroded over centuries to become the sand dunes of **Little Sahara State Park,** another geological surprise in northwest Oklahoma. The dunes have been called The Walking Hills for more than a century in homage to the Oklahoma wind that can move an entire dune 20 feet in one year. The shifting winds sculpt dunes that range from 10 feet to 7 stories high and change overnight. Approximately 1,500 acres of the dunes have been set aside for the state park, which is 10 miles north of the intersection of US 412 and US 281. The park is on the west side of the highway. There are forty-five campsites at the park and a nature trail along the eastern edge of the dunes. Don't expect much peace and quiet, especially on weekends, because the dunes are a magnet for the owners of off-road vehicles and dune buggies. A cable and a barbed-wire fence cordon off the trail area, but the sounds of engines revving can be heard far into the night, despite the 11:00 P.M. to 7:00 A.M. "quiet hours" regulation. Bring your own dune buggy, or Little Sahara Tourism Rentals, (580) 824–0569, www.lspsonline.com, operates six-passenger vehicles used to squire visitors up and down the dunes for forty-minute rides. The dune buggy operation is open on weekdays from 9:00 A.M.

to 6:00 P.M. and on weekends from 8:00 A.M. to 5:00 P.M. Come early; the sand gets very hot, and there is often a waiting list for the dune buggy rides. The park telephone number is (580) 824–1471.

From Waynoka travel north on Highway 15 for 15 miles and pick up the westward track of US 64. Approximately 14 miles down the road is *Freedom,* www.freedomokla.org, population 254, a town that holds its Western heritage proudly. A few decades ago, merchants even covered storefronts with false wooden fronts and rough cedar in the fashion of a movie set. A huge granite monument, 10 feet long and 4 feet high, in the city park at the east end of Main Street, maps out the huge historic ranches that operated in the area in the nineteenth century and is engraved with their old cattle brands and the names of the cowhands who worked them. Each August, about 1,000 people attend the *Old Cowhand Reunion,* where one old cowhand is singled out for having "lived the life." Organizers treat everyone to a free beef-and-bean dinner, held at noon at the city park, and, that afternoon, locals stage the Great Freedom Bank Robbery and Shoot-out, based on a historical event. Participants, many of whom work for the local bank, take quite a lot of poetic license with the details. The Cowhand Reunion coincides with the annual Freedom Rodeo, which began in 1937. The rodeo starts at dusk, and dances are held afterward at the American Legion Building. For information call Freedom Chamber of Commerce, (580) 621–3276.

Just a few miles south of the Cimarron River on Highway 50 is a great place to cool off in the summer. The pink-and-white gypsum caves in *Alabaster Caverns State Park* average a chilly 50 degrees year-round. The 200-acre park is built around what's thought to be the largest gypsum cave in the world open to the public. Alabaster Caverns and other caves in the area were formed within the sedimentary layers of gypsum, shale, and dolomite deposited in the area during the Permian age, 250 million years ago. Through natural upheavals of the rock deposits, cracks were formed in different layers. Water began flowing through the cracks and formed tunnels and, finally, caves. Hourly tours are conducted through a ¾-mile-long route in the main cavern, which is lighted to show off pink, white, and rare black alabaster walls sparkling with selenite crystals. Rock steps have been cut into the floor in many places, and the route is not demanding.

Five other natural caves are open for exploration from May through November. Would-be spelunkers must sign a release at the park office and have the following gear: a hard hat, three light sources per person (matches and extra batteries count), a group first-aid kit, long-sleeved shirt, pants, gloves, and water. The five caves offer varying degrees of difficulty, ranging from 200-foot-long Owl Cave to the challenging Hoe Handle and Ice Stalactite Caves.

The park is tiny, with eleven RV campsites and ten tent campsites. Some of the latter, along with a swimming pool, are in the ½-mile-long Cedar Canyon, which is looped with nature trails. The park telephone number is (580) 621–3381.

Farther west on Highway 50 is **Boiling Springs State Park,** the shadiest place in summer for miles around, thanks to the hundreds of trees planted by Civilian Conservation Corps crews when they built the park during the 1930s. The park's namesake springs don't actually boil; they bubble up along the banks of the North Canadian River, where cottonwood, elm, ash, hackberry, oak, locust, and willow trees grow. There are four cabins, a pool, and numerous tent and RV campsites at the park. The Boiling Springs park office can be reached at (580) 256–7664.

Woodward, (580) 256–7411 or www.woodwardok.com, population 13,500 and northwest Oklahoma's second-largest metropolitan area, is 6 miles west of Boiling Springs. Head on out in mid-July, because that's when the Woodward Elks Club holds its annual four-day-long rodeo. The rodeo, which began in 1929, is affiliated with the Professional Rodeo Cowboys Association, which means a winner's earnings may help him get a spot at the National Finals Rodeo. All of Woodward makes a big deal out of the rodeo, decorating downtown storefronts, coming out for the Saturday parade, and treating Friday-night rodeo attendees to a free hamburger dinner. The rodeo is held at the Woodward County Fairgrounds Rodeo Arena at Crystal Beach Park. From the Woodward Fire Department on US 412, go 1 mile east to First Street, then 1½ miles south on First Street. The park and fairgrounds are on the east side of the road.

The rodeo also set off another tradition: A local Woodward couple began to make Western clothing for their daughters to wear during rodeo-queen and barrel-racing competitions, then they branched off into Western-cut suits. The

Selman Bat Cave

Think of it as a bat nursery—a gypsum cave north of the state park where a half million migratory Mexican free-tailed bats (Tadarida brasiliensis) come each spring to give birth. Each adult bat typically gives birth to one baby bat. The newborn bat can use its feet to cling to its mother or to roost when the mother leaves the cave to hunt for insects. After about a month, mothers and babies—a million in all—leave the cave each night in search of insects. The Oklahoma Department of Wildlife, which has purchased the cave to protect the bat's habitat, escorts visitors to view the nightly flight during July and August. In May and June, the area is strictly off-limits to visitors, because when mother bats become excited, they often fly off and jerk the young bats from the roosts, causing them to fall to their deaths. For information about escorted bat-viewing times, call the Wildlife Diversity Program at (405) 424–0099.

Cheyenne Memories

In 1867 the Cheyenne, who hunted buffalo on the plains, were assigned to a reservation in Indian Territory south of the Cherokee Outlet and north of the Washita River. There were not enough buffalo to support the Cheyenne there, and the U.S. government issued tribal members work clothes and plows and determined to teach them to farm.

"When [the Cheyenne] first learned to plow in Oklahoma the farmer told them to get ready and come to a certain place and he would show them. They did not understand. They thought 'get ready' meant fancy costumes and not their new pants and shirts. So everybody had feathers on their heads and necklaces and leggings and fancy moccasins. It looked like a dance, not a farming lesson. And all the women and children went along to see them."

—John Stands in Timber,
Cheyenne Memories

business opened as Trego's Westwear in the 1930s, and over the years it has suited up customers including President Dwight D. Eisenhower, Roy Rogers, and country singer Vince Gill. The flagship downtown store has closed, but a factory outlet is open at 2215 South Oklahoma, where you can get bargains on pearl-button shirts and yoked sports coats.

Even travelers who generally don't like historical museums should consider stopping at the **Plains Indians and Pioneers Museum,** www.pipml .org, which illustrates both the Native American and non-Indian settlement of the area. The artifacts at the museum aren't particularly remarkable—Cheyenne beadwork, early twentieth-century furniture, old agricultural equipment—but the interpretation is. Murals painted on the walls show the changing landscape, and museum curators have assembled stunning old photographs and, best of all, have combed newspapers, old journals, and other written records and pulled out quotes so that area history is told through the words of the people who lived it. A farmer living through the 1930s Dust Bowl gamely jokes that his carrots are beginning to grow upwards and a poignant letter from a Cheyenne chief addressed to a local lawyer shows how bewildering the concept of land ownership was to the Plains Indians. The museum is at 2009 Williams Avenue, also Highway 270, a mile south of its intersection with US 412. It's open Tuesday through Saturday from 10:00 A.M. to 5:00 P.M.; (580) 256–6136.

Travelers through western Oklahoma will notice literally hundreds of windmills dotting pastures; the development of a mass-produced steel windmill in the nineteenth century made farming possible in the Great Plains. At the outdoor **Shattuck Windmill Museum,** at the junction of Highway 15 and U.S. Highway 283, dozens of brightly painted restored windmills, dating from 1850 to 1950, swirl in the wind like giant pinwheels. Shattuck residents have also built a dugout into the side of a hill; many early settlers in the area lived in dugouts on treeless plains for the first year or two. If you call ahead to the Shattuck Chamber of

Shattuck Windmill Museum

Commerce, a guide can meet you at the park and explain the various technological advances represented. The chamber's number is (580) 938–2818.

From Woodward, U.S. Highway 270 North takes travelers toward the Panhandle and **Fort Supply Military Park.** First known as Camp Supply, the fort was established in 1868 along the Beaver River as a winter camp for soldiers on expedition against the Plains Indians. Colonel George Custer, for example, led the surprise attack of the Seventh Cavalry against the Cheyenne camped along the Washita River. The fort was attacked several times by Indian bands; roll call was at 4:00 A.M. because of the dawn attacks. Soldiers later protected a military road from Fort Dodge, Kansas, into Indian Territory, which was used to haul provisions for the Plains tribes on southern reservations. Fort Supply soldiers also policed the cattlemen who leased land from the Cherokee and negotiated rights-of-way through Cheyenne-Arapaho country. Before the Cherokee Outlet was opened, they also patrolled for Sooners who sneaked into the territory before the official opening. The fort was closed in 1894, after the railroads began to be built through the territory. Five historic structures remain at the site, including an 1879 officers' quarters, an 1892 brick guardhouse, and log cabins. The original 1869 log stockade has been reconstructed on the property, with most of the labor done by inmates at a nearby federal correctional facility. Historical photographs, artists' renderings of the fort, and artifacts that have been found at the site are displayed inside a visitors' center, which is open Tuesday through Saturday from 9:00 A.M. to 4:00 P.M. Call (580) 766–3767 for information.

No Man's Land

The Beaver County line is 30 miles west of Fort Supply and marks the eastern edge of the flat high plains of the Panhandle. The Panhandle's nickname is "No Man's Land," but since 1682, three countries and the Republic of Texas have alternately claimed the area. France first claimed the land as part of the Louisiana Purchase, then returned it to Spain in 1819. It was then transferred to Mexico in 1824, and tacked onto the Republic of Texas in 1836. Texas relinquished the land in 1845, and the borders of New Mexico Territory, Kansas, and Colorado were fixed along lines that left a strip 167 miles long and 37 miles wide. From 1861 to 1890 the area was unclaimed and filled with ranchers, squatters, Indian bands, and outlaws fleeing nearby jurisdictions. The strip formally organized itself into "Cimarron Territory" in 1887; in 1890 when Oklahoma Territory was organized, No Man's Land was attached to it, and it became the Oklahoma Panhandle.

More than a century later, the three counties in the Panhandle are still the most sparsely populated in the state, and the rules still are a little different. Between October and April, motorists should carry food, water, and extra blankets in the car, because sudden winter storms can cause whiteouts, where it's literally impossible to see beyond the hood of your car. The isolation of the residents has caused them to stick together in ways that are often heartwarming: It's the rare pickup that will pass you on the highway without the driver giving you a wave hello. Drive west through Slapout (which got its name, the story goes, because the storekeeper there was always "slap out" of everything) on US 270/Highway 3, then north on Highway 23. About 15 miles north on 23 is the little town of *Beaver,* the former capital of Cimarron Territory. A plaque downtown marks the site of the territory's two-story capitol building on Main Street, which roughly follows the track of the Jones and Plummer cattle trail. The independent streak that marks Panhandle residents was evident early on in

jimpowersjunk artmuseum

You don't have to watch too closely for the entrance to *Jim Powers Junk Art Museum,* what with the dinosaur built from tire rims in the front yard. Powers, a genial man who wears a big straw cowboy hat, owned a salvage yard for years before he began to weld together scrap metal into surprising and expressive forms. Imaginative, whimsical, and occasionally stunning, Powers's sculptures are arranged behind his shop in a kind of environmental folk art garden. He's happy to show visitors around if he's in. The museum is at the intersection of Highways 15 and 46 in Gage.

Beaver; when the MK&T Railroad cut off the county seat and went 7 miles north of town to Forgan, Beaver residents built their own rail line, which they made so profitable that the rival MK&T bought them out.

Beaver is known to radio disc jockeys throughout the country, who check in with the town during its annual World Championship Cow Chip Throw and Cimarron Territory Celebration, held in April. It's a contest that rewards long-distance tossing of, well, cow patties. The festival has historical roots, because homesteaders burned chips for fuel during long winters. During the festivities a 14-foot fiberglass beaver holding a 2-foot-wide cow patty presides over Main Street. For information, call the Beaver Chamber of Commerce, (580) 625–4726.

The shortgrass plains break into sand dunes in the 520-acre **Beaver State Park,** (580) 625–3373, across the Beaver River. Although off-road vehicles and dune buggies are allowed on the dunes, they are much less heavily used than those in Little Sahara State Park. A trail takes hikers along the fringes of the dunes. Campsites surround a small lake. The county road west of Beaver takes travelers to the **Beaver River Wildlife Management Area,** where two prairie-dog towns flourish, along with burrowing owls, foxes, prairie chickens, and songbirds. Camping is allowed in the wildlife management area, but it is closed to nonhunters between October 1 and February 1.

pickin'upchips

Buffalo were long gone from the plains by the time homesteaders arrived in the latter part of the nineteeth century, but a plentiful supply of their dried bones and manure remained. There were few trees, and many pioneers survived by burning buffalo patties. One verse of a folk song went:

"Pickin' up bones to keep from starving,

Pickin' up chips to keep from freezing,

Pickin' up courage to keep from leaving,

Way out West in No Man's Land."

You'll have to go back through Beaver to get to Highway 3; it's about another hour west to **Guymon,** (580) 338–3376, www.guymoncofc.com, where cattle are fattened on huge feedlots before they are shipped to slaughterhouses. Guymon is the largest city in the Panhandle and is home to the annual Pioneer Days Rodeo, the largest Professional Rodeo Cowboy Association event in the state and the third largest in the country. The event is held the first weekend in May, and, along with traditional rodeo events like steer roping and bronco riding, events include a parade, trail rides, a sunrise breakfast, square dancing, a carnival, barbecue, and country music.

Guymon's **Thompson Park** is built around a fishing lake with picnic tables, campgrounds, and a swimming pool and has a nearby game reserve.

The park is at the west end of First Street. From Guymon, angle southwest to Goodwell, where the approximately 1,200 students of Panhandle State University outnumber the less-than-a-thousand local residents. The ***No Man's Land Historical Museum,*** (580) 349–2670, at 207 West Sewell, Goodwell, is well marked and easy to find once you're within the city limits. The exhibits at the museum are as unique as the history of the area: documents related to feuds that broke out before local governments were established, a collection of carved alabaster miniatures, lamps, jewelry made by two brothers and a sister who lived on adjoining area ranches, and a stuffed two-headed calf, brought by a local rancher to a taxidermy class conducted at the college in the 1930s. The museum also holds regional pioneer histories, a barbed-wire collection, arrowheads, quillwork, quilts, and two desks used by the Panhandle representatives to the Oklahoma Constitutional Convention. (There have been several drives to secede from the state since then, although none has been in earnest.) Hours are Tuesday through Saturday from 10:00 A.M. to noon and 1:00 to 3:00 P.M.

A statue at the southwest end of town, *The Plainsman,* marks the entrance to the university. The county highway that leads north back to Highway 3 crosses the Beaver River and goes through areas broken up by canyons and dotted by cedar.

Black Mesa Country

Forty miles west is ***Boise City*** (*Boise,* in this case, rhymes with *voice*), one of only two incorporated towns in Cimarron County. The county is the only one in the United States to be surrounded by four different states: Kansas, New Mexico, Texas, and Oklahoma.

The path of the old ***Santa Fe Trail*** angles across the Panhandle and crosses both Highway 3, 20 miles north of Boise City, and Highway 325, at a point 20 miles west of Boise City. This portion of the Santa Fe Trail was known as the "Cimarron Cut-off," a shortcut dared by those willing to risk greater numbers of Indians and less water than encountered along the trail in Colorado. Wagons traveled three abreast along the trail, and the wales they've left behind are visible south of a historical marker on Highway 325. (The marks are quite dim and appear as discolorations in the prairie grasses.) Many historic sites related to the trail are on private land; an ideal opportunity to see them comes around each June during Santa Fe Trail Daze, when Cimarron County residents escort visitors on field trips to the sites. Among the most impressive are ***Autograph Rock,*** where signatures of nearly 200 travelers dating from the 1840s are carved, and the ruins of Camp Nichols, built in 1865 to protect travelers

The Bombing of Boise City

A monument on the courthouse lawn in Boise City pays tribute to the night of July 5, 1945, when Boise City became the only town in the continental United States to be bombed, and by U.S. troops. That night a crew took off from Dalhart Air Force Base in Texas on a training mission, armed with ten sand bombs and headed for a bombing range in the Texas Panhandle. The crew's regular navigator had a cold, and his replacement steered the crew 40 miles farther north, which put them over Boise City. Unfortunately, the four streetlights on the courthouse square were eerily similar to the bombing range target lights, so the crew dropped six one-hundred-pound bombs on Boise City. Nobody was hurt, and the damage was calculated to be one roof, a church wall, a sidewalk, and three lawns. Back at Dalhart, the plane's crew woke up to banners that read, "Remember the Alamo. Remember the *Maine*. Remember Pearl Harbor, and for God's Sake, Remember Boise City!" Boise City residents unveiled the memorial, one of the bombs nestled in a cement crater, pointed back toward Dalhart, on the fiftieth anniversary of the bombing.

along the route. At other times of the year, call the Cimarron County Chamber of Commerce to make arrangements, (580) 544–3344. The **Cimarron Heritage Center,** www.ptsi.net/users/museum, which holds area history, has an exhibit about the trail, including information about ten stops along the 70 miles of trail in Oklahoma. The museum is at 1300 North Cimarron, on U.S. Highway 287 on the north side of Boise City. The museum is open Monday through Saturday from 10:00 A.M. to noon and 1:00 to 4:00 P.M. The telephone number is (580) 544–3479.

Ever think you should have been a cowboy? The **Hitching Post** gives visitors the chance to see if they have what it takes. Located 36 miles west of Boise City, this working ranch has fences to mend, calves to brand, and cows to move, and they let guests help with all the chores. Guests can stay in a trailer home, log cabin, or in the ranch house. If guests get tired or are not interested in ranch work, they can enjoy hiking, fishing, hunting, or historical tours. Cattle drives, overnight trail rides, and cookouts can be arranged. If sightseeing is of interest, there are the Old Mummy Cave, the Dinosaur Quarry, and Black Mesa to visit. For more information call (580) 261–7413 or visit the Hitching Post Web site at www.blackmesacountry.com.

In the Panhandle, the best really is saved for last: Black Mesa, topped with black lava from a now-extinct volcano, is the high point of Oklahoma's most intriguing and beautiful landscapes. On the way, stop at **Black Mesa State Park,** built around Lake Carl Etling, where both RV and tent campsites are available. A rustic handful of cabins is usually reserved for groups, but individuals can rent a cabin if it's available, first come first served. (There's no plumbing or bedding, although bathrooms with hot showers are nearby.) Nearly eighteen tons of fossilized dinosaur bones have been quarried in Cimarron County since the 1930s, but there are still plenty left. Keep an eye out as you hike around the park for fossils and petrified wood. Maps to the hiking trail up Black Mesa are available at the park. The park's telephone number is (580) 426–2222. As you drive north along Highway 325 from the park, look for a looming Dakota sandstone formation, known locally as The Three Sisters.

The trailhead to the Black Mesa Trail is east of Kenton; the ***Kenton Mercantile,*** (580) 261–7447, is the perfect place to stock up on water and picnic supplies. The little cafe/gas station/general store was established in 1898 and still functions as the heart of the community. Dinosaur fossils and old jars and bottles are tucked in among the other merchandise. Don't worry if it suddenly seems like your watch is running slow: Kenton sets its clocks by Mountain Standard Time.

One last detour: As you drive toward the mesa, you'll see a sign painted with the outline of a dinosaur. Travel back east to a dry creek bed, where dinosaur tracks are fossilized. There is a parking lot for hikers to the north of Black Mesa, owned by the Nature Conservancy, which leases it back to the state tourism department. The 4-mile trail to the top can be walked in about four to five hours round-trip; hikers easily make a day trip of it. Eight rare animals and twenty-three rare plants are preserved on the mesa, where hikers pass junipers, piñon, mountain mahogany, and lemon sumac, along with cholla cactus and numerous wildflowers. Golden eagles are often sighted, as are

The Three Sisters at Black Mesa State Park

pronghorn elk, bobcats, and piñon jays. You'll know you've reached the top when you spot an 11-foot-tall granite obelisk, marking the elevation at 4,972 feet: Oklahoma's highest spot.

Places to Stay in the High Plains

CHEROKEE

Cherokee Inn
1720 South Grand
(580) 596–2828

ENID

Comfort Inn
202 North Van Buren
(580) 234–1200

Days Inn
2901 South Van Buren
(580) 237–6000

Ramada Inn
3005 West Garriott
(580) 234–0440

GUYMON

Econolodge
923 Highway 54 East
(580) 338–5431

Super 8 Motel
1201 Highway 54 East
(580) 338–0507

WATONGA

Noble House Bed and Breakfast
112 North Noble
(580) 623–2559

Redbud Manor Bed and Breakfast Inn
900 North Burford Street
(580) 623–8587

WOODWARD

Days Inn Woodward
1212 US 270
(580) 256–1546

Neeley's Inn at the Park
32 Boiling Springs Estate
(580) 254–3830

Places to Eat in the High Plains

BOISE CITY

La Mesa
901 East Main
(580) 544–2997

CHEROKEE

Dottie's Cafe
115 South Grand Avenue
(580) 596–5699

ENID

Chat & Chew
213 West Willow
(580) 234–8490

City Boots
800 West Broadway Avenue
(580) 242–3663

Garfield Grill
2101 West Garriott
(580) 234–1031

La Luna Blu
115 East Main
(508) 242–6673

Port Lugano
(soup and sandwiches)
813 South Van Buren
(580) 233–6012

The Sage Room
(fine dining)
1927 South Van Buren
(580) 233–1212

Tia Juana Restaurant
2327 North Grand Avenue
(580) 237–5268

The Wooden Nickel
410 West Walnut Avenue
(580) 237–5554

FAIRVIEW

Frank's Country Kitchen
508 South Main
(580) 227–2242

GUYMON

Eddie's Steak House
421 Village Shopping Center
(580) 338–5330

LeAnn's Restaurant
(family style)
205 Southeast Second Street
(580) 338–8025

Marla's
402 East Highway 54
(580) 338–1820

Naifeh's Steakhouse
704 Northeast Twelfth
(580) 338–5355

WATONGA

Hernandez (Mexican)
301 South Noble
(580) 623–2631

Noble House Restaurant
112 North Noble
(580) 623–2559

WOODWARD

El Sol Mexican Restaurant
920 Main
(580) 254–3300

K-Bob's Steakhouse
3113 Williams Avenue
(580) 256–9413

Wagg's Bar-B-Q
123 Seventh Street
(580) 256–6721

FOR MORE INFORMATION

Cimarron County Chamber of Commerce
6 Northeast Square
Box 1027
Boise City 73933
(580) 544–3344
www.ccccok.org

Great Salt Plains Recreational Development Association
111 South Grand
Cherokee 73728
(580) 596–3053
www.greatsaltplains.com

Guymon Convention and Tourism Bureau
219 Northwest Fourth Street
Guymon 73942
(580) 338–5838
www.guymonok.org

Red Carpet Country
Drawer B
Alva 73717
(580) 327–4918, (800) 447–2698
www.redcarpetcountry.com

Woodward Chamber of Commerce
1006 Oklahoma Avenue
Woodward 73802
(580) 256–7411, (800) 364–5352
www.woodwardchamber.com

Index

About the Author

Deborah Bouziden was born in Oklahoma and has lived there all her life. She began writing and publishing in 1985. Since that time she has had hundreds of articles published in not only Oklahoma publications but also national magazines such as *Writer's Digest* and *Woman's Day*. Bouziden teaches creative writing and speaks at conferences across the country. To learn more about her, visit her Web site at www.deborahbouziden.com.